I0827710

IMAGES
of America

Las Villas of Plattekill and Ulster County

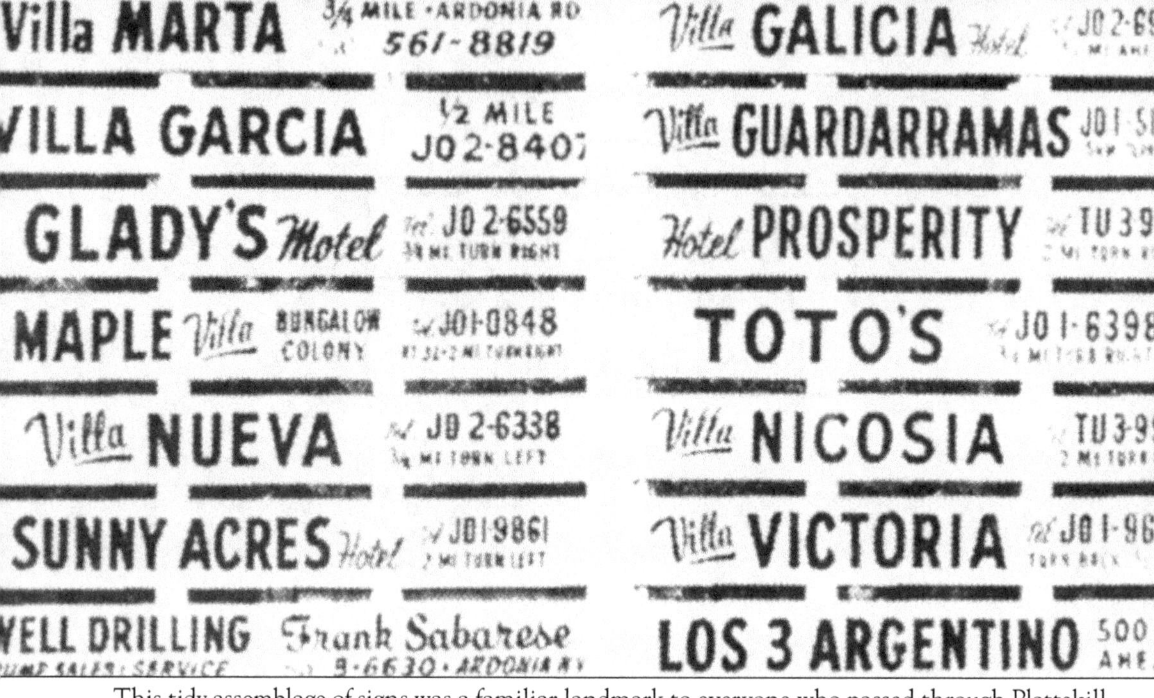

This tidy assemblage of signs was a familiar landmark to everyone who passed through Plattekill in the 1960s and 1970s, as it was located at the center of the village where the Plattekill Ardonia Road intersected with State Route 32. It was very similar to a sign that was located in the same general area as this one in the 1940s. (Courtesy of Sonny Wager.)

On the Cover: Los Jovenes Estrellas de Cuba (The Young Stars of Cuba) was a band that was actually made up of musicians from several different Latin American countries. The location of the photograph was at Sunny Acres, the villa where the band performed on summer weekends in the late 1950s and the early 1960s. The leader of the band was Ernie ?, pictured in front of the car. (Courtesy of the Martinez family collection.)

IMAGES
of America

Las Villas of Plattekill and Ulster County

Ismael "Ish" Martinez Jr.
Foreword by Tito Puente Jr.

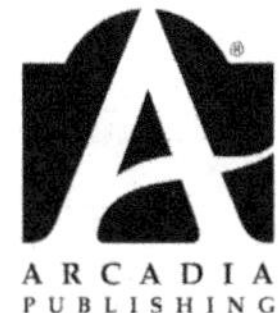

ISBN 9781531699192

Published by Arcadia Publishing
Charleston, South Carolina

Library of Congress Control Number: 2016935115

For all general information, please contact Arcadia Publishing:
Telephone 843-853-2070
Fax 843-853-0044
E-mail sales@arcadiapublishing.com
For customer service and orders:
Toll-Free 1-888-313-2665

Visit us on the Internet at www.arcadiapublishing.com

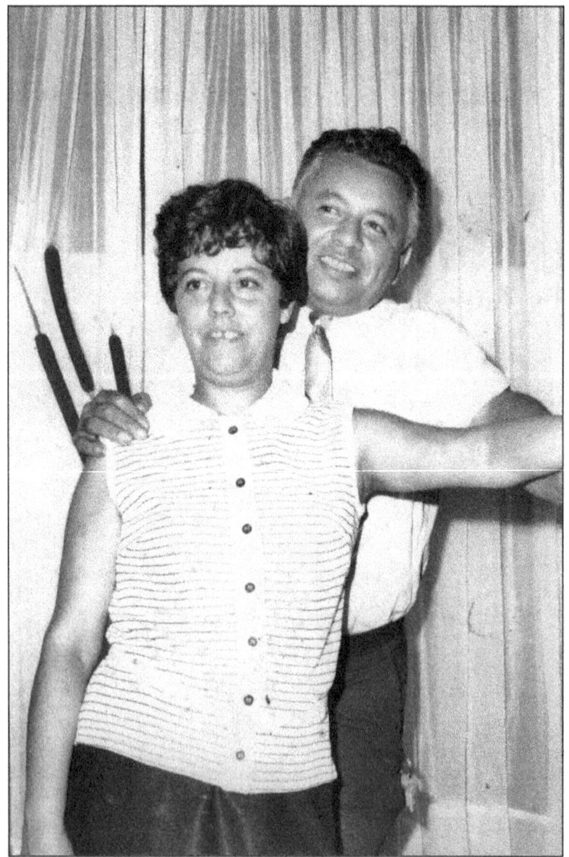

To the memory of my parents, Shorty and Lucy, whose love for Plattekill and Las Villas was only surpassed by the love for their family (Courtesy of the Martinez family collection.)

Contents

Foreword

Growing up in New York was something special to me. The summertime is what I truly remember about my youth. I spent countless hours outdoors with friends, and looking and searching for the next water source seemed to be the thing I yearned for the most at that time. Hot summer days and warm, sticky nights were the norm in New York City, but I always wanted hot days and cool summer nights. I wanted to be able to spend time with friends and family close to home and not have to fly far away to find a place like that. To this day, one place that stays in my mind is Las Villas in Upstate New York. A 90-minute drive north of Manhattan Island for a true New Yorker was considered "upstate" back then. This place had both hot summer days and cool nights, *and* something else—Latin music. My father, Tito Puente, knew of this place because, as a musician, he spent many summers there, playing music with his band. He took me to this place of great fun, music, friends, and family. It had everything a kid from New York could ever want during a New York summer! That unforgettable place was Las Villas of Plattekill, New York!

—Tito Puente Jr.

ACKNOWLEDGEMENTS

A book of this type could not be accomplished without the generous exchange of information by all of those who took the time to share their photographs, stories, and knowledge of this topic with me. I am forever grateful to my Plattekill friends and neighbors from today and from back in the day. It has been a tremendous experience for me to have reconnected with the many wonderful people from my past and to have met so many new people while on this journey.

I would like to thank my title manager at Arcadia, Stacia Bannerman, for her patience and for keeping me on track throughout this process.

I am especially grateful to Tito Puente Jr. for his unselfish willingness to write the foreword, which clearly enhances the appeal of this book. Tito is universally thought of as being a person of class, from a family of class.

I am indebted to the Plattekill Historical Society and the Town of Plattekill historian, Elizabeth Werlau, for taking an interest in this book and for sharing her experiences and photographs. I would also like to thank Shirley Anson for sharing her extensive collection of photographs and for her willingness to meet with me and make accessible the facilities of the Plattekill Historical Society.

James Fernandez, as well as his Facebook page Spanish Immigrants in the United States, has been an invaluable asset to me. I am thankful for his willingness to share his resources regarding the Hispanic experience in this country, which he has so painstakingly and meticulously researched and documented.

A special thank-you goes to my sister Carla Martinez Ramos for reawakening my enthusiasm for this project by creating the Facebook page Las Villas of Plattekill, New York, and for providing me with key photographs. Thanks go to my brothers Ron and Larry Martinez, who have joyfully shared their memories, stories, and pictures with me.

Finally, heartfelt thanks go to my family and to my wife, Maryann, who, through difficult times, has exhibited endless patience and has always supported and encouraged me in this endeavor.

INTRODUCTION

Las Villas of Plattekill and the Ulster County region of New York State was a vibrant and eclectic cluster of large and small summer resorts. These villas catered to mostly Spanish, Puerto Rican, Cuban, Dominican, South American, and other ethnic groups from the Hispanic communities of the New York City metropolitan area. The history of Las Villas was an inimitable era that we can trace back to the early part of the 20th century. The golden era of Las Villas spanned over 60 years at which time it was the destination of choice for a great many Hispanic families.

Beginning in the 1920s, Spanish immigrants in New York City and its environs felt the need to relocate to more rural surroundings. They wanted to get back to their roots and to escape the often crowded and unwholesome conditions that existed in many of the larger cities around that time. The Hudson Valley town of Plattekill, as well as most of Ulster County, was primarily a region of hundreds of small private apple orchards and dairy farms.

Just as many other European immigrants had done at the turn of the 20th century, Spanish immigrants had come to America searching for jobs, greater opportunities, and a better life and future for their children. Some of the Spanish villa owners, like Alejandro Rodriguez, the owner of the Villa Rodriguez, had been cigar makers in Cuba, the Florida Keys, or Ybor City, a Spanish enclave within the city of Tampa, before settling in Plattekill. By most accounts, Alejandro was the first Spaniard to buy a working farm in the town of Plattekill and transform it into a villa.

Many villas were soon to follow in Plattekill and in other Ulster county towns, like Wallkill, Phoenicia, Rifton, Allaben, Shokan, Shandaken, and Ellenville. At first, like many other villa owners, Alejandro primarily operated his property as a farm and supplemented it by taking in summertime tourists. Eventually, most of the owners of villas operating as both a farm and a villa put all their energies into running them exclusively as villas. Their guests liked the fact that they could find in these resorts the authentic Spanish food and music they cherished. The accommodations in the early years were basic, but they were also very affordable.

Another appealing aspect of the villas for most families was that the area was a relatively short drive by car, about an hour or two. The villas could also be reached by some combination of train, car, and boat. By the late 1940s and early1950s, a sizeable number of Hispanic families, mostly Puerto Ricans—or Boricuas, as they sometimes refer to themselves—began to relocate to Plattekill from New York City. After having vacationed there themselves, they found the area to be a desirable place to live. Some of these families started up villas of their own or purchased villas that had previously been owned by Spaniards. Much like the Spanish, the Puerto Ricans who relocated to the region were attracted to the area because of the bucolic setting and the natural beauty of the terrain, which reminded them of their beloved island.

What was once a popular area for boardinghouses that served as residences for the locals and provided rooms for summer guests eventually became a mecca of Spanish and Puerto Rican resorts. The villas were an eclectic mix of establishments that ranged in size from the tiny one-room bar, dining room, and dance hall to the more sumptuous hotels that offered scores of rooms to rent and lots of amenities.

By the 1960s, Puerto Ricans made up the most prevalent group visiting Las Villas, and during these years, tourism peaked and was a thriving industry. The increase in visitors to the villas also added much more traffic than small towns like Plattekill had ever seen. On summer weekends, the influx of tourists would quadruple the town's population. Not only were there more cars traveling bumper to bumper along the small winding back roads that led to the various villas, but there were also many charter buses, called jiras, that added to the congestion on the roads. The jiras were organized by agencies and other social groups who sold tickets to individuals that included a bus ride to the villas, free live music, and a hearty meal, usually consisting of *arroz con gandules* (rice with pigeon peas), *lechon asado* (roasted pork), *tostones* (fried plantains), and a salad. Not all villas took in jiras, but the ones that did were able to offer many people a very popular and affordable way to visit Las Villas.

Other Hispanic groups, such as Cubans, Dominicans, and South Americans, also flocked to the region, where the similarities in language, music, food, and customs brought them together for enjoyable excursions and memorable family vacations. Some people chose to return to the same villa year after year, becoming loyal customers, while others preferred to go "villa hopping," visiting multiple villas in the course of a day or weekend. There were vacationers who preferred the peaceful and quiet surroundings of certain villas, and there were other villa-goers who sought a more active experience and selected villas that offered activities like picnicking, swimming, boating, horseback riding, movies, and other recreational sports.

The region became so popular during the 1960s and 1970s that a number of articles appeared in the *New York Times* detailing the activities at Las Villas and referring to the area as the Spanish Alps or the Puerto Rican Alps because of the Spanish influence and its proximity to the Catskills. A common adage from the people who experienced the social life at Las Villas goes as follows: "It was the Latin version of the movie *Dirty Dancing*."

In the 60 years or more of their existence, the villas entertained tens of thousands of guests from the tristate area. With the growing trend in the 1980s of affordable fly-away vacations and the younger generation seeking other forms of recreation and entertainment, Las Villas became less popular and interest waned such that only a couple of villas remained in operation by the year 2000.

This is now a bygone era of a vacation destination for Hispanic families that had not existed in this country prior to this time. Based on how the villas came to be, it is highly unlikely that we will ever see anything quite like it again. The history of Las Villas is not only a part of the history of Plattekill and Ulster County, but it is also a part of the history and culture of all the Hispanic groups that found their way to this cluster of distinctive villa resorts.

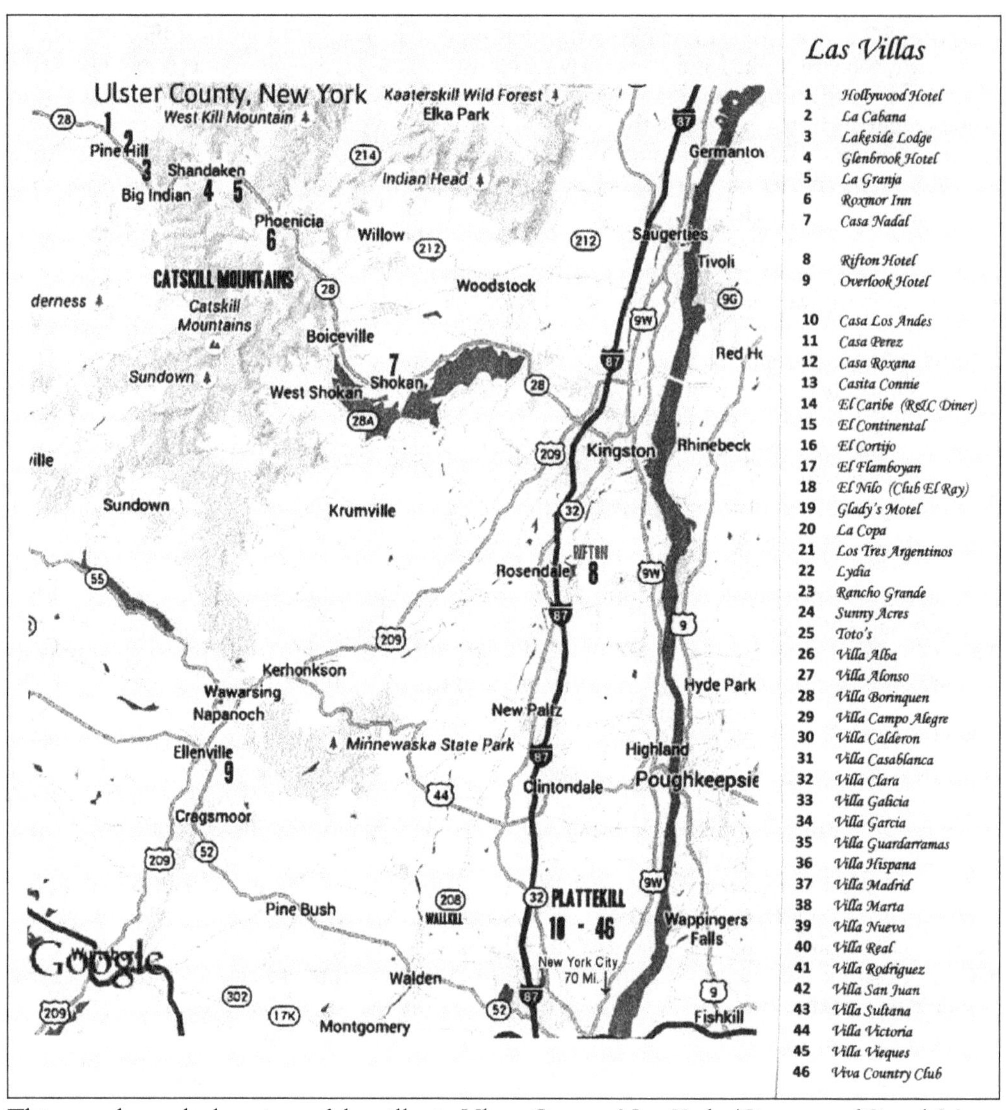

This map shows the locations of the villas in Ulster County, New York. (Courtesy of GoogleMaps, edited by the author.)

One

"Vamos a Las Villas"

"Let's Go to The Villas"

Las Villas, as they were collectively known, was a string of summer resorts, hotels, and restaurants that catered primarily to Hispanics and existed in the decades between 1920 and 2000. There were two main areas where these villas were clustered. The villas in and around Plattekill, New York, were 70 miles north of New York City, and another group that had developed in the Catskill Mountains was 40 to 50 miles farther north. In the years prior to World War II, visitors to Las Villas could drive by car or charter a bus if traveling with a large group. The terrain in the region of Las Villas, whether in the town of Plattekill or on the Route 28 corridor of the Catskill Mountains, was quite rural. The town of Plattekill is made up of gently rolling hills and woodland, while the Route 28 corridor of the Catskills ran through a valley that was heavily wooded and mountainous. During the time of the villa boom, small private farms dotted the landscape. It was from some of these farms that many of the villa owners fulfilled a dream of owning their own little piece of heaven and created their resorts. By 1970, the number of Hispanic villas had peaked at about 50 to 60. The majority of these villas were located on Route 32, Plattekill Ardonia Road, and Unionville Road in the Plattekill area. In the region of the Catskill Mountains, they were mostly located on Route 28, but there were also a couple in Rifton and Elenville. Weekdays at the villas were generally quiet. Guests tended to take walks, swim in the pool, row a boat, or just work on getting a tan. On weekends, the pace picked up considerably as large crowds of people inundated the area and filled the dining rooms, dance halls, and bars. One of the biggest draws for people was the lively weekend music that could be heard throughout the summer at many of the villas. The large crowds and heavy traffic caused by Las Villas congested the roads and created some headaches for the local residents and the small police forces in the towns. On the upside, though, there is no doubt they were a huge boost to the local economy, which other businesses in the community also benefitted from. On the whole, villa owners were good neighbors and well-respected members of the community and left a legacy that will be fondly remembered for many years to come.

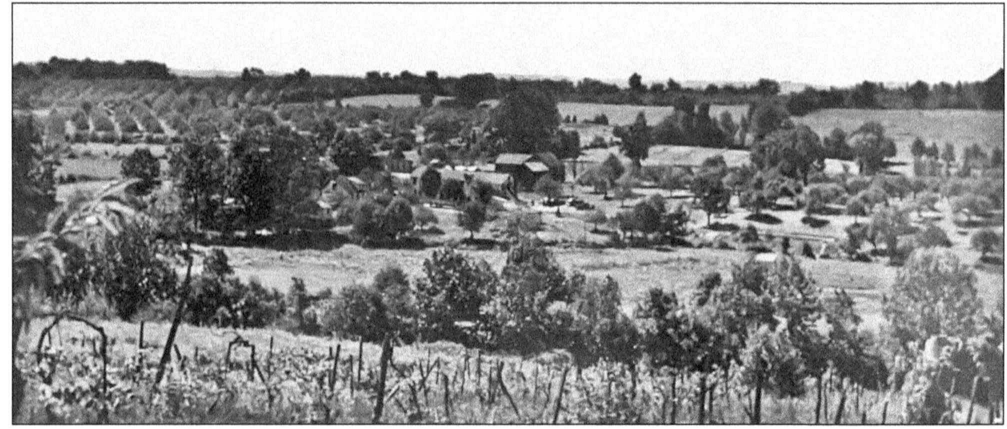

Here is a panoramic view of the Plattekill as it looked at the time when many of the early villas were established, first as farms and then as vacation resorts. For Spanish immigrants, their new life was a realized dream come true, and for many Puerto Ricans, the region's rolling hills brought back fond memories of their beloved island. (Courtesy of Shirley Anson.)

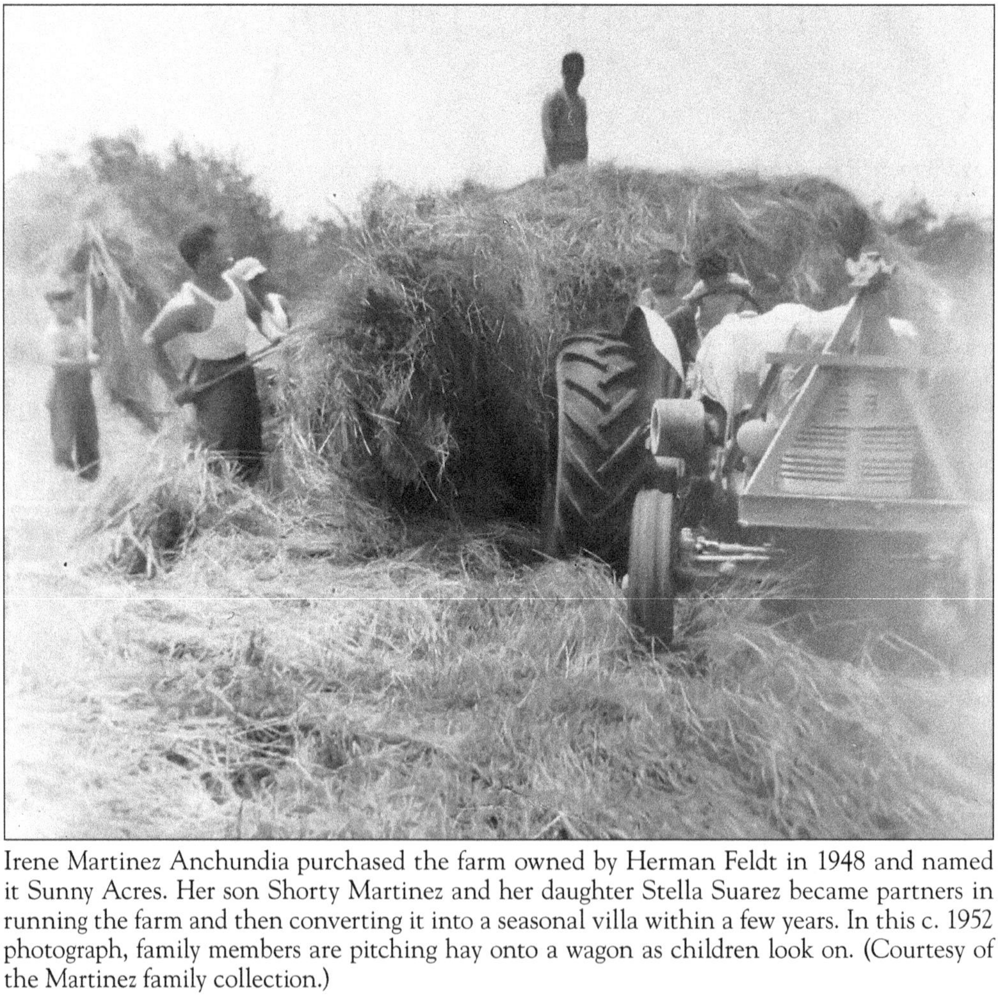

Irene Martinez Anchundia purchased the farm owned by Herman Feldt in 1948 and named it Sunny Acres. Her son Shorty Martinez and her daughter Stella Suarez became partners in running the farm and then converting it into a seasonal villa within a few years. In this c. 1952 photograph, family members are pitching hay onto a wagon as children look on. (Courtesy of the Martinez family collection.)

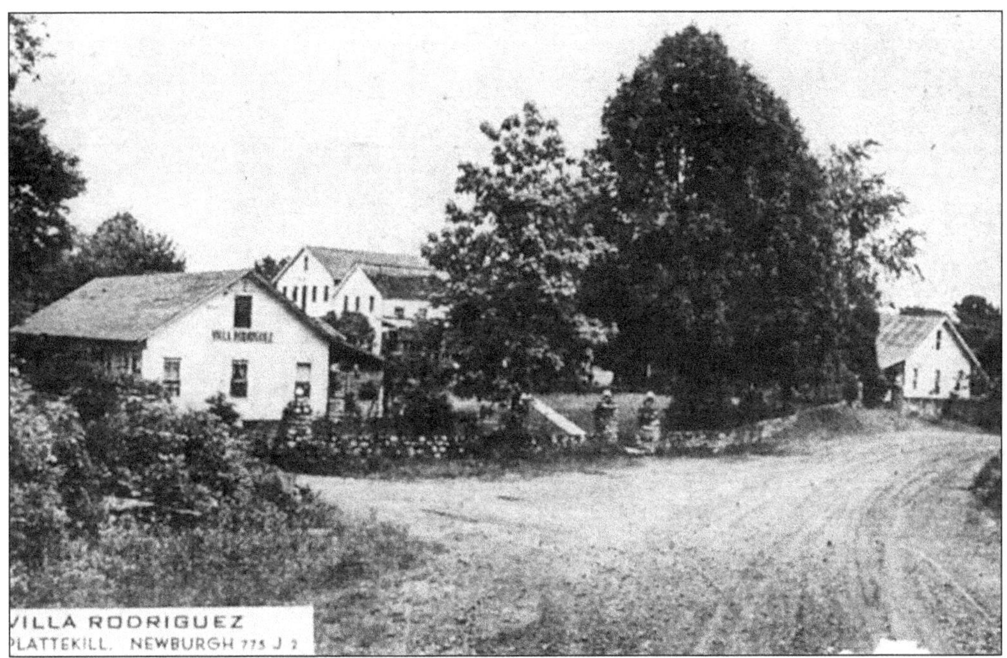

Villa Rodriguez was located on Unionville Road and was the first of several Spanish villas to be established in and around the town of Plattekill in the 1920s and 1930s. Alejandro Rodriguez, the owner and operator of the Villa Rodriguez, had emigrated from Asturias, Spain, to Ybor City in Tampa, Florida, where he had been a cigar maker. He moved to New York and bought a farm in Plattekill, which was soon transformed into the villa. (Courtesy of Anthony Patino.)

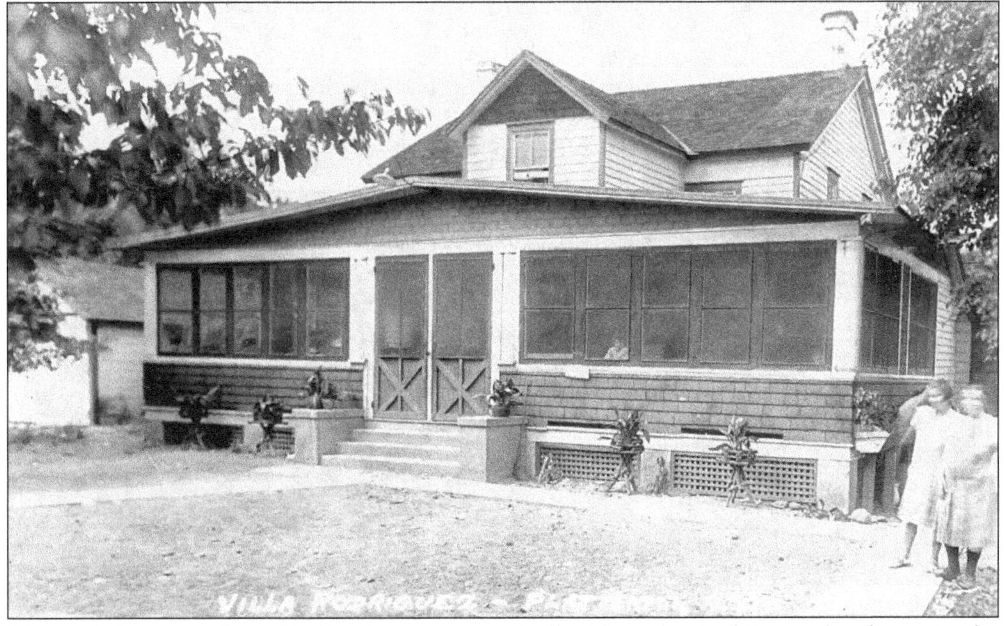

The main house at the Villa Rodriguez was originally Alejandro Rodriguez's farmhouse in the early to mid-1920s. The farm soon doubled as a villa as Alejandro started renting rooms on the farm to Spanish relatives and friends who wanted to spend some time in the country. (Courtesy of Shirley Anson.)

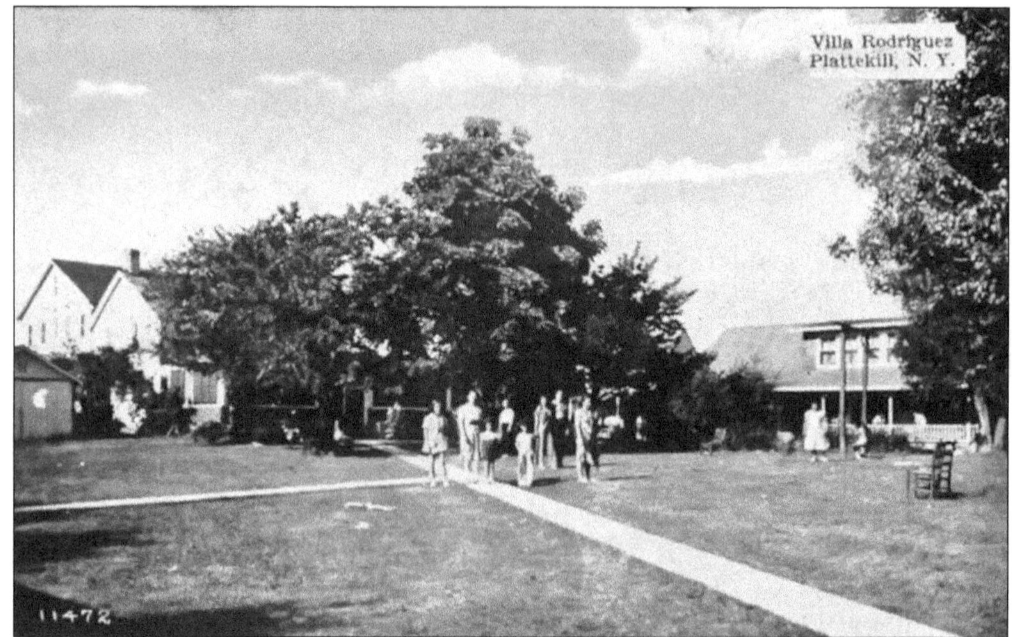

At the center of the Villa Rodriguez, the main house with its green was an area where guests could get together to play games or to sit and enjoy a relaxing conversation. Early records indicate that the 78-acre property could accommodate 55 guests. (Courtesy of Elizabeth Werlau.)

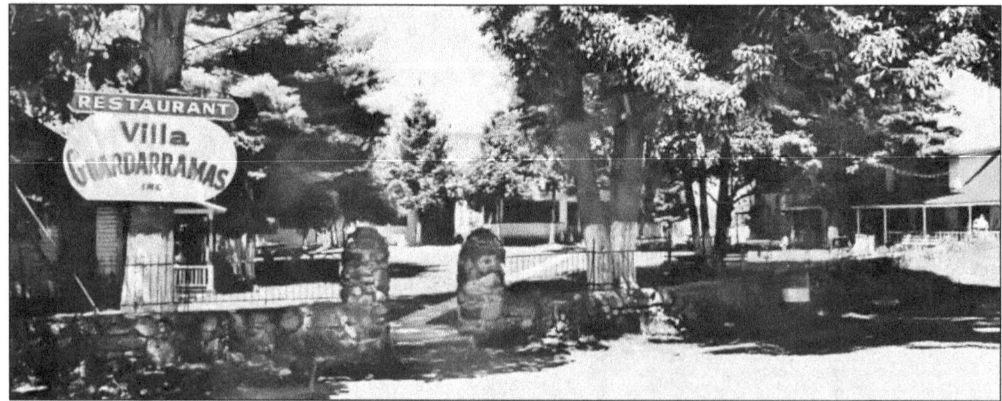

The Villa Guardarramas was formerly called Villa Rodriguez, but in 1957, it was bought by two Puerto Rican families from New York City. Pedro and Gonzala Guardarramas, along with Pedro's brother Gabriel, incorporated the villa in partnership with Raul and Carmen Correa. Several years later, Raul and Carmen would sell their stake in the business and start a restaurant up the road called the R&C Diner. (Courtesy of Norma Guardarramas.)

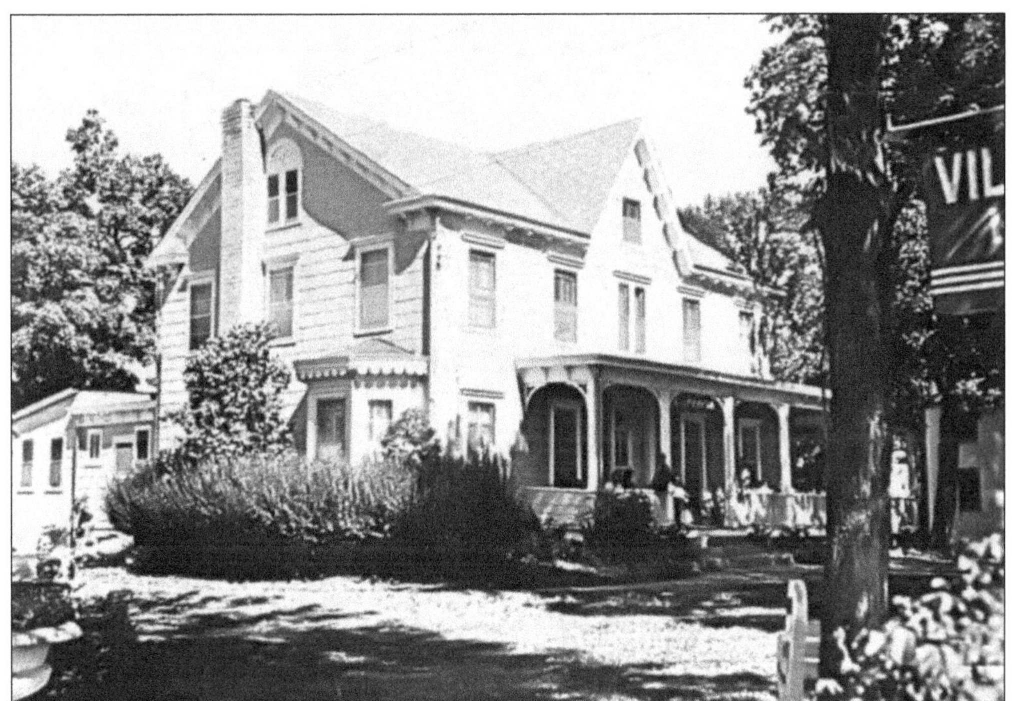

The main house at the Villa Garcia was the most identifiable building in the resort and the hub for all activities that occurred within the complex. The villa was also a working farm that had been purchased in the mid-1920s by Celestino and Flora Garcia, who had emigrated from Asturias, Spain. (Courtesy of the Office of the Plattekill Historian.)

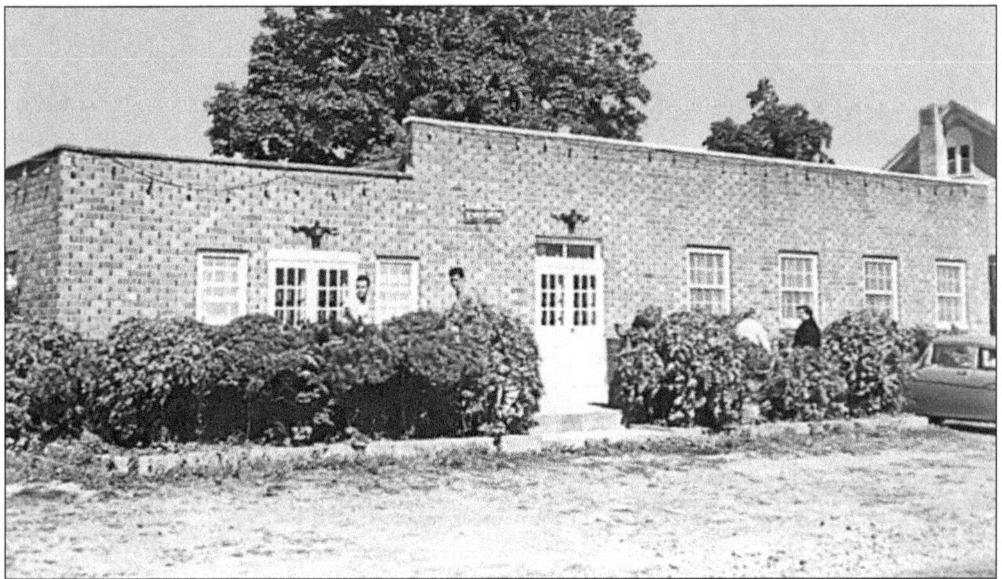

The building that housed the bar and dance hall at the Villa Garcia, seen around 1958, stood to the left of the main house. The peak of the main house can be seen at the extreme right-hand side of this photograph. The bar area was at the leftmost part of the building where the roofline is lower than the rest. It was typical for many of the villas to have the bar and dance hall in a separate building, which was sometimes referred to as the casino. (Courtesy of Shirley Anson.)

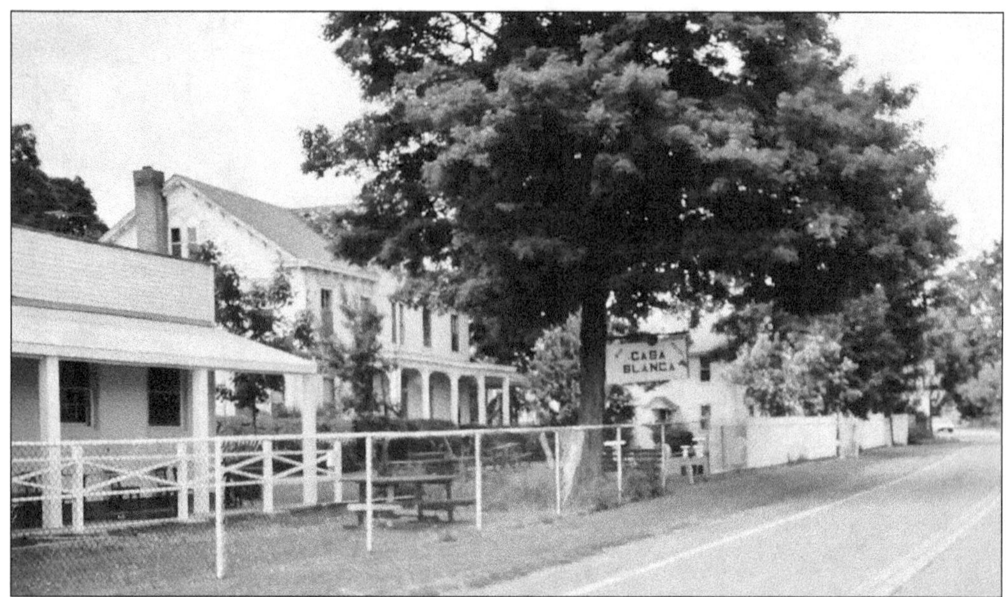

Villa Casablanca was previously called Villa Garcia before it was purchased by Clemente and Judy Rodriguez in 1982. At that point, it was one of the most active of the remaining villas. Clemente brought in popular salsa bands as the demographics of the tourists to the villas had gradually shifted from predominantly Spanish prior to 1960 to mostly Puerto Rican and other Hispanics thereafter. (Courtesy of Elizabeth Werlau.)

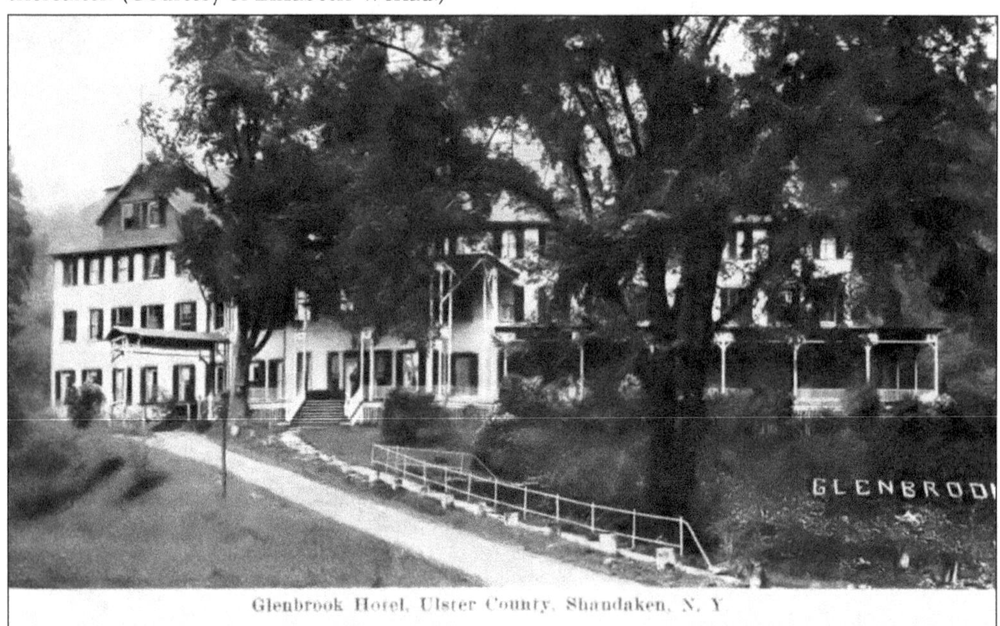

The Glenbrook Hotel was located in the Catskill Mountains just off of Route 28 in Shandaken, New York. In 1937, it was owned by Ricardo Gil, Carmen L. Garcia, and her mother, Dolores G. Lopez. In 1939, a dispute between Gil and the other two partners developed over Gil making the hotel his permanent residence. They were unable to resolve the dispute, and a lawsuit was filed by Gil against Garcia and Lopez, which went all the way to the New York State Supreme Court. (Courtesy of the Martinez family collection.)

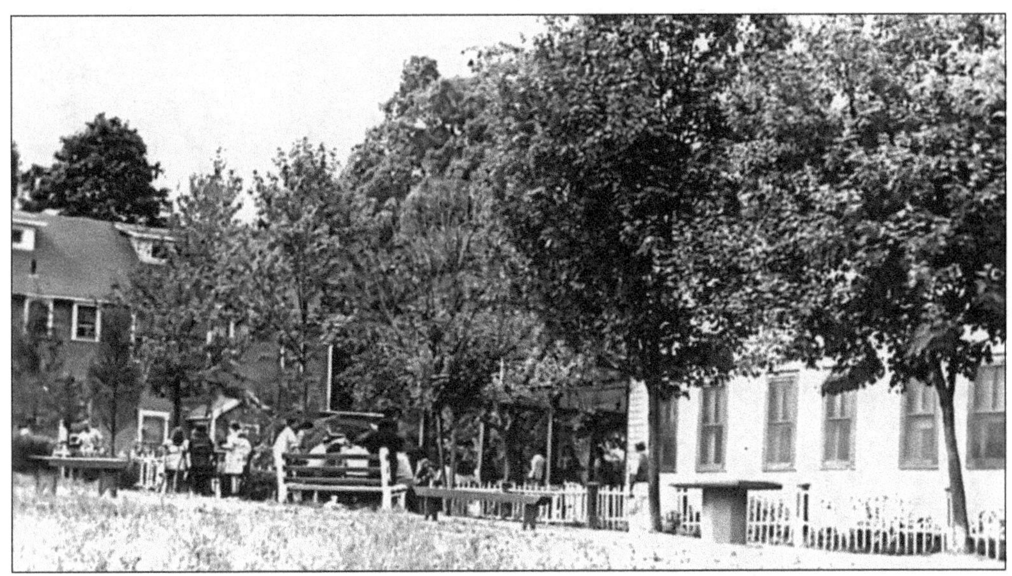

The area between the main house (left side of photograph) and the dining room of the Villa Nueva was a common gathering point for people to sit and socialize while enjoying the pleasant, scenic surroundings of the villa. Through word of mouth and extensive advertising, the resort was one of the most widely known villas in the tristate area's large Hispanic community. (Courtesy of Shirley Anson.)

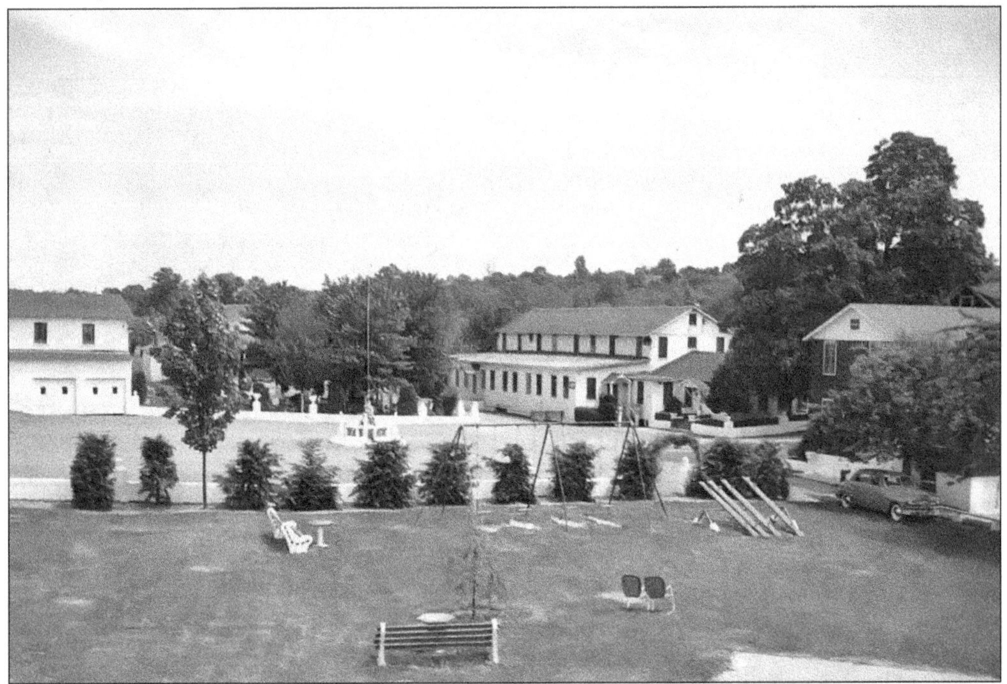

A playground and meticulously manicured lawns are seen in front of the main hotel building of the Villa Nueva in this c. 1952 photograph. Villa Nueva, referred to at times as "Queen of the Spanish Alps," was perhaps the largest of the villas in the Ulster County region of New York State. Only four or five other villas were in operation in this area when Severino and Amor Garcia purchased the property, along with an existing farmhouse, around 1930. (Courtesy of Shirley Anson.)

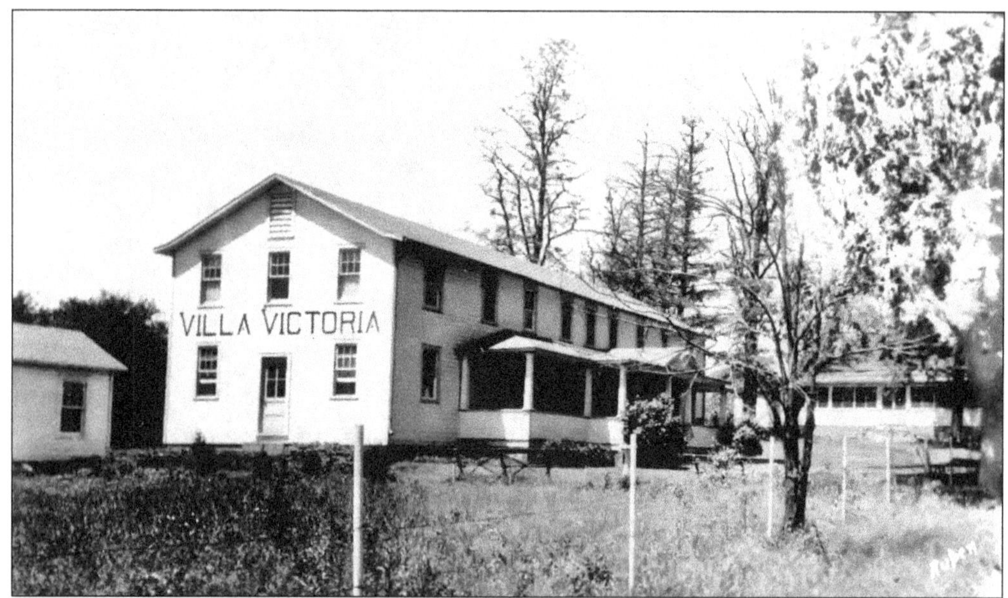

Some of the guest accommodations at the Villa Victoria were in this building, which was located to the right of the bar and dance hall. Painted on the side of the building in large lettering, the name of the villa was visible to motorists approaching from the south on Route 32 in the town of Plattekill. (Courtesy of Shirley Anson.)

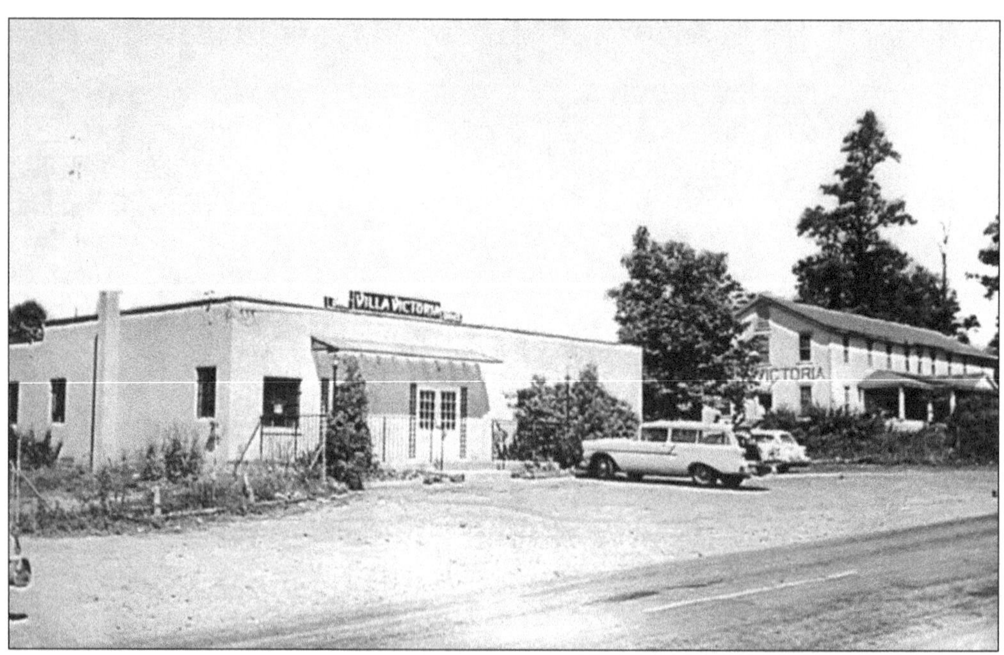

The Villa Victoria, pictured around 1957, was on Route 32 in Plattekill; it was owned by Joe and Rita Vega. Joe's family was from Cadiz, Spain, while Rita was born in Cabo Rojo, Puerto Rico. Joe's mother, Anna, and an uncle had purchased the property around 1927 for $8,000 when it was a farm with 88 acres of land, 24 cows, and a bull. (Courtesy of the Office of the Plattekill Historian.)

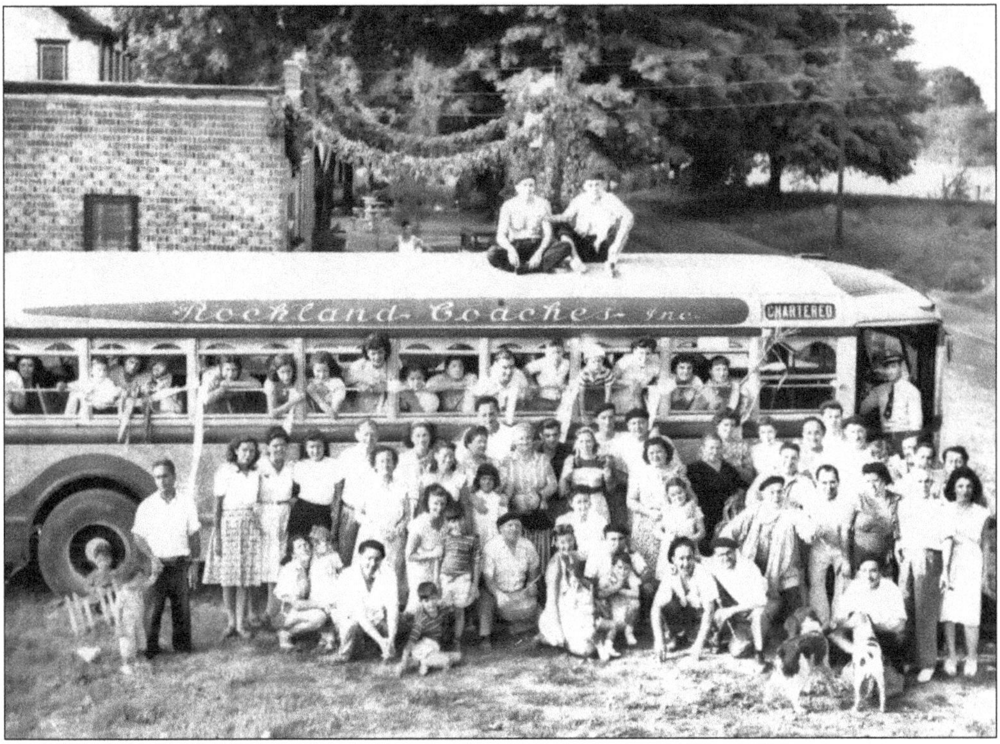

Charter bus trips by Spanish, Puerto Rican, and other Hispanic clubs or groups were common occurrences for practically the entire era that the villas were in existence. In this photograph, a Basque outing at the Villa Garcia on Labor Day 1947 was one of many activities organized by the Centro (Vasco), a social organization of Basque immigrants. (Courtesy of Marina Rios Frees.)

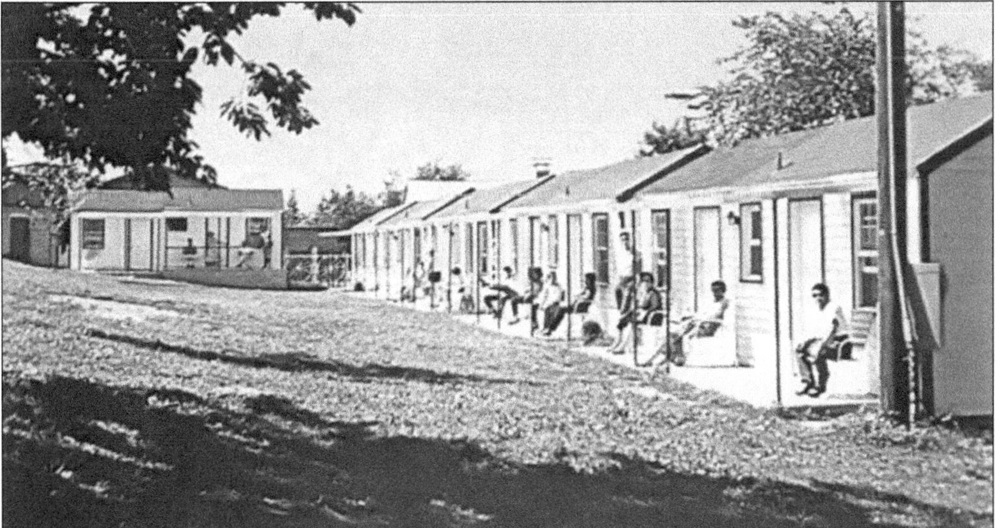

The popular bungalows at the Villa Garcia stood directly behind the building that contained the dance hall and bar. From where the guests are sitting, the live music coming from the dance hall could easily be heard. Bungalows were a common fixture, not only in the Spanish villas but also at many other summer resorts in the Hudson Valley that catered to Italians, Irish, and Jewish tourists among others. (Courtesy of Shirley Anson.)

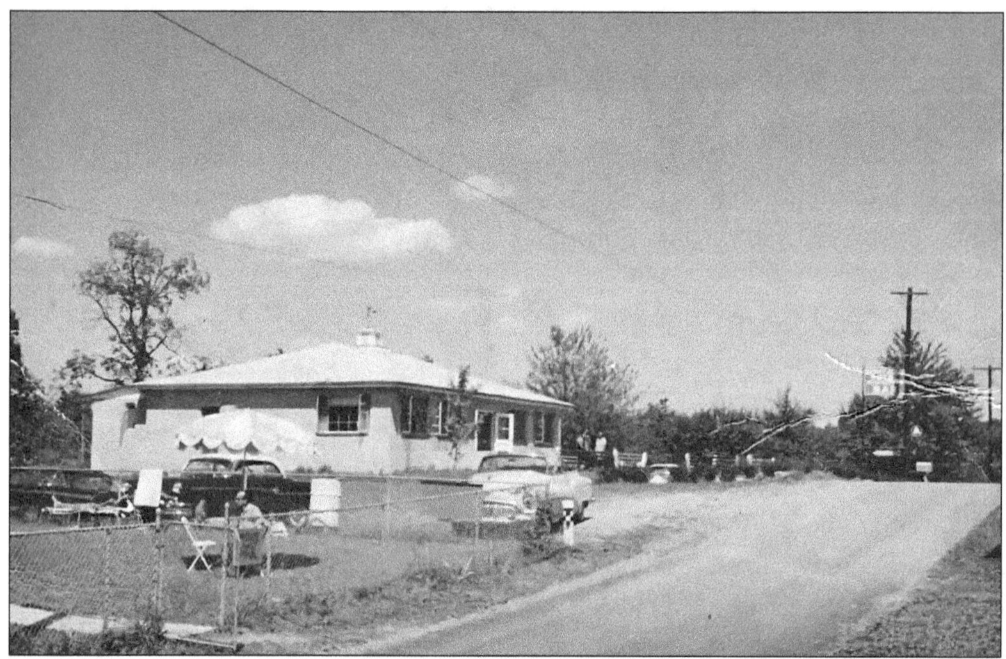

Villa Sunny Acres' dance hall and bar is seen around 1960, which was prior to the addition of a new dining wing at one end of the building and the new bar on the opposite end. Sunny Acres incorporated in 1965, making Irene Martinez Anchundia and her children Shorty Martinez and Stella Suarez equal partners. (Courtesy of the Martinez family collection.)

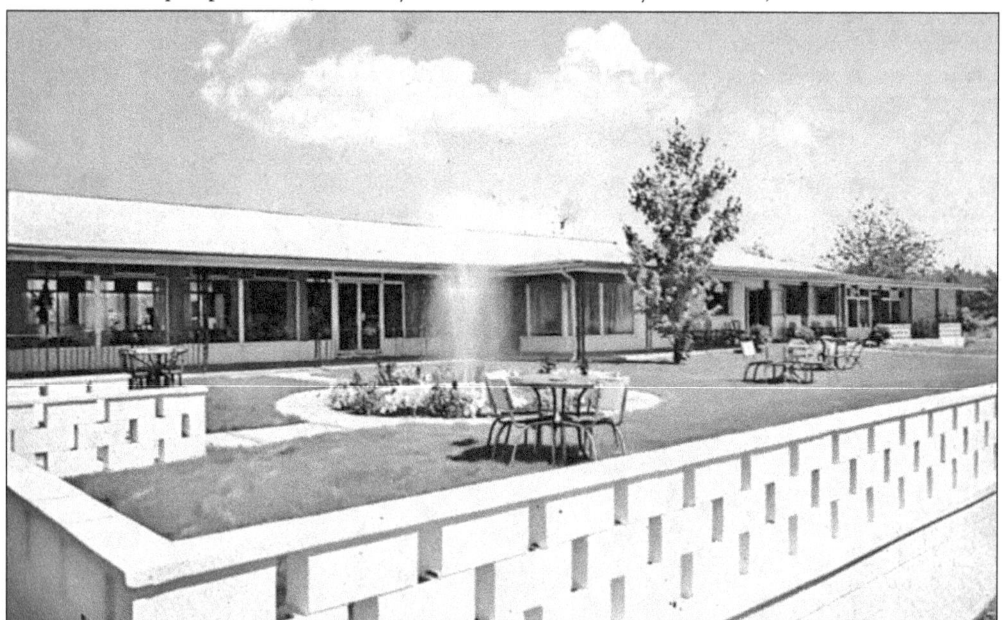

Here is Sunny Acres around 1967; note the addition of the new dining room on the left of the dance hall in the center and the new bar on the far end of the photograph. The building was built by the owner, Shorty Martinez, who also operated his own construction company, Martinez Construction, in the off-season and built a number of homes in the town. (Courtesy of the Martinez family collection.)

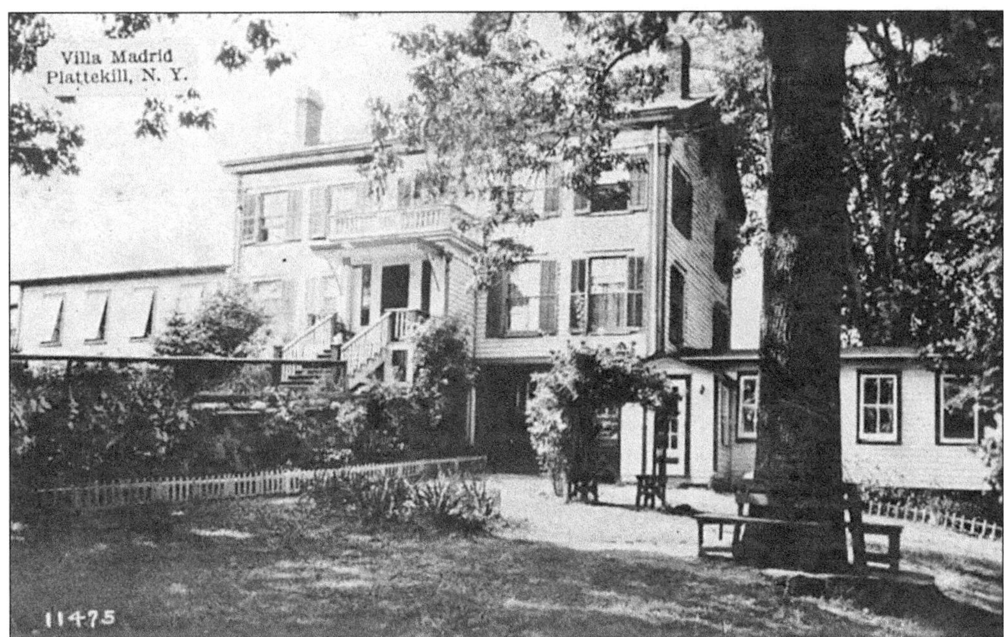

Villa Madrid was one of the earliest of the Spanish villas to be established in the town of Plattekill. Manuel and Pilar Tafall of Madrid, Spain, opened it in the late 1920s. After having been in operation for over 30 years, the villa was still a low-key resort by the 1960s. The main building was destroyed by a fire on April 3, 1968. (Courtesy of Shirley Anson.)

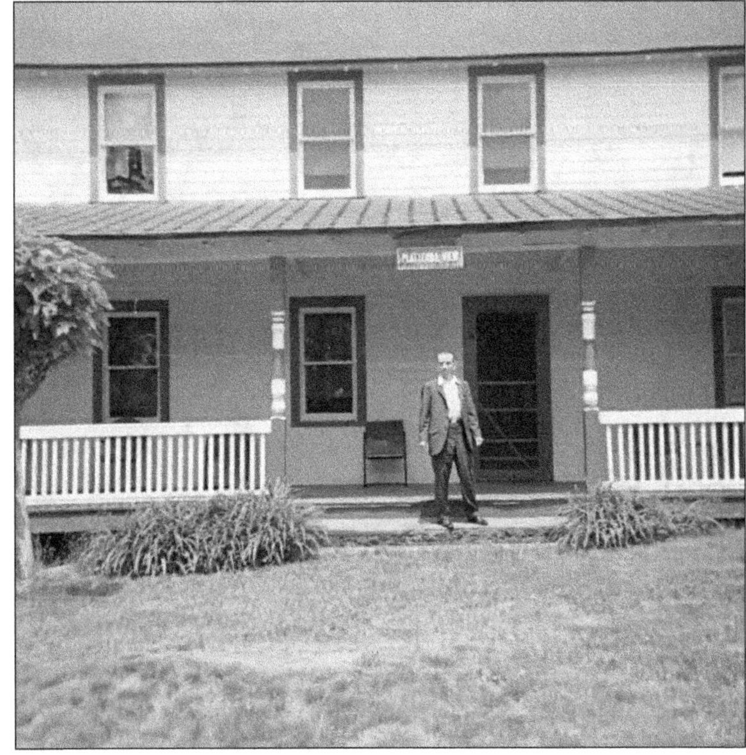

The boardinghouse at the Villa Madrid was where the majority of the guests stayed while vacationing at the villa. The sign above the gentleman's head reads, "Plattekill View," because from the vantage point of the porch, the guests had a panoramic view of the scenic Plattekill countryside. (Courtesy of Sue and Bill Rodriguez.)

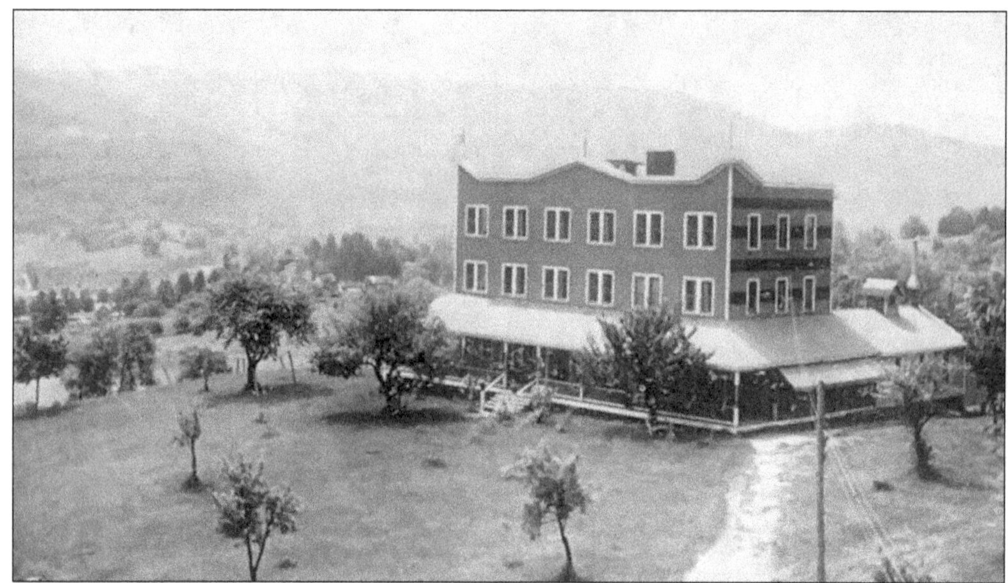

As reported in the May 10, 1946, edition of the *Brooklyn Daily Eagle*, the Overlook Hotel, previously owned by Louis Drucker, a Russian immigrant, was purchased by Daniel E. Colman, Waldo Colmelo, and Claudio Diaz. Included in the sale of the 100-acre property were the main hotel building and accessory structures, a swimming pool, an athletic field, and a casino. (Courtesy of the Ellenville Public Library and Museum.)

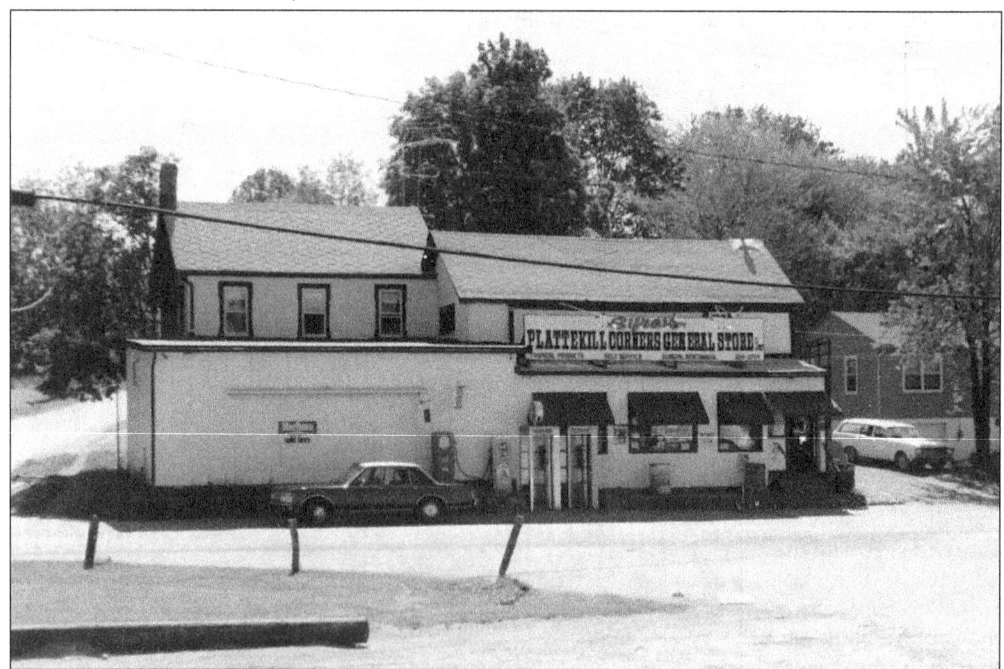

The Plattekill Corners General Store is a mainstay in town and has had a number of owners over the years. It is located at the intersection of Route 32, Huckleberry Turnpike, and the Plattekill Ardonia Road. During the era of Las Villas, it was most commonly known as Sisti's and, later, as Sifre's. Almost everyone visiting Las Villas would pass it and frequently avail themselves of the vast assortment of everyday items offered. (Courtesy of the Martinez family collection.)

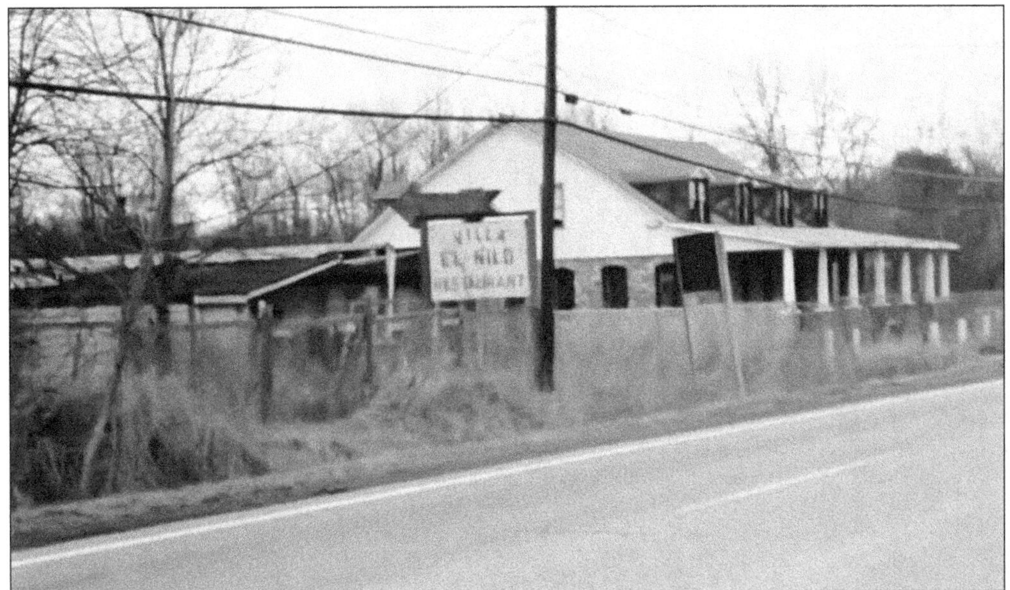

The Villa El Nilo sign stands as a mute reminder to the hundreds of buses and thousands of customers that had passed through its gates over the many years it was in operation. At the time of this photograph, the business had closed down for good, as evidenced by the chain-link fence that enclosed the property. The now neglected building on the left-hand side of the picture was where the pig roasts took place. (Courtesy of Elizabeth Werlau.)

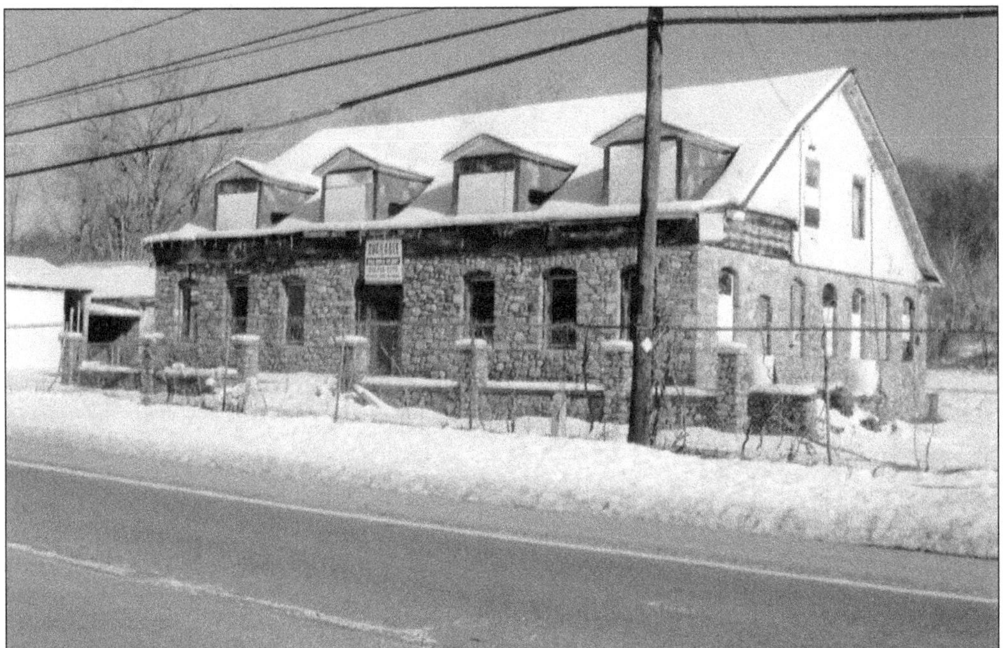

The main building at Villa El Nilo is seen shortly before it was razed around 2006. The trademark front porch had already been torn down, and only parts of the columns can be seen. A sign over the front door indicates that the space is available, but nothing further was ever done with the premises. At the present time, the spot that was once occupied by this building is just a big empty lot. (Courtesy of the Martinez family collection.)

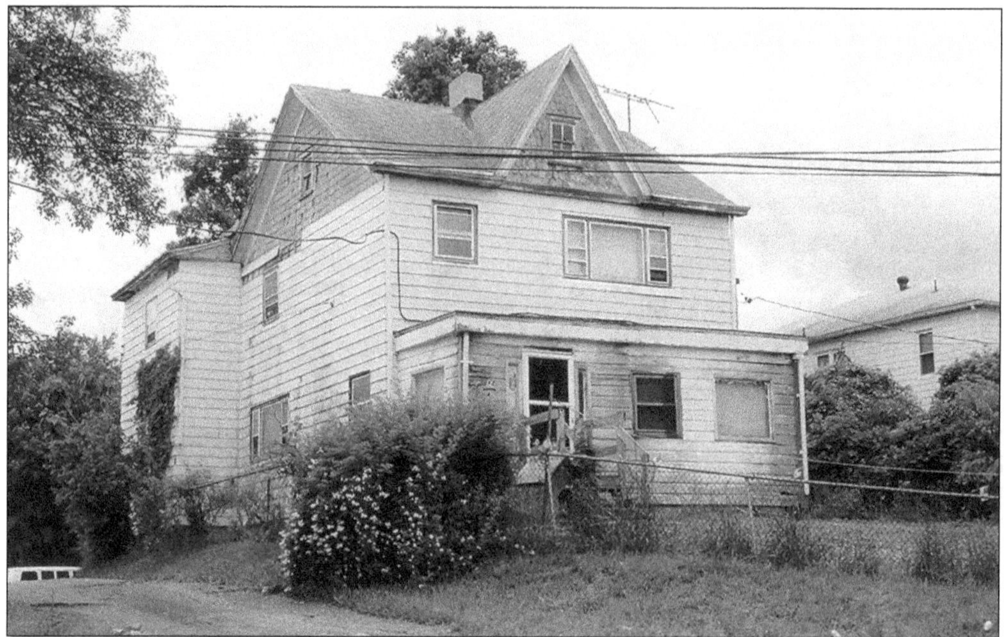

The deteriorating condition is evident in this 2009 photograph of Los Tres Argentinos, located on Plattekill Ardonia Road. Henry and Mercedes Cuney, who were originally from Spain, owned the villa. In the 1960s, Henry started a meat-canning business that he ran in the off-season. His primary product was canned roasted pork, much like the seasoned pork he served his guests at the villa during the summer season. (Courtesy of the Martinez family collection.)

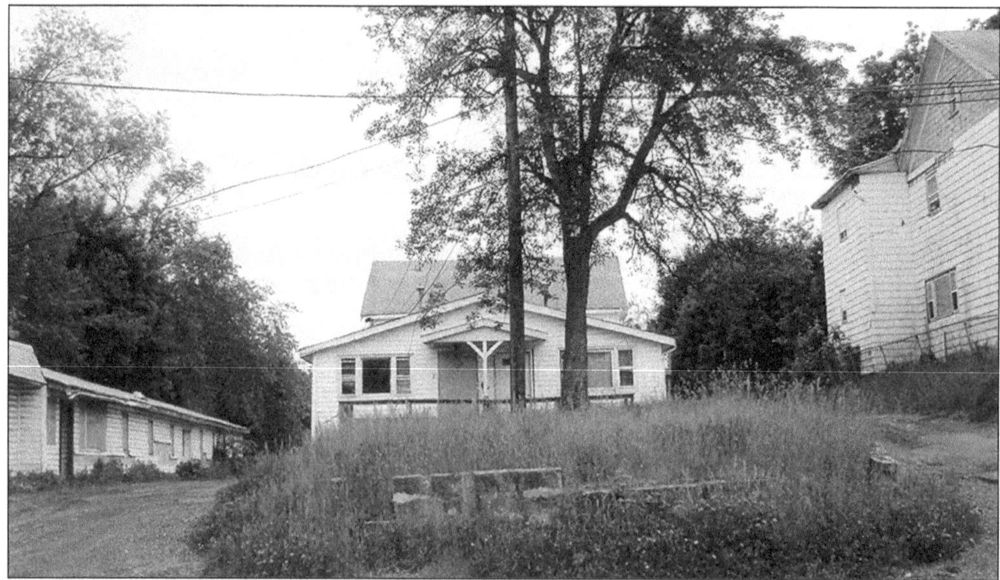

Los Tres Argentinos was noted for the roasted pigs turned on a spit located in the buildings on the left, which at that time were open sheds lined with cement blocks. People who visited the villa or drove by while pigs were being roasted will say that the aroma from the roasted pork was both tantalizing and unforgettable. There had to be enough pork to feed the large number of guests who frequently arrived in buses (jiras), so multiple pigs would be roasted at one time. (Courtesy of the Martinez family collection.)

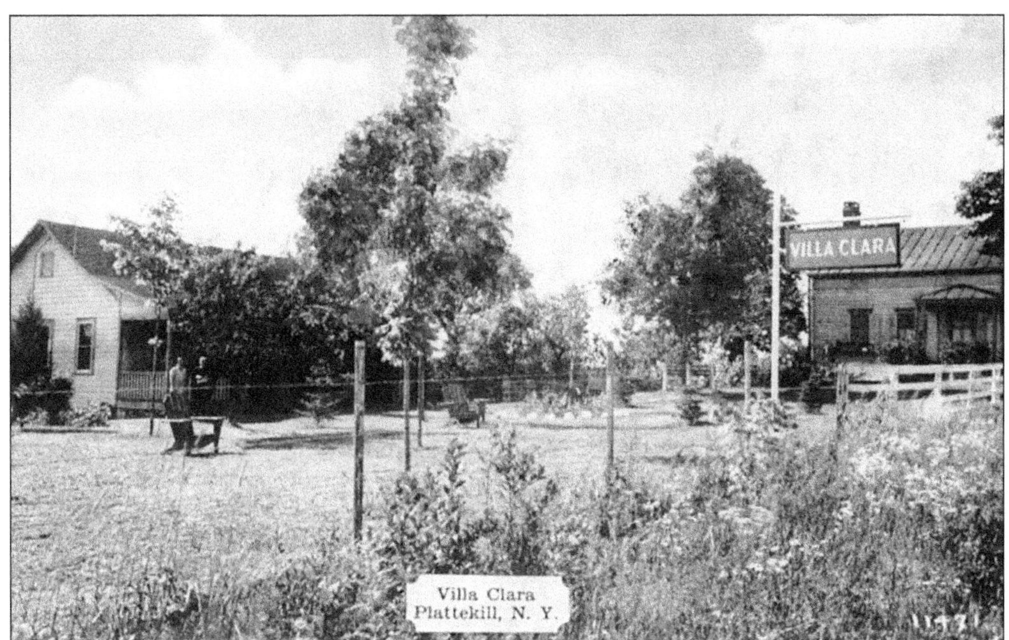

Ramon and Clara Blanco from Spain owned the Villa Clara. Quaint and low-key, the villa appealed to those who were looking for a good place to relax and just enjoy being out in the country. The Blancos also had a daughter named Gloria. Villa Clara was located on the left-hand side of Route 32 as one approached the town of Plattekill from the south. (Courtesy of Shirley Anson.)

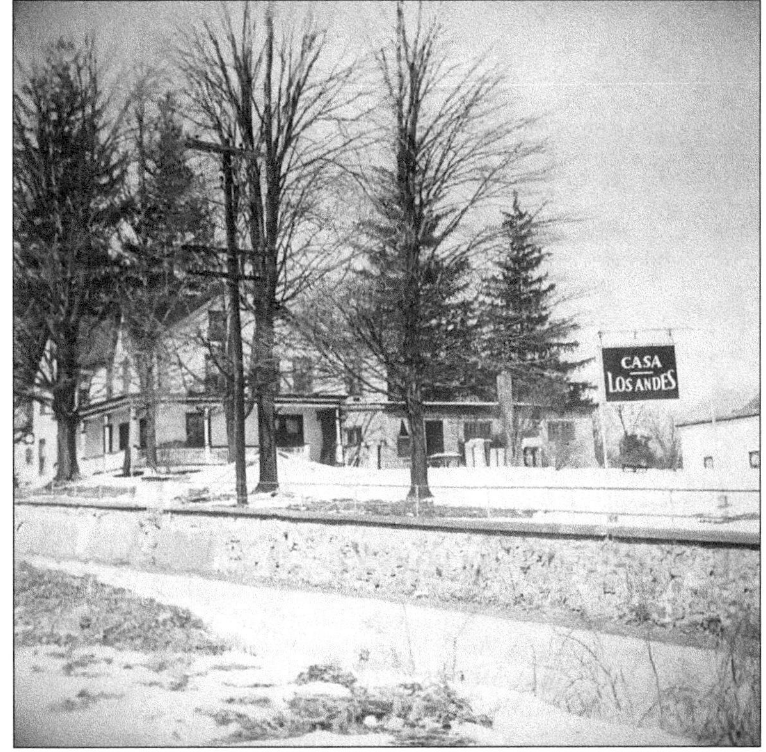

The Romero family owned Casa Los Andes, located on Route 32 in the village of Plattekill, just north of Flemings General Store and Post Office. In the mid-1950s, the construction of the New York State Thruway bisected the Romeros' villa property right about where the sign is in this photograph. The Romeros sold the business a short time later. (Courtesy of Shirley Anson.)

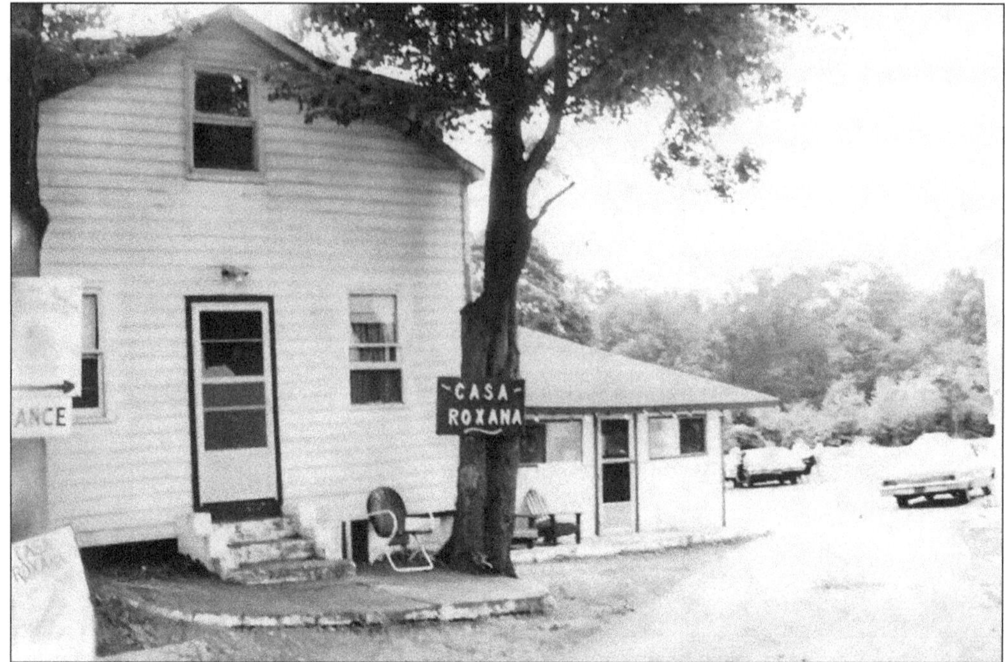

The Casa Roxana, located on Unionville Road, was owned by Josefina and Radames Santiago. Though small in comparison to some of the other villas, it did offer sleeping accommodations and delicious Puerto Rican–style cooking. Their guests could enjoy playing cards or dominoes while relaxing and taking in the countryside's fresh air. (Courtesy of Roxy Santiago.)

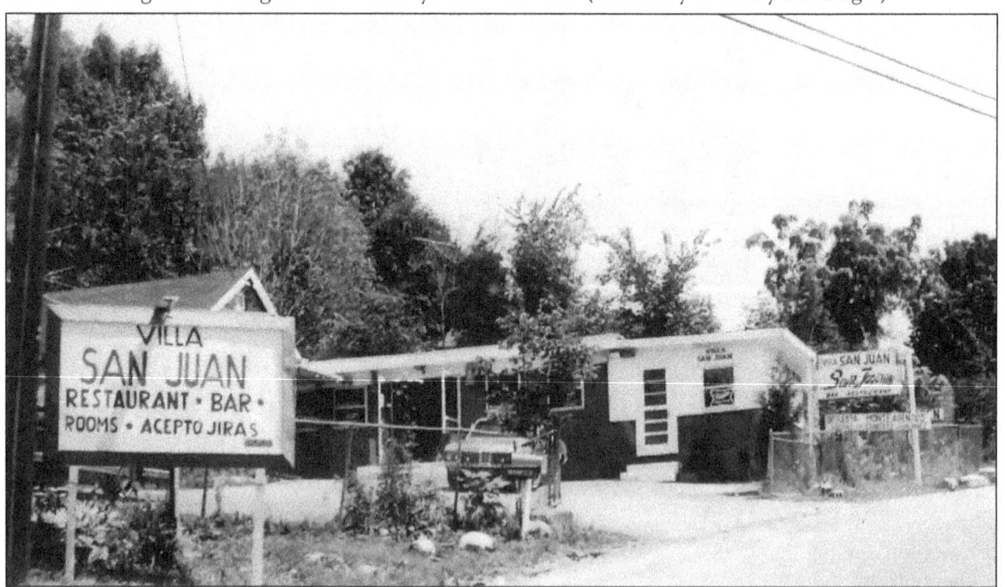

This c. 1968 photograph depicts Villa San Juan, owned by Willie and Tula Ortiz. The villa was located on Unionville Road in the town of Plattekill. In terms of size, it was one of the smaller and more intimate establishments, but it still provided live music, food, and limited accommodations. It was named for the capital of Puerto Rico, an indication of where Willie and Tula were originally from. Most of those who worked and visited Las Villas were bilingual, as evident in the Villa San Juan sign, which is in both English and Spanish. (Courtesy of Roxy Santiago.)

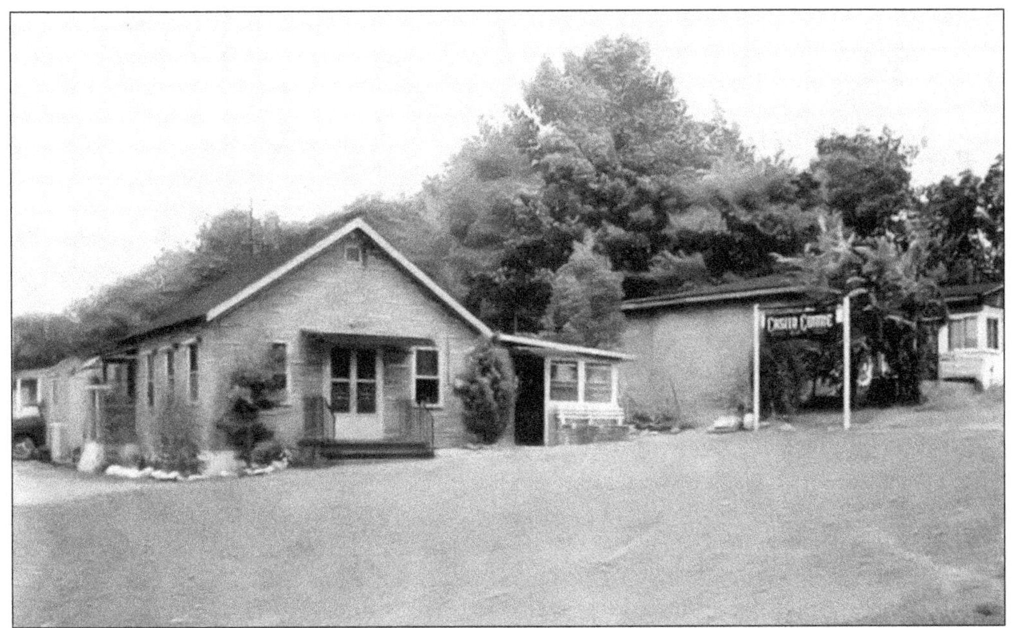

The Casita Connie was a small cluster of rustic buildings on Unionville Road and was owned by Connie Santiago, the sister of Radames Santiago, the owner of Casa Roxana just down the road. Casita Connie was bought by Puerto Rican couple Willie and Tula Ortiz, who changed the name to El San Juan. (Courtesy of Roxy Santiago.)

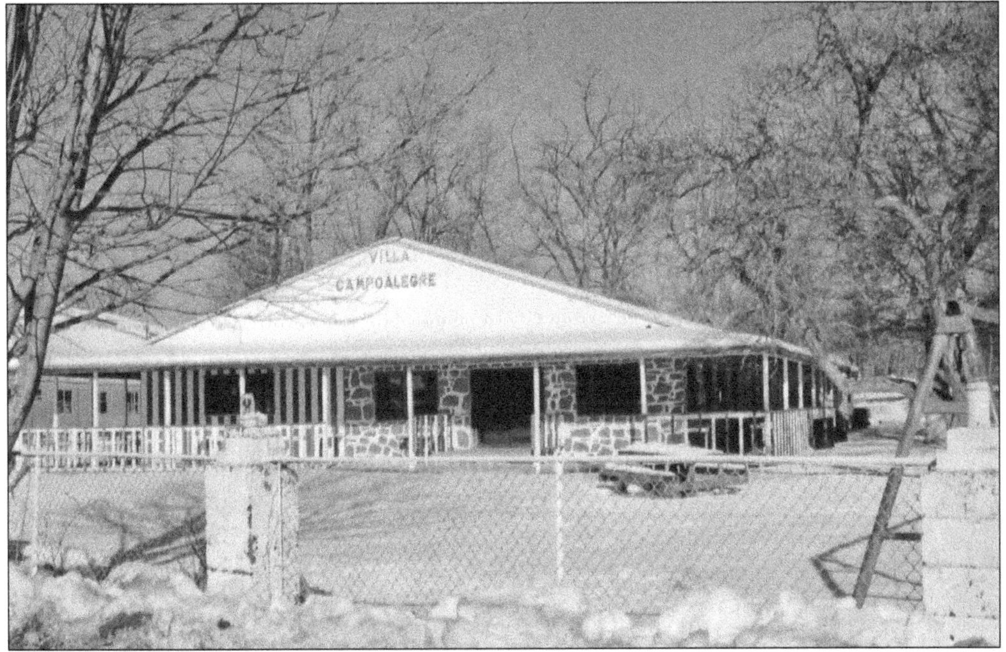

The Villa Campo Alegre, like the majority of the villas in the off-season, is quiet and desolate in this wintertime photograph. But once spring arrived, the owners and their families would get excited anticipating the start of another vibrant tourist season. Previously called Casa Perez, Villa Campo Alegre was owned and operated for many years by Andres Figueroa. (Courtesy of the Martinez family collection.)

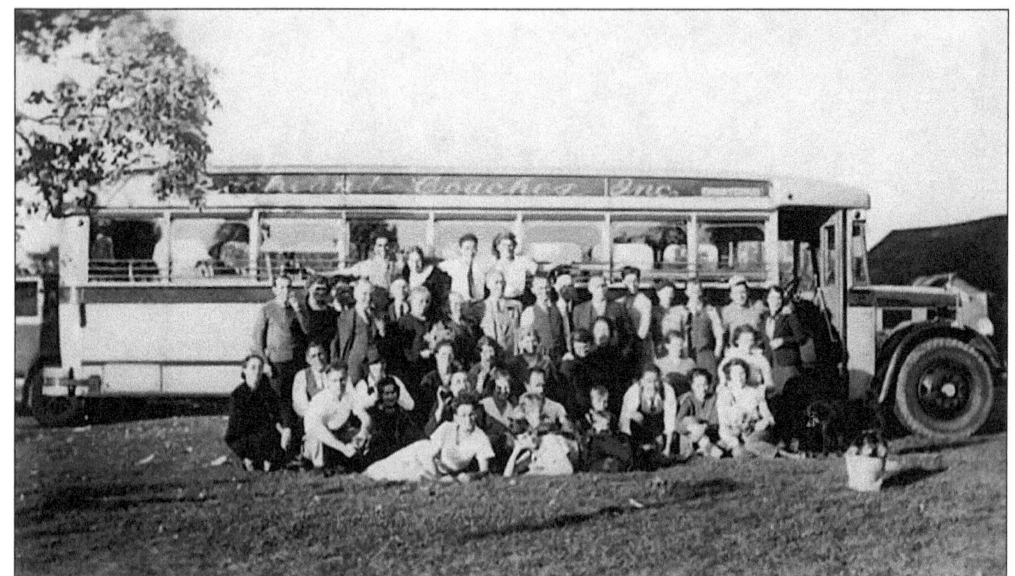

An autumn tour group to the Villa Alonso is pictured here around 1935. Villa Alonso was a small, no-frills summer resort owned by Angel Alonso and his wife, Consuelo Suarez, from Nevares, Asturias, Spain. Angel's homemade apple cider was so popular that people came from all over the area to buy it. (Courtesy of the Alonso-Sanchez family.)

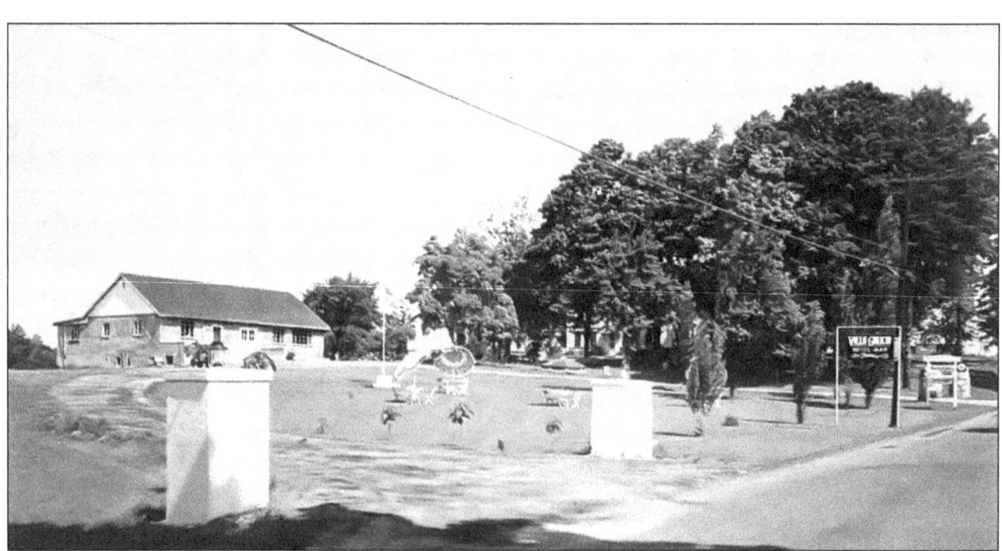

The Villa Galicia was started around 1947 by Fred and Mary Somoza, who were from the northern region of Spain. The property was previously owned by the Ruggiero family, and prior to that, it was known as Waite's Boardinghouse. In 1968, the Somozas sold the villa to Roberto and Fela Gomez and opened a liquor store on the adjoining property. (Courtesy of Shirley Anson.)

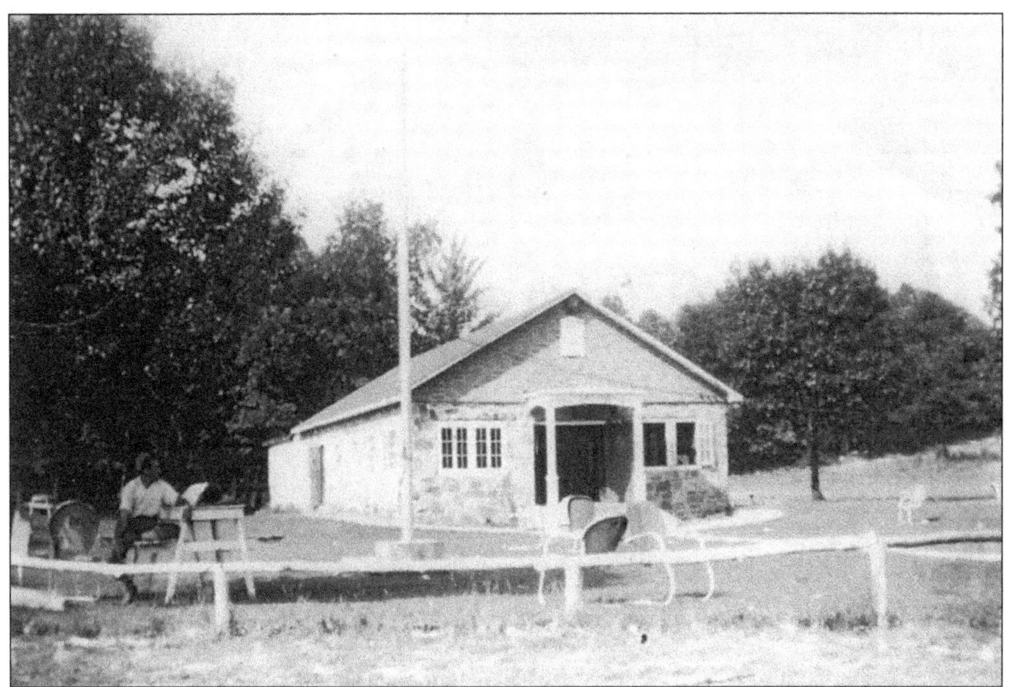

The building containing the dance hall and bar at the Casa Perez, pictured around 1950, was called the casino. The building was later expanded to include a dining area and a wraparound porch. The villa was later sold to Andres Figueroa and was renamed Villa Campoalegre. (Courtesy of Roxy Santiago.)

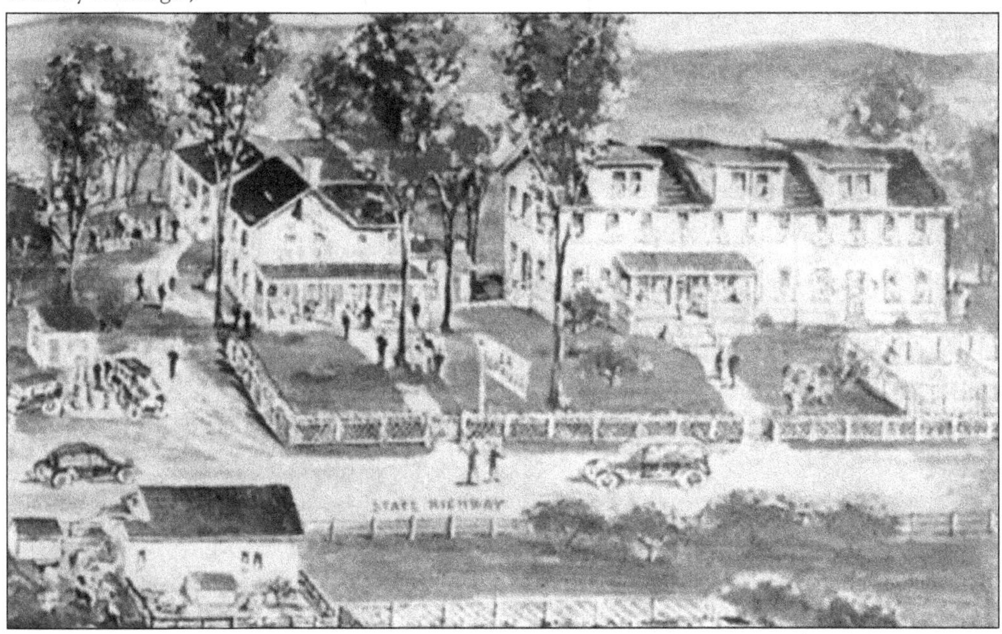

La Granja was a farm turned villa in Allaben, New York, within the town of Shandaken. By 1930, it was valued at $16,000 and owned by Spaniards Raimundo Marcos, Manuel Rodriguez, and Jose Fuentes. By 1940, the resort had grown considerably, and Fuentes was then sharing ownership with Joseph Regines. (Courtesy of James Fernandez.)

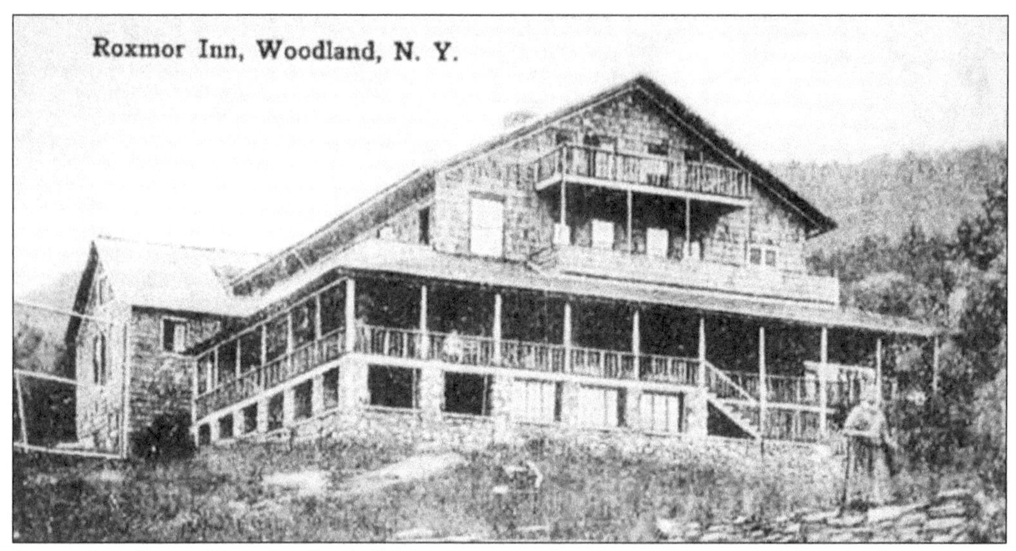

Located on Route 28 in the Catskill Mountains in the 1930s, 1940s and 1950s, the Roxmor Inn was in Woodland-Phoenicia, New York, and was operated by a Spanish Basque couple, Avelino Castanos Garay and his wife, Rosita Cuadrado Herrera, along with the Anieas family. Avelino was born on November 10, 1893, in La Cuadra, a town near Bilbao, Spain. Rosita was born August 30, 1909, in the Panama Canal Zone during the canal's construction by the United States of America. Her parents were "pucelanos," a term used for people from Valladolid, Spain. Avelino and Rosita also owned and operated a restaurant called La Bilbaina on Fourteenth Street in New York City. (Courtesy of Rafael Quinones.)

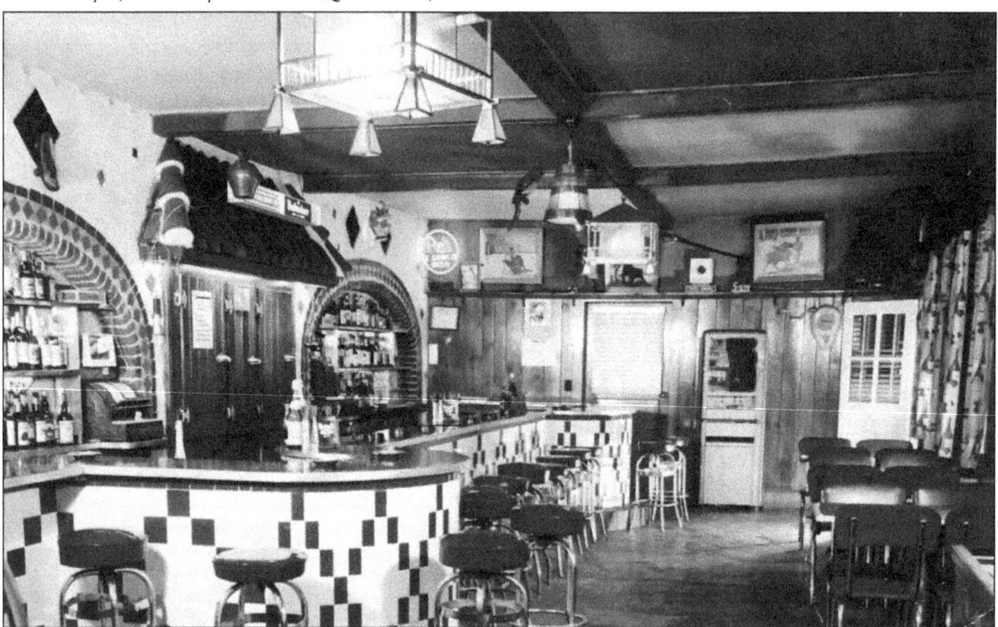

The traditional Spanish decor and ambiance of the bar at the Villa Nueva is reminiscent of the architecture of Asturias, the region of Spain that the owners, Severino and Amor Garcia, had emigrated from. At the far end of the bar, note the cigarette machine with a mirror on the upper part of the cabinet; the mirror was a typical feature of cigarette machines of the 1950s and 1960s. (Courtesy of Shirley Anson.)

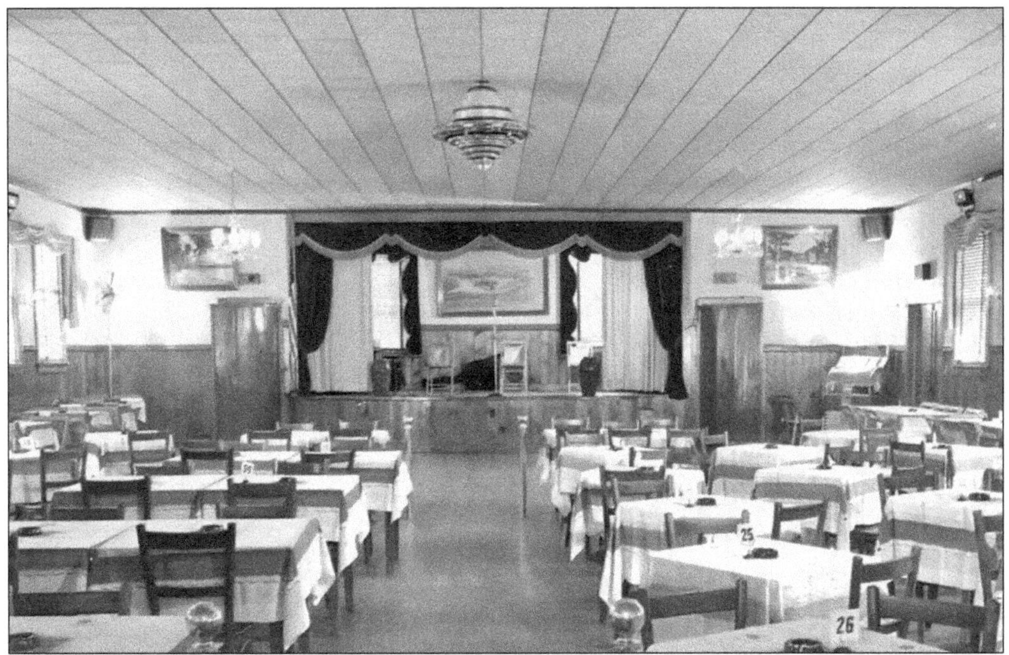

The room called the casino at the Villa Nueva was not a gambling casino but rather a dance hall where music and other forms of nighttime entertainment were performed. The band or entertainer would perform on the stage seen here located at the front of the room. Guests would dance in the area right in front of the stage. (Courtesy of Shirley Anson.)

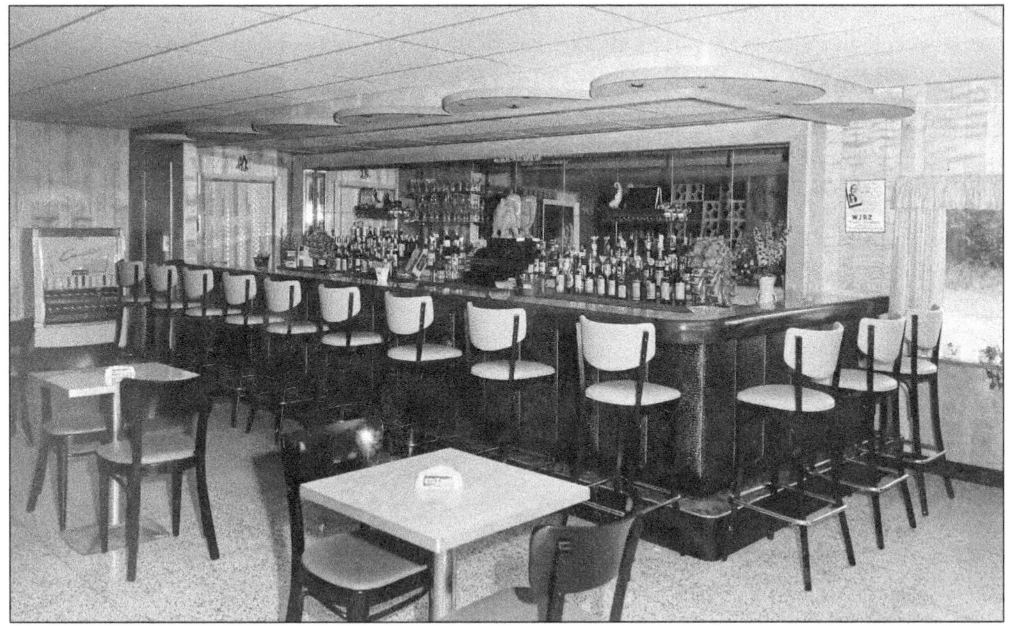

This photograph of the well-appointed bar area at the Villa Sunny Acres was taken in June 1963, when the building containing the dance hall was expanded with a new addition for the bar. As the business grew in size, the bar was rebuilt in different areas of the villa. The first bar was in a building erected in 1950, and that one was followed by one built within the new dance hall building in 1956. (Photograph by Frank V. Zadroga, courtesy of the Martinez family collection.)

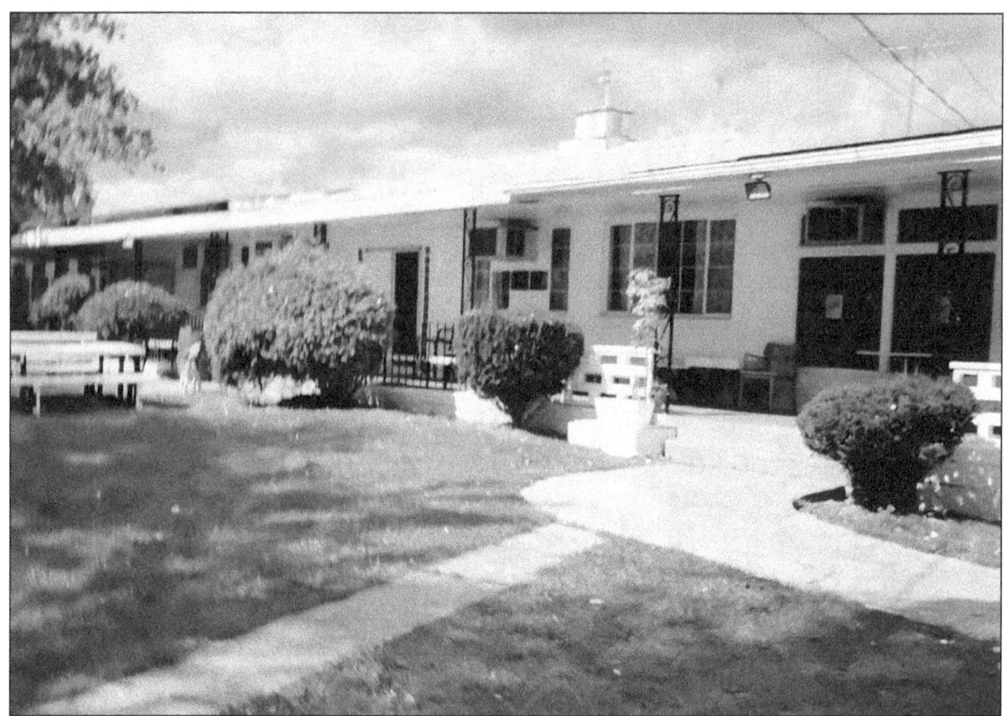

Pictured is the front entrance to the main building at Villa Sunny Acres in August 1997. The resort had always operated as a seasonal business, but as the villas became less popular as a summer weekend destination, Sunny Acres began to host private parties, graduations, and other special events in order to remain profitable. Fire destroyed the entire building on May 31, 2008. (Courtesy of the Martinez family collection.)

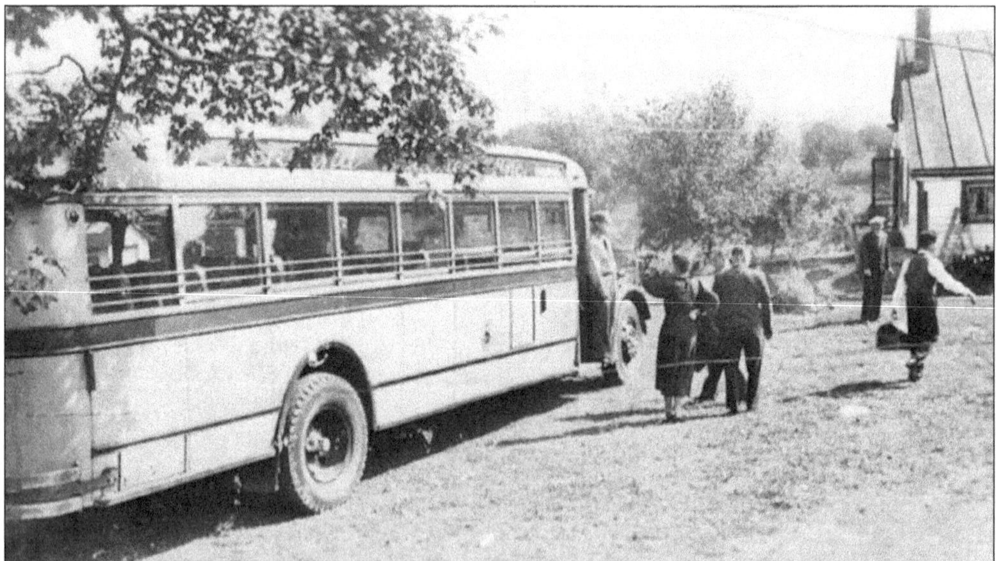

A busload of tourists arrives in the Hudson Valley at the Villa Alonso in this c. 1935 photograph. This was one of the early rustic farms owned by Spaniards who also took in boarders to supplement what they earned from selling apples, cider, and hay. The first tourists to Las Villas were content to just spend time being in the country. (Courtesy of the Alonso family.)

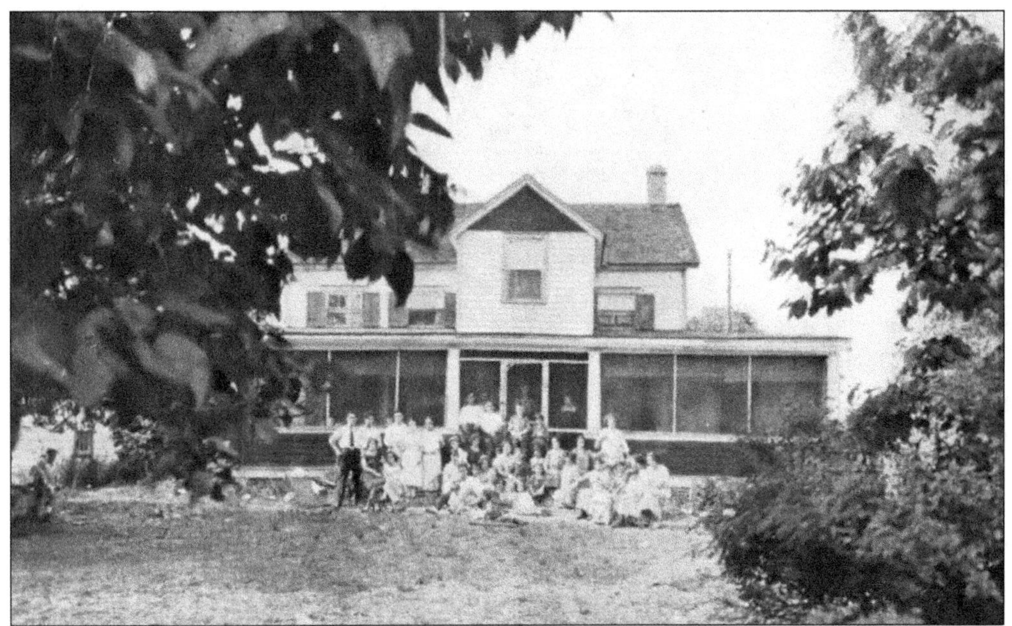

Guests gather in front of the main house for a photograph at the Villa Rodriguez around 1935. The villa is believed to have been the first of many that sprouted up in the town of Plattekill in the 1920s and 1930s. Another area that saw a similar but somewhat smaller development of Spanish villas was the Route 28 corridor of the Catskill Mountains. (Courtesy of Shirley Anson.)

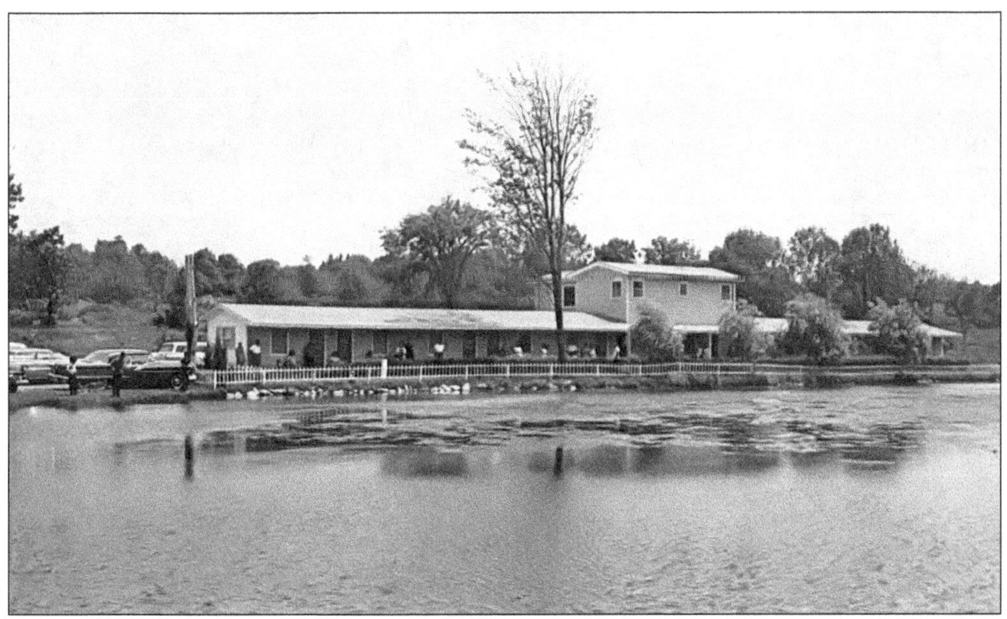

Gladys' Motel was owned and operated by Frank and Gladys Piniero. Seen here in this early-1960s photograph, the business took advantage of the overflow from villas that did not have rooms to rent or from the overflow of the villas that could not accommodate all their guests. The motel was located on a small lake, directly across from the Villa Toto on Old Unionville Road. (Courtesy of the Martinez family collection.)

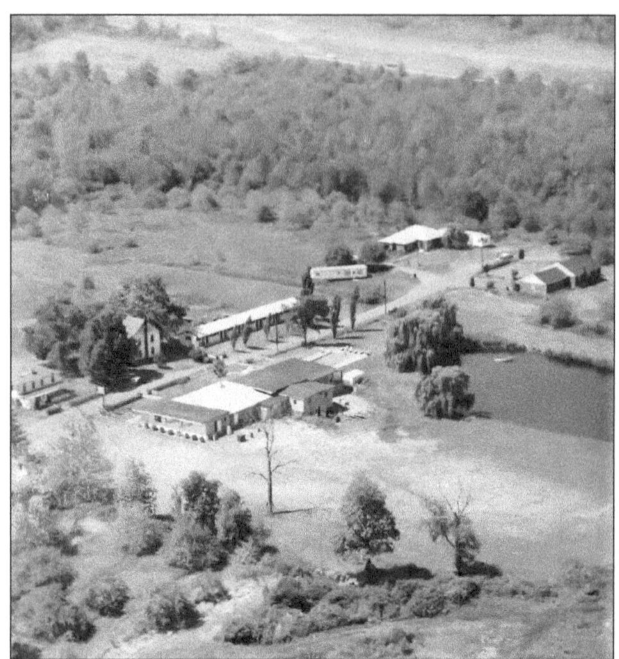

Here is a c. 1965 aerial view of Sunny Acres. The villa was transformed in the early 1950s from a 24-acre farm that had chickens, cows, pigs, and an apple orchard. The man-made pond on the right of the photograph was originally a swampy area of the property. The two houses at the top right of the photograph were the homes of the villa owners. (Courtesy of the Martinez family collection.)

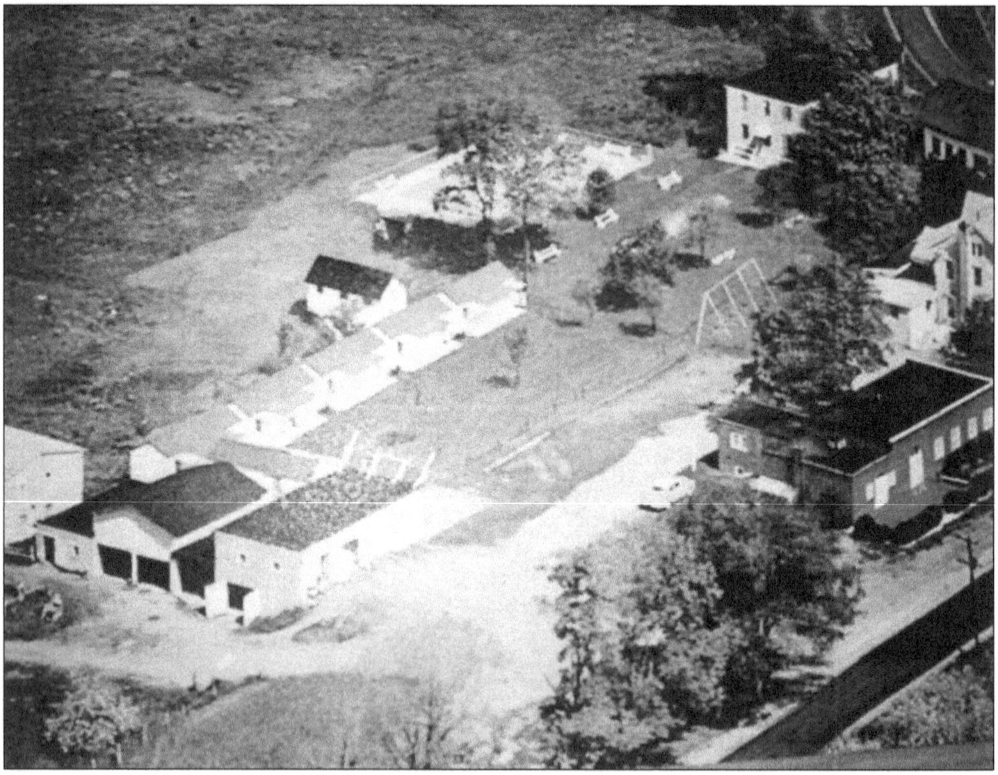

Here is a c. 1958 aerial view of Villa Garcia, with the garages at the lower left of the photograph. In the center of the photograph are the bungalows, and on the right is the building that housed the bar and dance hall. Just above that are the main house and other hotel buildings. (Courtesy of Judy Rodriguez-Gallagher.)

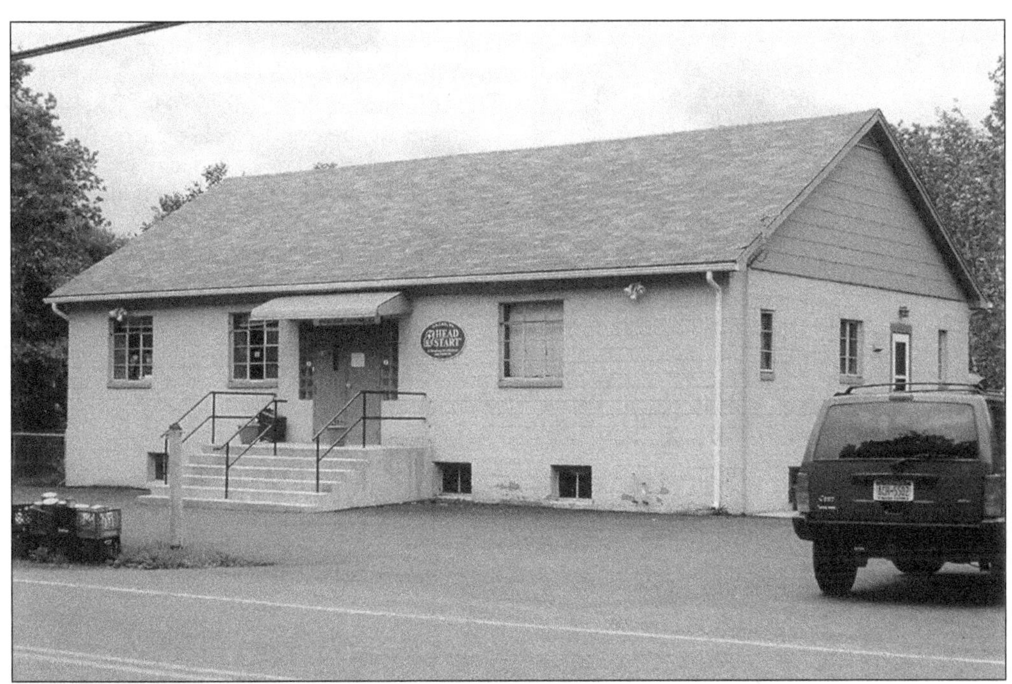

As they had done in the communities where they lived before moving to Plattekill, the Spanish residents formed an organization called the Spanish-American Social Club. During the era of Las Villas, this building was the club's home. The Spanish-American Social Club hosted many dinners, dances, and other functions for the enjoyment of the local residents. (Courtesy of the Martinez family collection.)

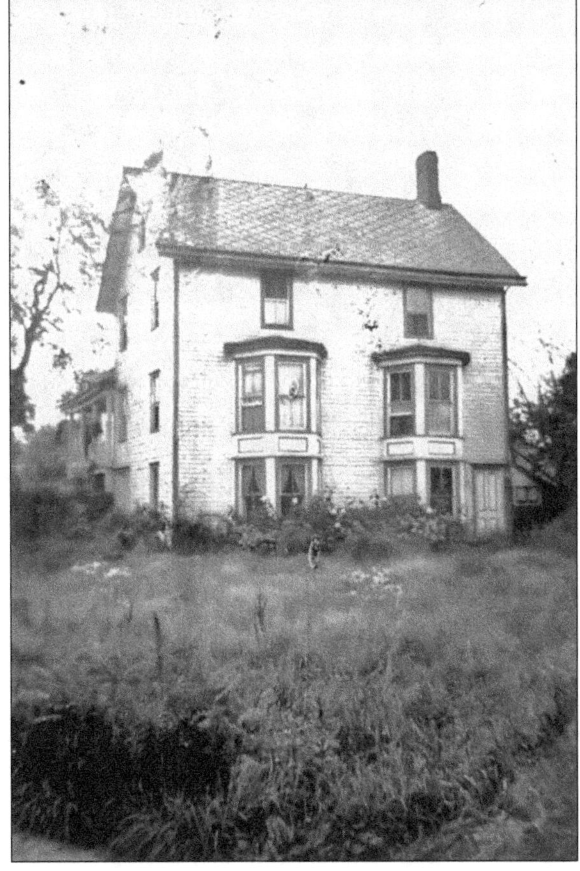

This is a backyard view of the main house at Villa Hispana, which was located on Quaker Street and owned by Alberto and Marta Gallardo. It was one of the more modest villa-farms that raised chickens and pigs but also took in boarders for the summer. Having been started in 1944, the villa had a relatively short run as the property was sold in 1952, after the unexpected passing of Alberto. (Courtesy of Nora Hammond Gallardo.)

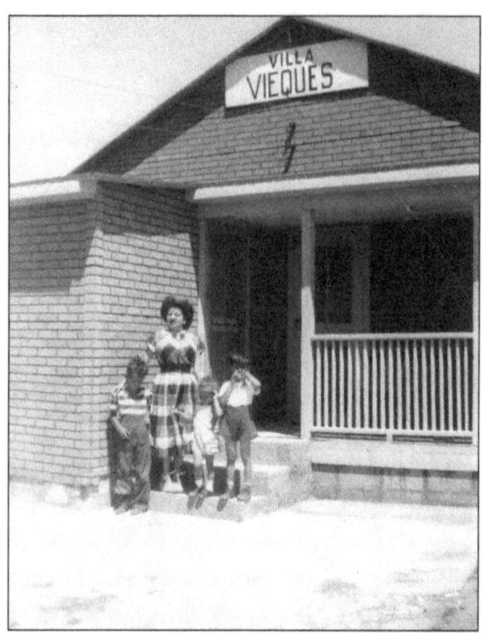

Frances Emeric stands on the front steps of the Villa Vieques with some family members. The children are, from left to right, Charlie Rodino, a nephew of the villa owners, Angelo and Leonci Flores; Frances's daughter Susan Emeric; and the villa owners' son Eddie Flores. Like most of the other villas, Villa Vieques was very much a family-run business. (Courtesy of Carmen Flores Brigham.)

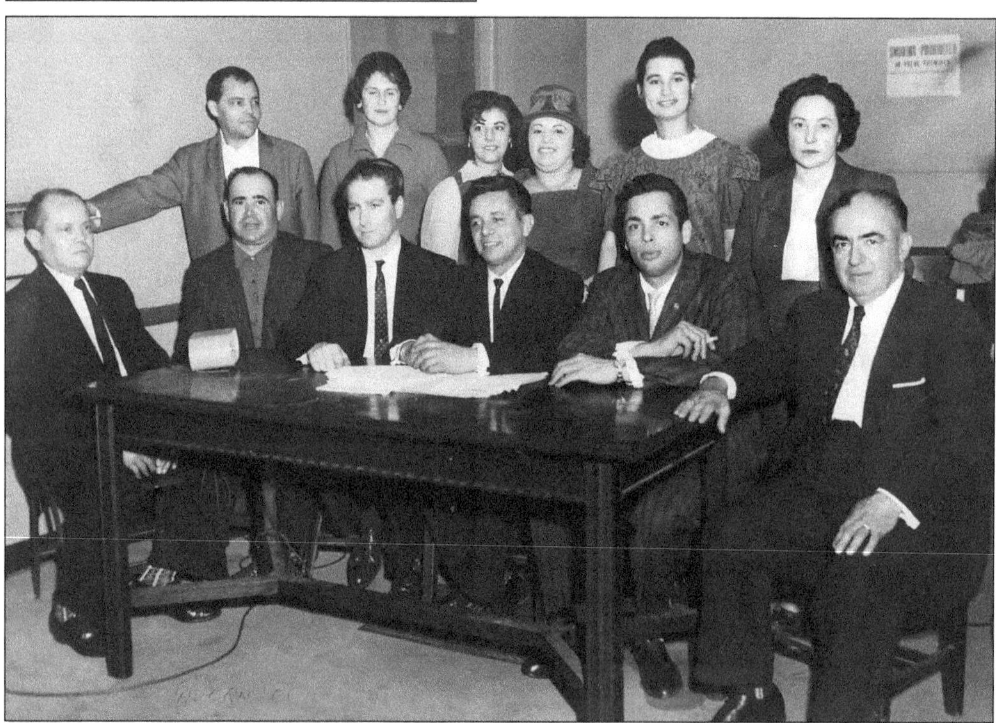

Pictured at a c. 1961 meeting, members of the Plattekill Tavern Owners Association, whose goal was to promote tourism to Las Villas, are, from left to right, (sitting) Pedro Guardarramas (Villa Guardarramas), Delfin Bilbao (Villa Garcia), Joe Vega (Villa Victoria), Shorty Martinez (Sunny Acres), Ralph Correa (R&C Drive-In Restaurant), and Daniel Perez (Casa Perez); (standing) Gabriel Guardarramas, Margaret Bilbao (Villa Garcia), Lucy Martinez and Stella Suarez (Sunny Acres), Carmen Correa (R&C Drive-in Restaurant), and Genoveva Perez (sister of Daniel Perez). (Courtesy of the Martinez family collection.)

Two

La Gente
The People

When talking about Las Villas, one must first mention the people who were its true heart and soul and made it all possible. The owners and their families, the musicians, the employees, and the tourists were all part of the fabric of what was a historically unique experience. Of all these, no one would dispute that the lifeblood of Las Villas was the owners. Their entrepreneurial spirit, hard work, dedication, and willingness to risk it all not only made this resort community possible but also made it thrive. Some were foreigners in a strange land while others were people of little means with nothing more than the promise of a dream. The majority of the owners were either Spanish or Puerto Rican; however, there were a few other Hispanic types and even an Irishman. Employees were also an integral part of the operation of any villa. At the larger villas, the owners often had to hire outside help because there was more work than the owners and their children could manage. Some villas would hire their employees for the entire summer season, and many of them would return year after year. The musicians were the entertainment and the main reason why many of the customers would make the trip to Las Villas. Many bands and entertainers also came back to perform at the same villa every year. The customers were the people who allowed the villas to make a profit and to grow. Over the next couple of decades, the customer base became much more diverse as New York City and other nearby urban areas became more of a melting pot for additional Latino groups. Puerto Ricans dominated the scene in the 1960s and 1970s, but Cubans, Dominicans, and South Americans were also well represented. As far as the other residents of the community were concerned, the villas were a mixed blessing. In the early years when the villas were small and the tourism was low, the impact to other local residents was minimal, but as the villas grew in size and the number of visitors to the region had significantly increased, the impact on the non-villa residents became more acute. Some situations or misunderstandings were brought on merely by a clash of languages and cultures. But on the whole, the villa owners got along very well with other residents of the town, both socially and in business.

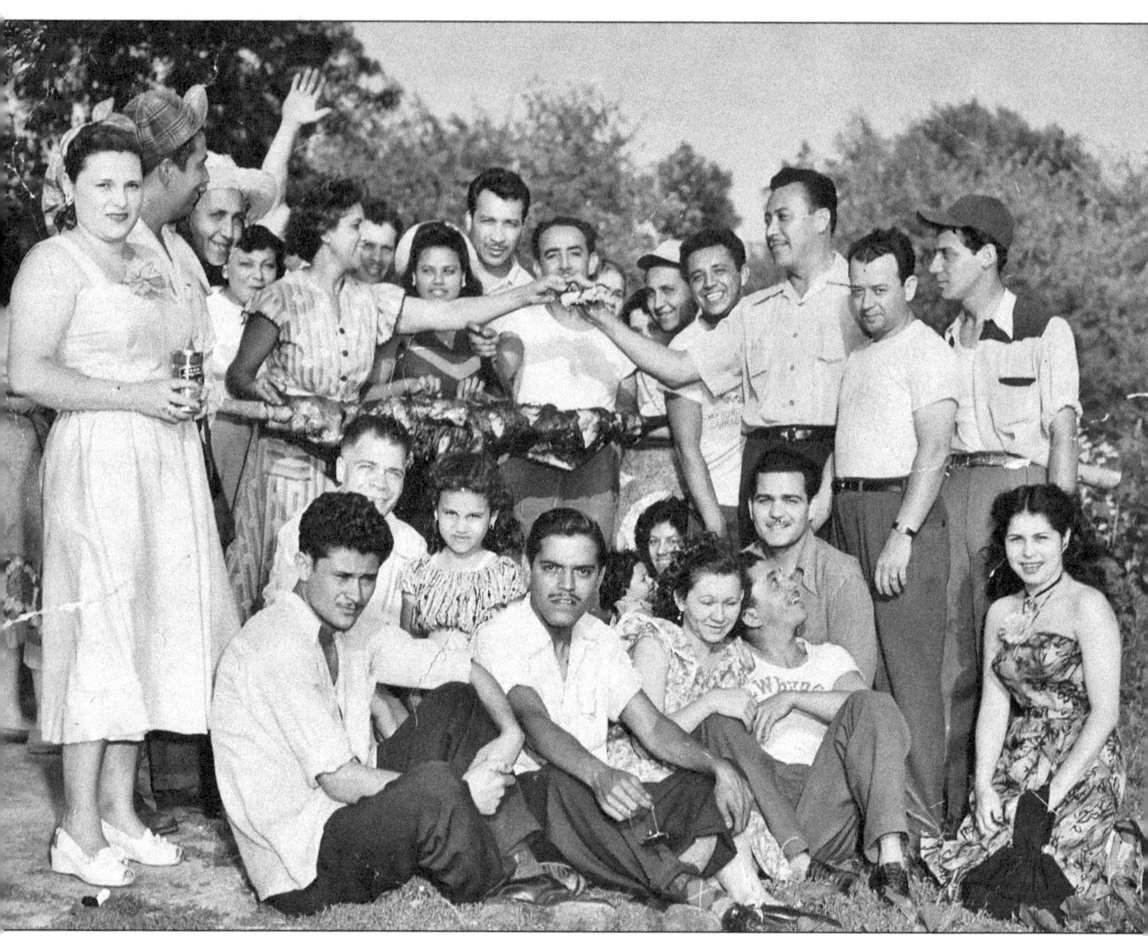

Seen around 1950, when the villa was transitioning from being a farm, members of the Martinez family are hosting a pig roast at Sunny Acres. Once the villa grew and the number of guests increased, pig roasts were no longer practical, and the pork was cooked in the kitchen and served in the dining room. The author of this book is the baby barely seen at the bottom center of the photograph. (Courtesy of the Martinėz family collection.)

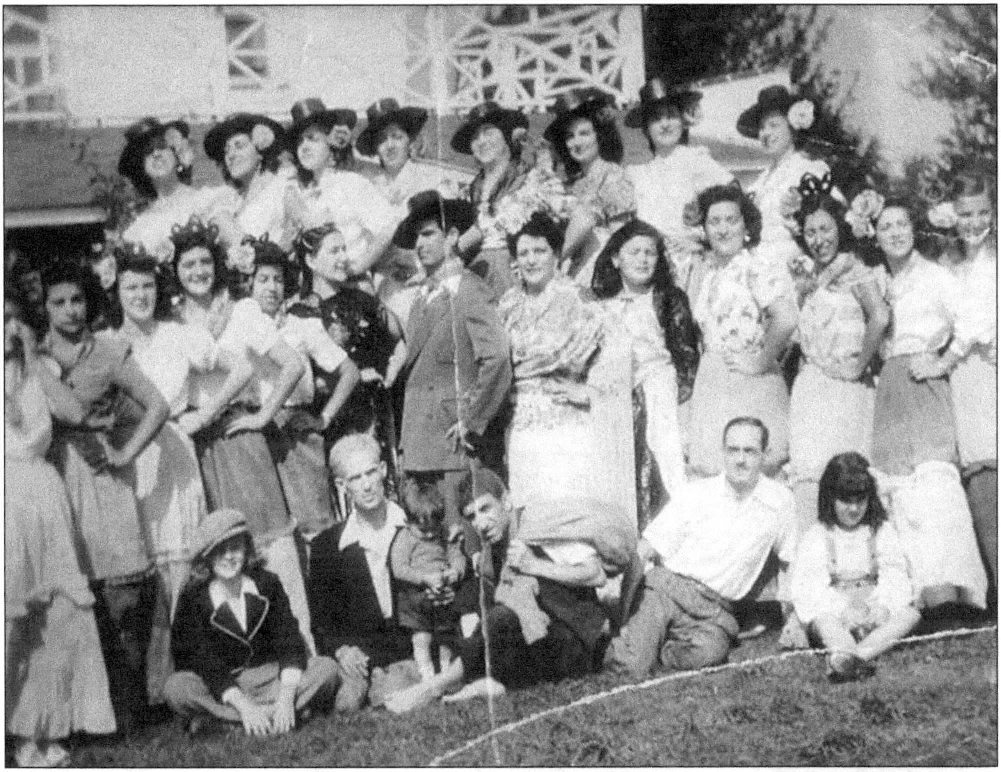

Juan Pliego, the owner of El Cortijo, is the gray-haired gentleman in the dark jacket sitting in front of this group of traditionally dressed Spaniards at his villa. Juan was from the Andalusian province of Cadiz and had previously worked as a cigar maker before starting the villa around 1940. One of Juan's friends was the great flamenco guitarist Sabicas, who also performed at El Cortijo. (Courtesy of Ronald Pliego.)

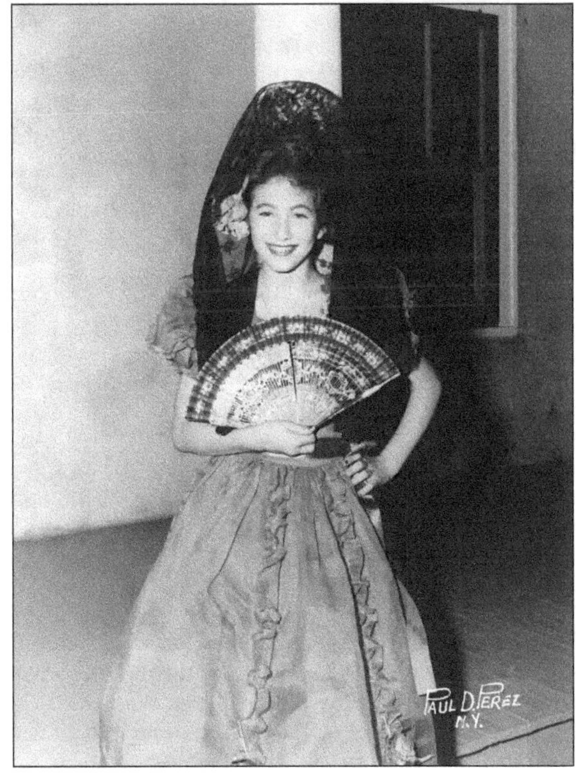

A guest at the Rifton Hotel, located in Rifton, New York, is seen in traditional Spanish dress. Alfredo Diaz and Pilar Montes Diaz, of Sama de Langreo, Spain, owned the villa; therefore, it is not surprising that many of the customs from their native country were passed on to the younger generations that visited the hotel, especially during certain holidays. (Photograph by Paul D. Perez, courtesy of Luz Damron.)

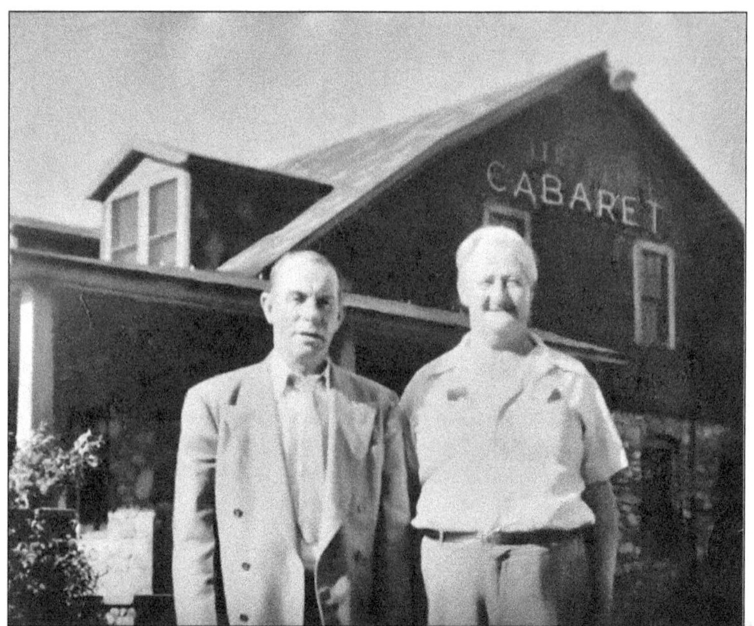

This c. 1958 photograph shows Ray Shea Sr. standing on the right; he is in front of his Villa El Nilo on Route 32 in the town of Plattekill. Shea had previously called the establishment Club El Ray when it operated as a nightclub and cabaret. The other gentleman in the picture is believed to be Shea's brother-in-law Raymond Manning. (Courtesy of the Office of the Plattekill Historian.)

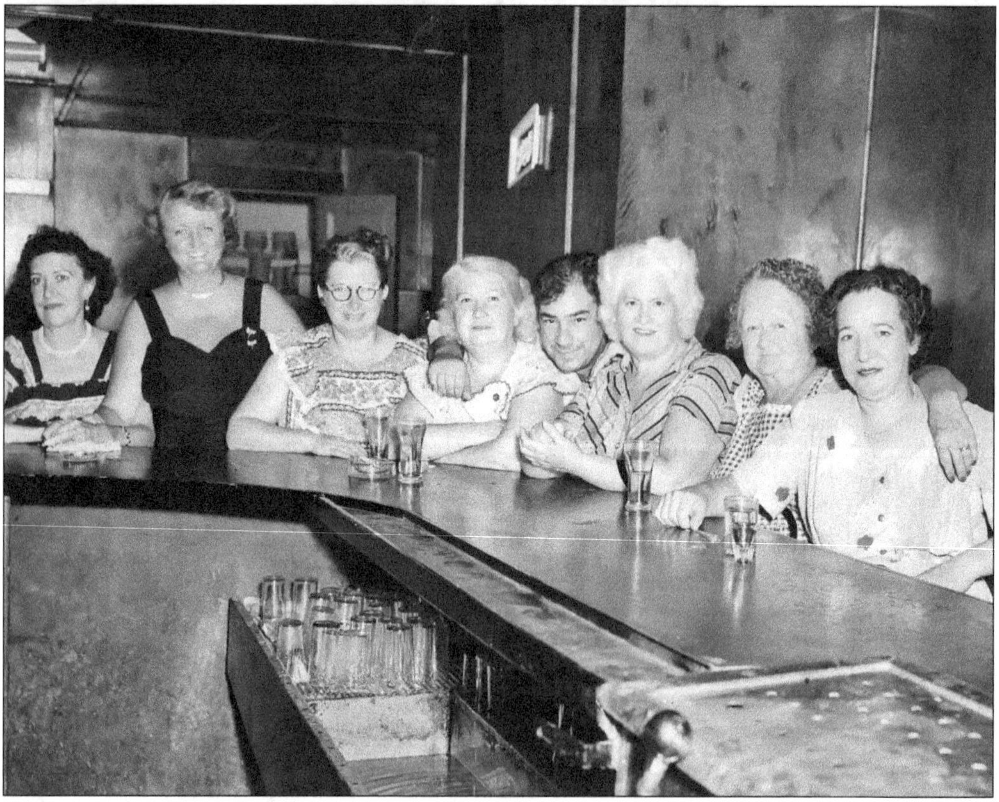

The bar at the Club El Ray/El Nilo in the 1940s was the first villa encountered as one entered the town of Plattekill from the south on Route 32. El Nilo was one of several villas that arranged for large jiras (charter bus groups) from New York City to come and enjoy a day of picnicking, listening to Latin music, and dancing. (Courtesy of Elizabeth Werlau.)

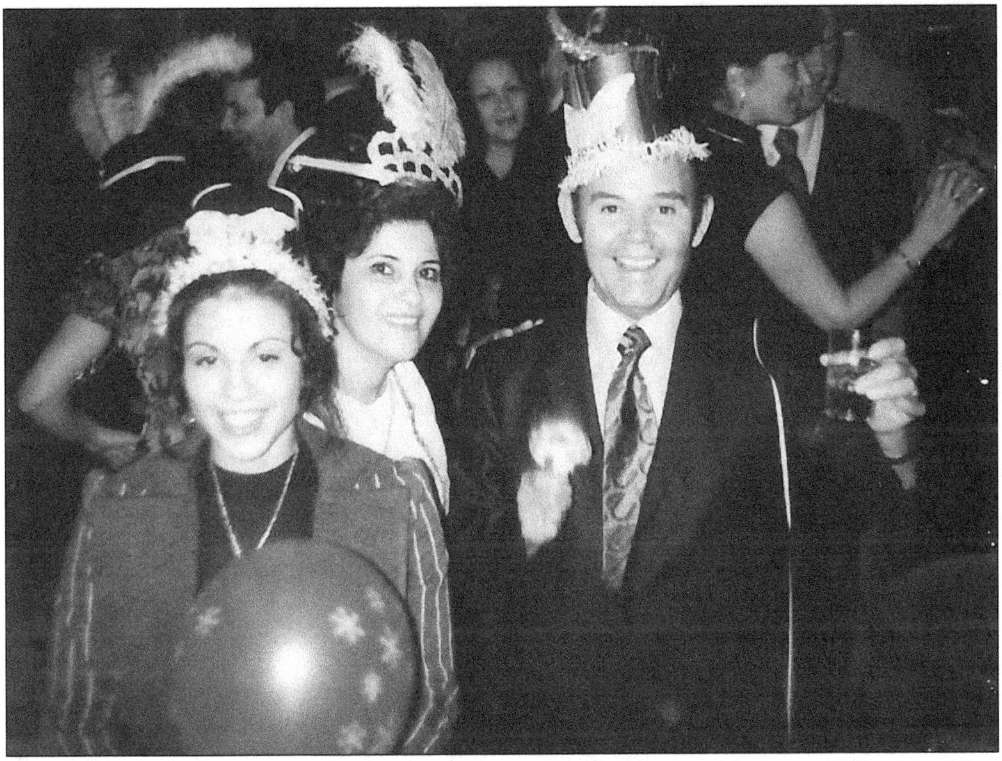

Pictured here is Brenda Charriez with her parents, Hilda and George Charriez, celebrating a New Year's Eve party at Villa Nueva, around 1972. Villa Nueva was one of the villas that became a year-round resort. After the summer vacation season was over in September, the owners would operate the business as a restaurant and catering venue. (Courtesy of Roland Charriez.)

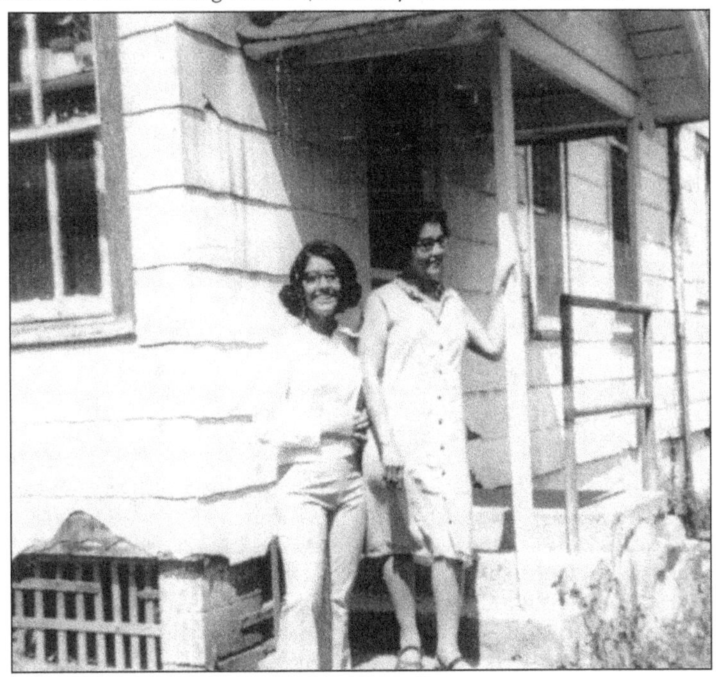

This late-1960s photograph shows Gonzala Guardarramas (on the right) and her daughter Norma outside the main house of the Villa Guardarramas. Gonzala and her husband, Pedro, owned the villa along with Pedro's brother Gabriel. Jennie, Gladys, and Iris were the other daughters of Pedro and Gonzala. (Courtesy of Norma Guardarramas.)

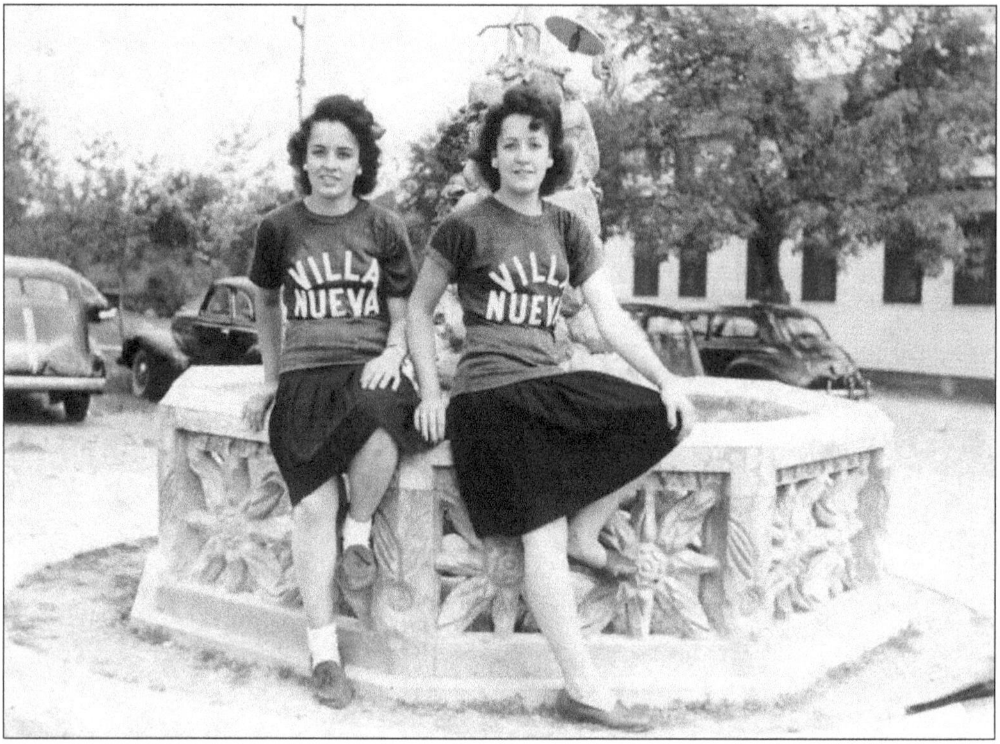

Sisters Louisa (left) and Amor "Chata" Garcia pose in front of the fountain at the Villa Nueva in the 1940s. The fountain was a very recognizable landmark at the villa, owned by their parents, Severino and Amor Garcia, originally from Asturias, Spain. Amor "Chata" Garcia would eventually become the face of the villa and very well known throughout the community. (Courtesy of Amor "Chata" Lasini.)

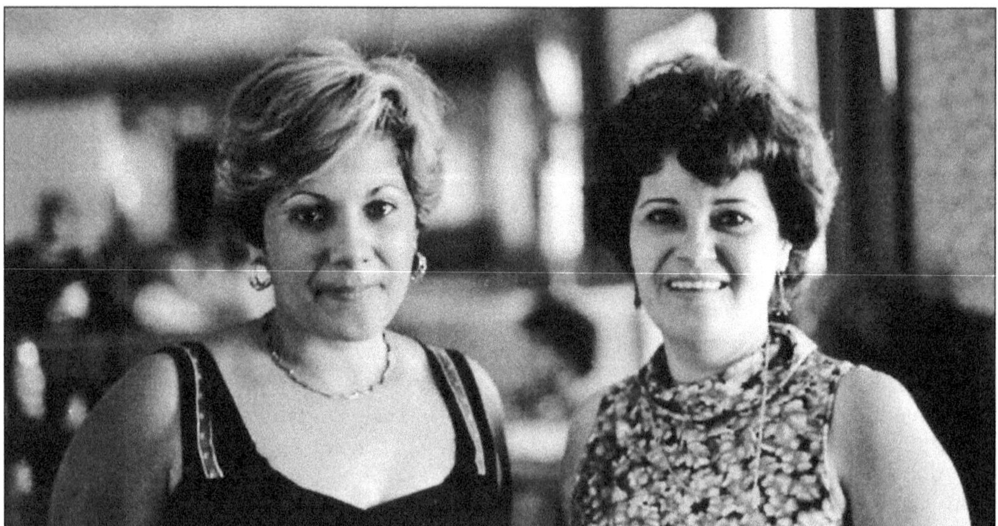

This c. 1974 picture shows Mildred Schlichting (left) with her cousin and Plattekill resident Hilda Charriez at the Villa Galicia. Many of the locals enjoyed spending the day with relatives at any one of the many villas where they could dance to the music, have a drink, and perhaps, catch a bite to eat. (Courtesy of Roland Charriez.)

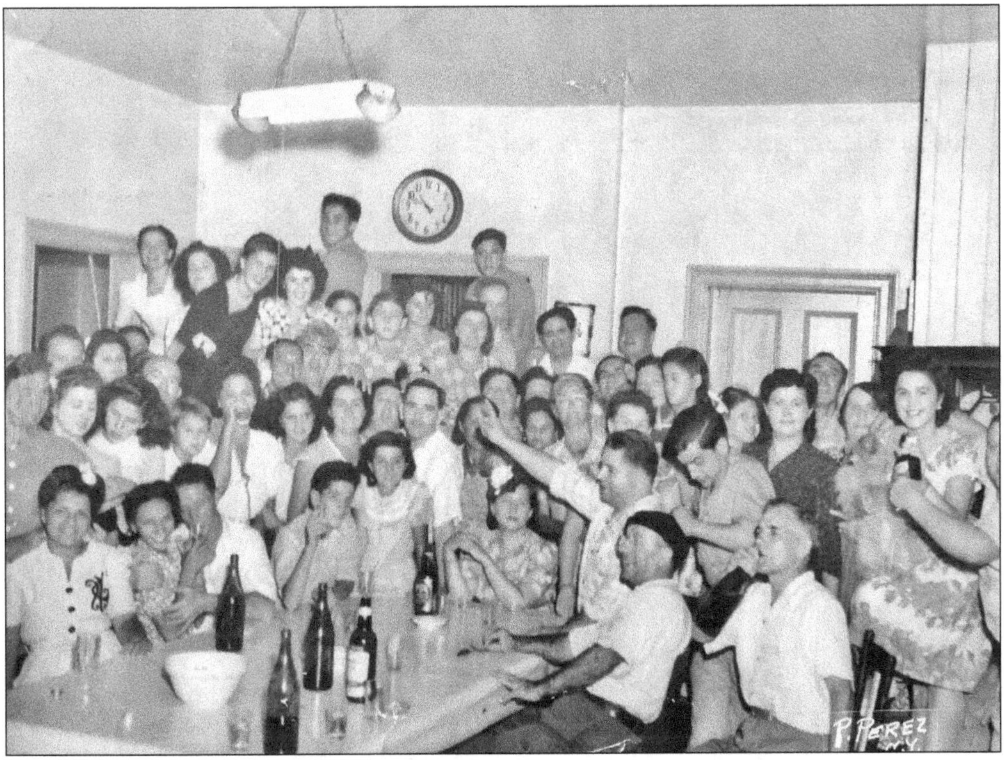

Guests at the Villa Garcia cram together in the villa's kitchen for a group photograph opportunity. The obvious familiarity of the group indicates that it was most likely made up of several families, possibly belonging to the same social club or organization. Margaret Bilbao, the daughter of the owners, Celestino and Flora Garcia, can be seen at the top of the picture in the black-and-white patterned dress. (Courtesy of Marina Rios Frees.)

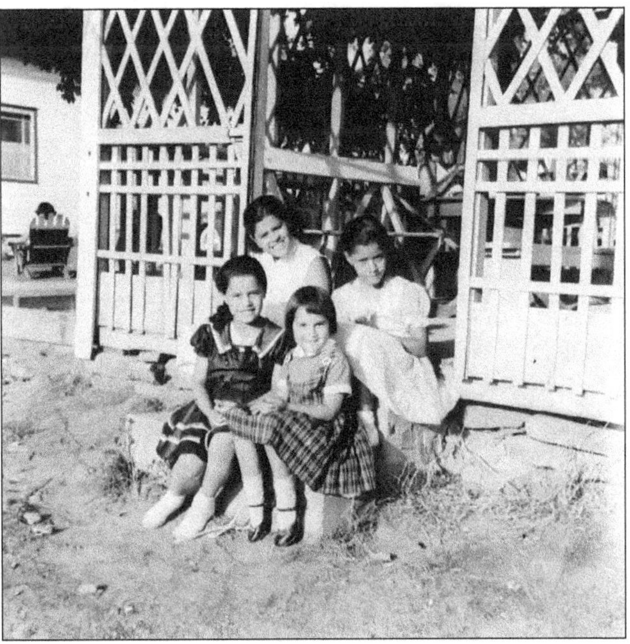

The Guardarramas and Correa families purchased the Villa Rodriguez on Unionville Road in 1957. While waiting for the deal to close, the families stayed at the Villa Garcia. Once purchased, the owners changed the name of the Villa Rodriguez to the Villa Guardarramas. The daughters of the new owners are, from left to right, (first row) Gladys Guardarramas and Yvonne Correa; (second row) Jennie Guardarramas and Norma Guardarramas. (Courtesy of Yvonne Correa Morales.)

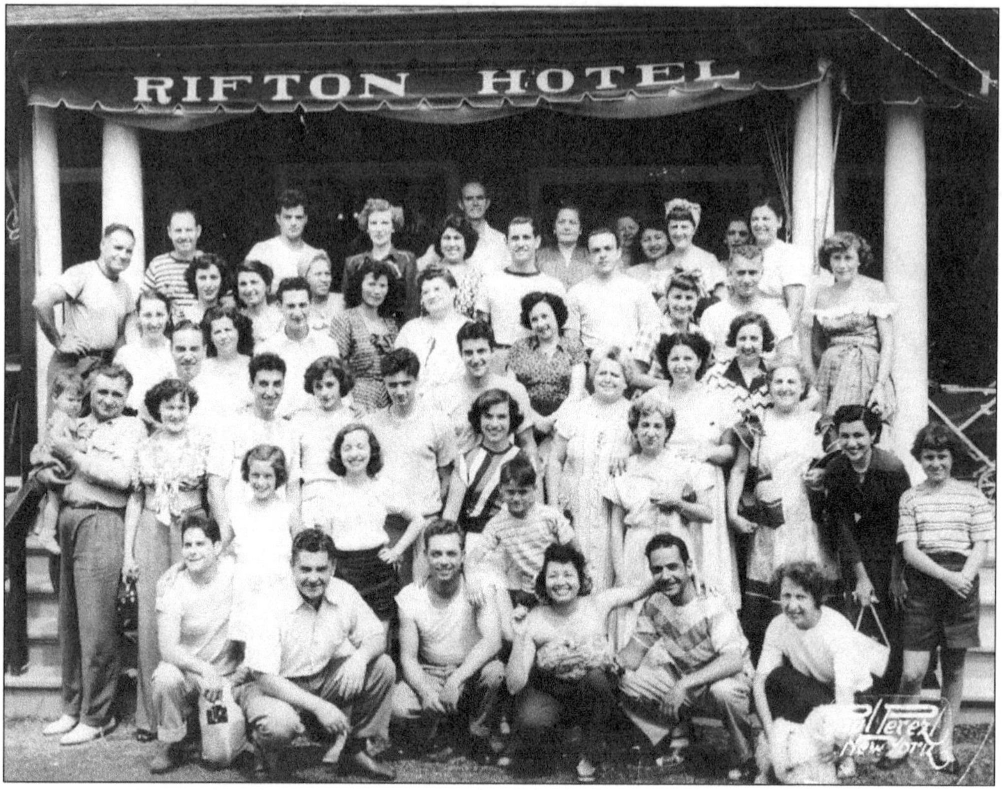

The Rifton Hotel in Rifton, New York, was an outlier of the Spanish villas in that it was located neither in Plattekill nor on the Route 28 corridor. Nonetheless, it was in the Hudson Valley and very similar to the other Hispanic villas. (Photograph by Paul D. Perez, courtesy of Luz Damron.)

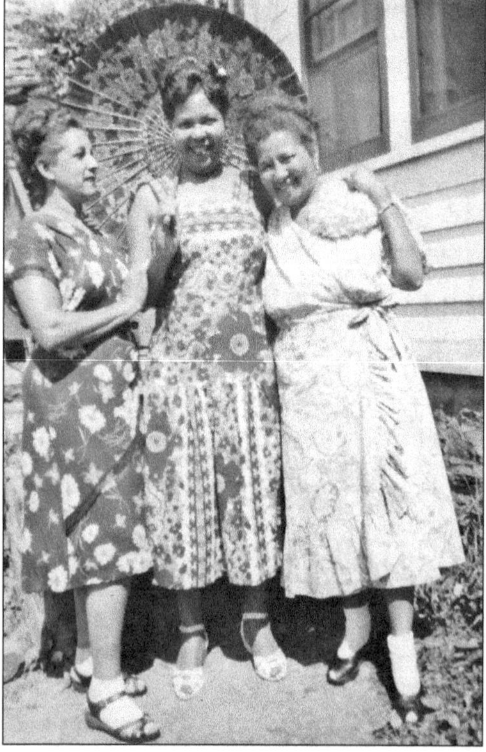

Enjoying the day at the Villa Hispana around 1943 are, from left to right, Irene Martinez, Ana Davoli, and unidentified. The farm-villa was located on Quaker Street between Mill Street and Church Street on the Plattekill town line. The decorative parasol being held by Davoli was used to shield oneself from the sun. This item is a throwback to the 19th century, when it was a common accoutrement for women. (Courtesy of Nora Gallardo.)

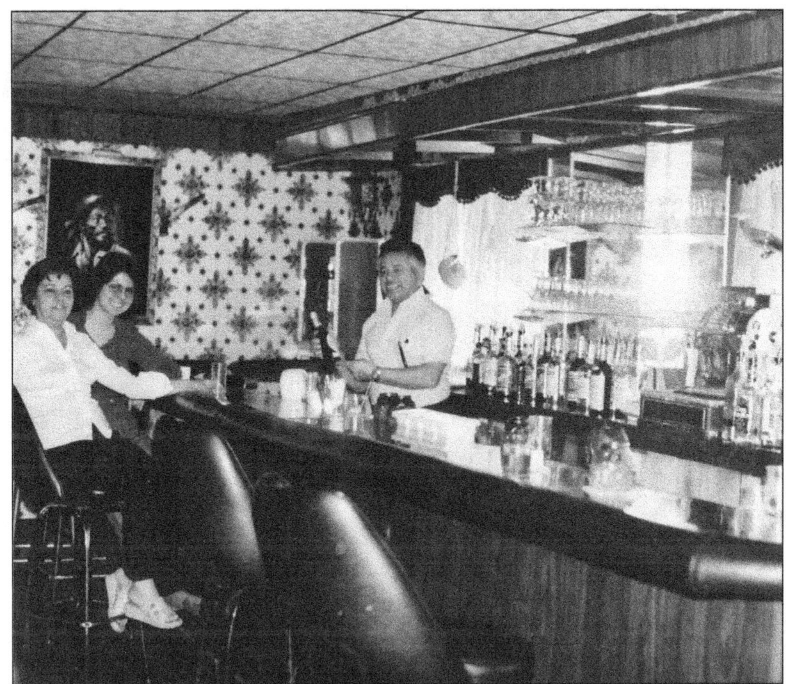

Seen around 1975, the bar at La Copa offered just about every variety of drink. The restaurant was open year-round, and, at times, featured live music suitable for casual dining. Though not a villa in the usual sense, it was centrally located in the village and offered the locals and visitors to the villas another dining alternative. (Courtesy of the Martinez family collection.)

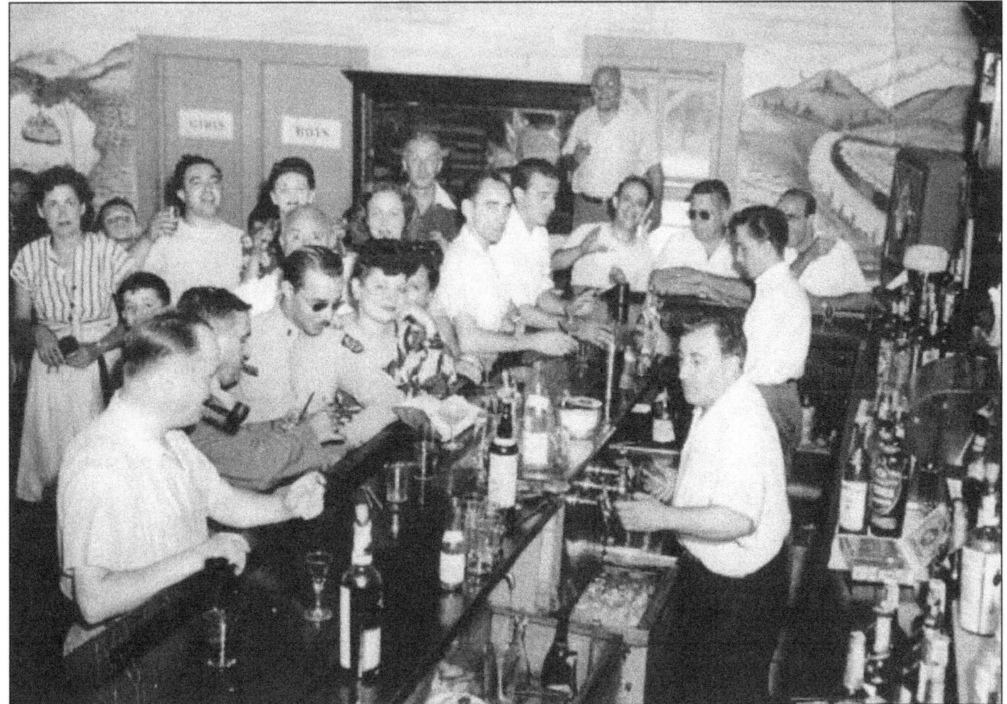

A busy bar area at the Rifton Hotel is depicted in this c. 1945 photograph. Note the uniformed serviceman with the dark glasses; his attire might indicate that World War II was still in progress. Though the hotel was mostly frequented by Spaniards, it also was an attractive getaway for Puerto Ricans, Cubans, and South Americans, among others. (Photograph by Paul D. Perez, courtesy of Luz Diaz Damron.)

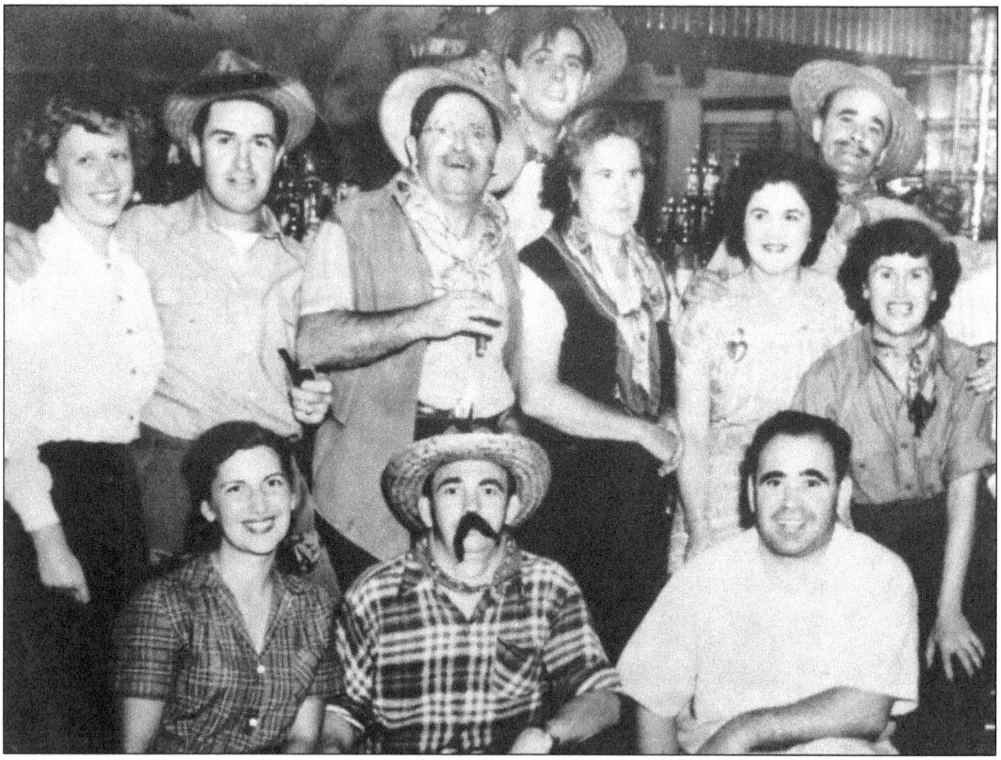

Celestino and Flora Garcia, standing at center with members of their family, were the owners of the Villa Garcia. To the right of Celestino are the Garcias' son Ralph and his wife, Millie. On the far right of the photograph is the Garcias' daughter Margaret, sitting behind her husband, Delfin Bilbao. (Courtesy of Denise Garcia-Cornog.)

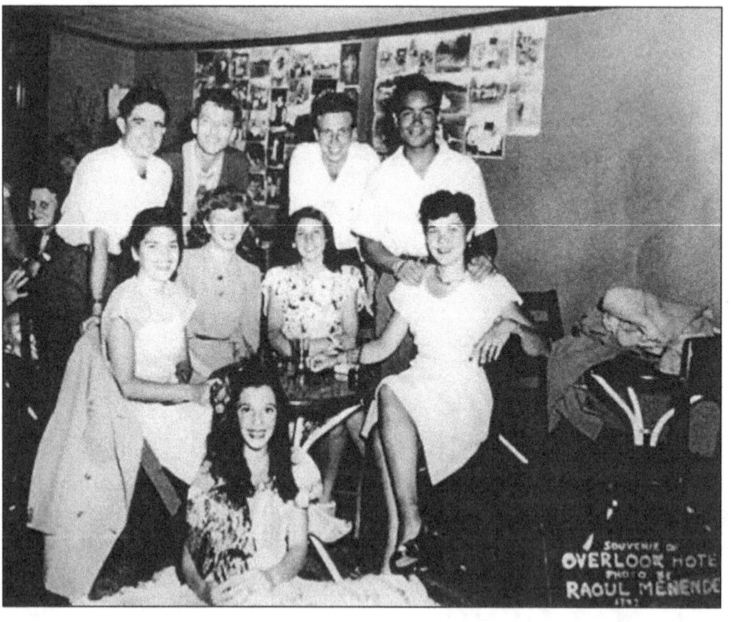

The Overlook Hotel was another outlier of the Spanish resorts, being neither in Plattekill nor on the Route 28 corridor but in Ellenville, New York. Identified in this photograph are Dolores Sanchez, sitting at the far left, and Manuel "Cuckie" Vazquez, standing at the far left. (Photograph by Raoul Menendez, courtesy of Nancy Vazquez-Camardo.)

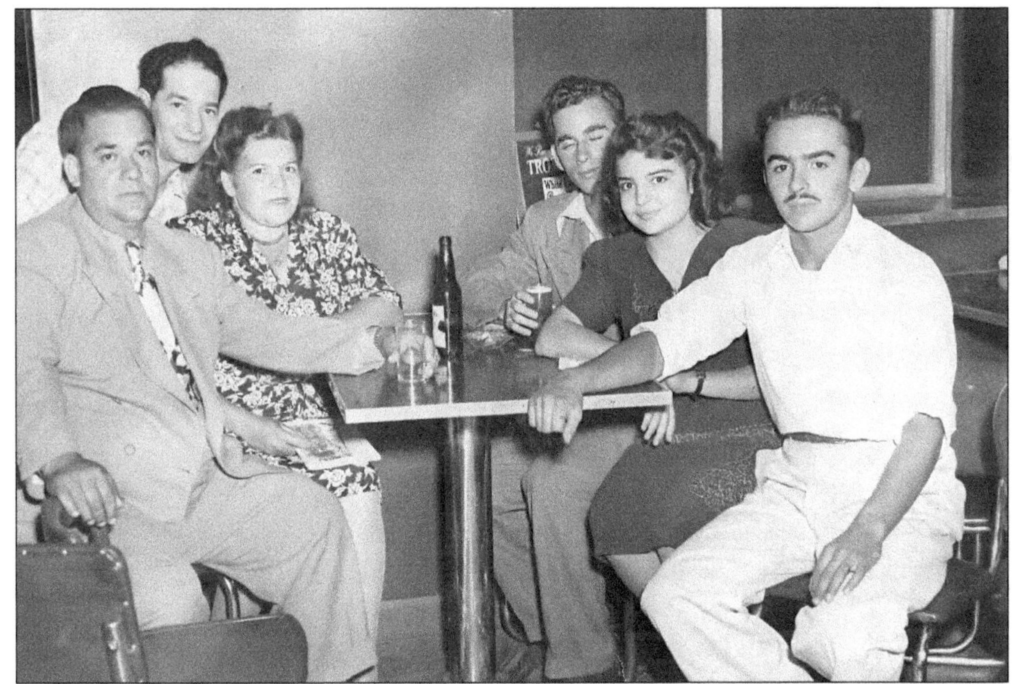

Radames Santiago, wearing the suit jacket on the left, and his wife, Josefina, owners of the Casa Roxana, enjoy a night out with some friends at the nearby Casa Perez. Unlike the Casa Roxana, the Casa Perez had live music and entertainment on the weekends, which drew many New York City guests as well as locals who enjoyed the sounds of Latin music. (Courtesy of Roxy Santiago.)

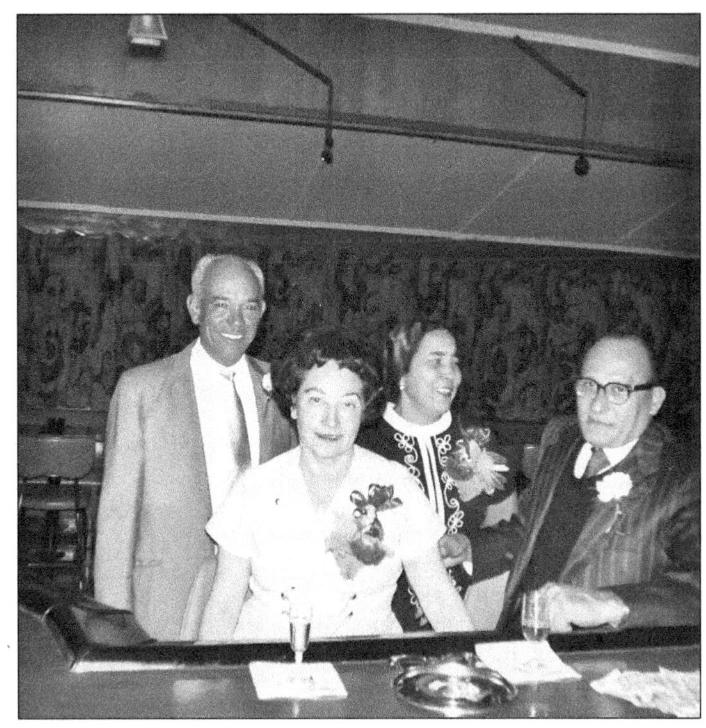

Every year, one of the villas would have a Mother's Day Dance, which, for the most part, kicked off the season for this resort area. The event was very popular and heavily attended by members of the community. Identified in this photograph: Frank Pineiro, standing behind Genoveva Perez, the sister of Daniel Perez, who owned Casa Perez. (Courtesy of the Martinez family collection.)

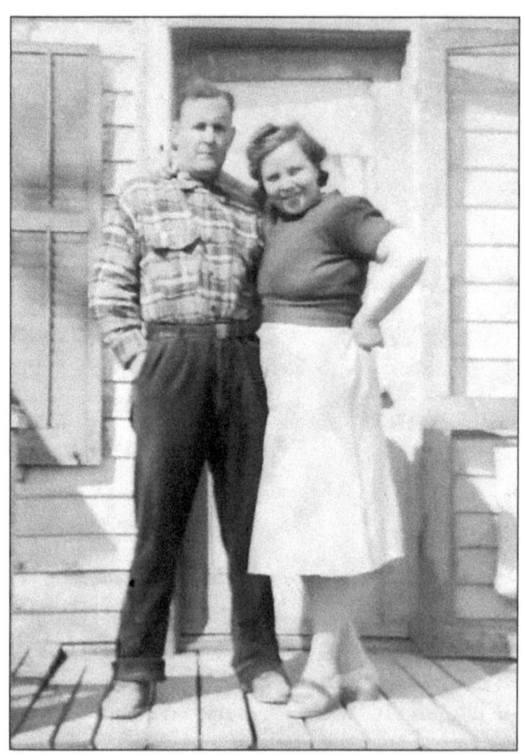

Isidoro and Elvira Romero owned and operated the Casa Los Andes from about 1941 until 1956. Isidoro was from Chile, and Elvira was originally from Argentina. At first, they catered to a clientele of Jewish and Italian tourists, but the resort eventually became a destination for South Americans and other Hispanic groups from the Greater New York City area. (Courtesy of Henry Romero.)

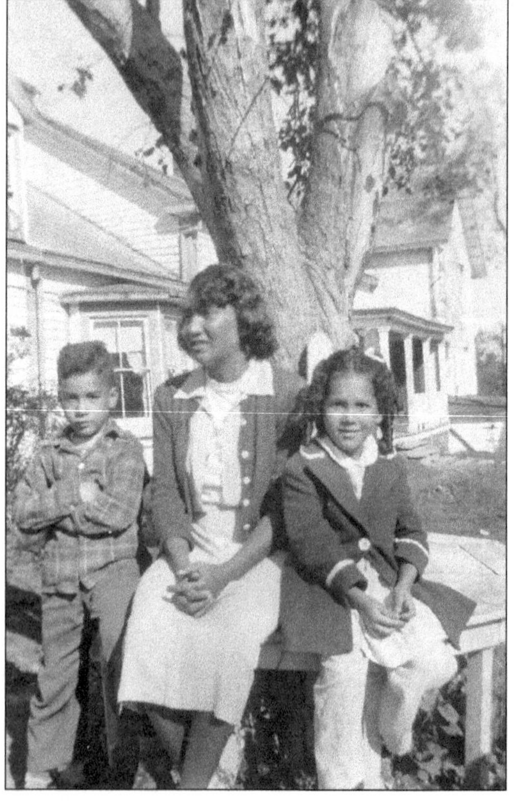

The children of Alberto and Marta Gallardo, owners of the Villa Hispana, are seen out in front of the main house. The Gallardos were originally from Cuba and purchased the farm around 1944 before operating it as both a villa and farm. They also raised pigs and usually roasted the pigs on a spit over an open wood-burning fire pit. The children are, from left to right, Alberto Gallardo Jr., Diana Gallardo, and Nora Gallardo. (Courtesy of Nora Hammond Gallardo.)

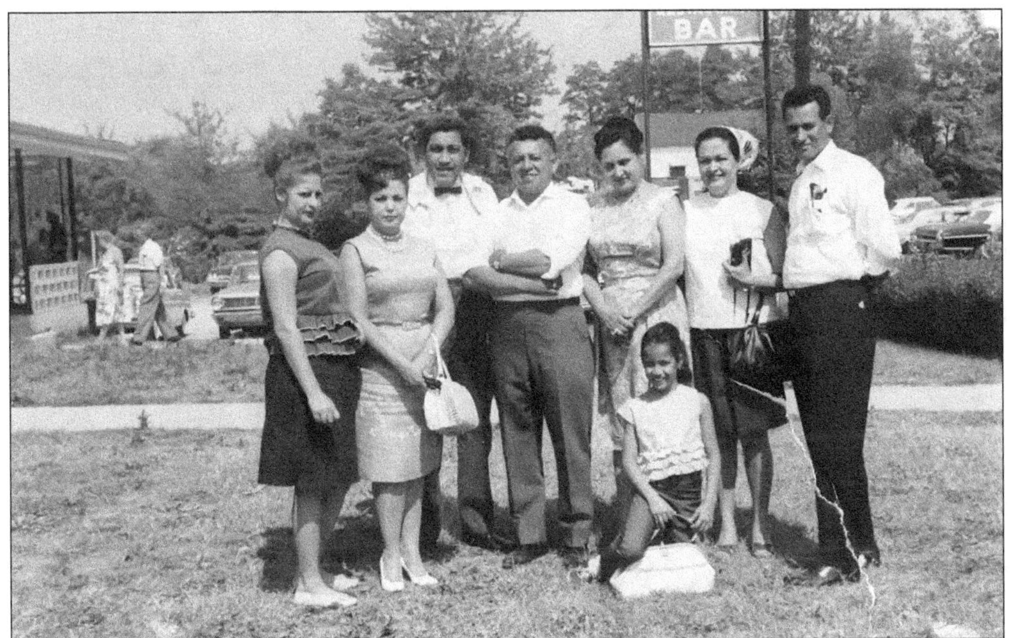

Shorty Martinez (center), the owner of the Sunny Acres Hotel, is seen around 1967 with guests. This picture was taken on the lawn in front of the dance hall, which would have been to the left of where they are standing. Shorty was a well-known personality, both at the villa and around town. He was always happy to oblige visitors, who frequently requested that he pose for pictures with them. (Courtesy of the Martinez family collection.)

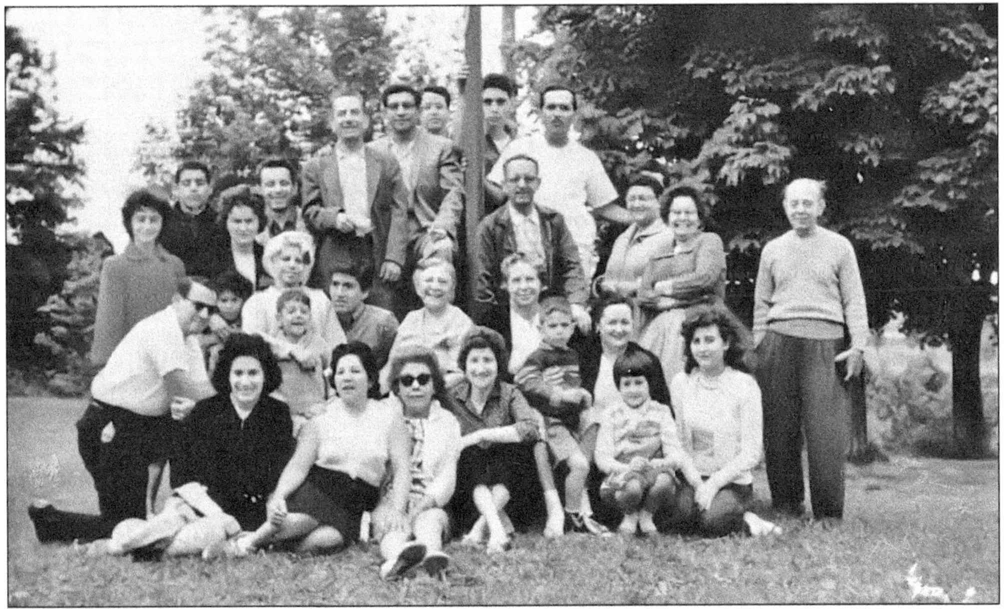

The Baldasarri, Rodriguez, Graniela, and Leoro families gather for a photograph by the iconic flagpole at the Villa Madrid around 1961. Villa owner Dona Pilar Tafall sits in the middle of the group, just to the left of the flagpole. Like other villas, the Villa Madrid had its share of loyal customers who came back year after year because they enjoyed the peaceful atmosphere of the resort. (Courtesy of Sue and Bill Rodriguez.)

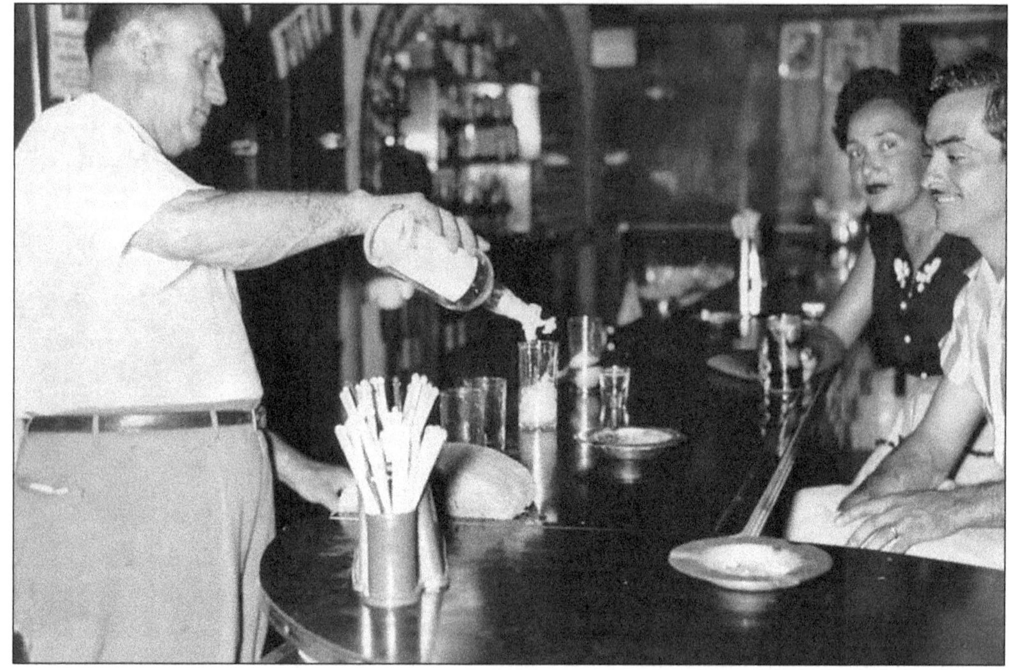

Antonia and Roberto Perez are being served a cocktail by bartender Julio Gonzalez at the Villa Nueva. The nightlife was a big part of the villa experience, and a fair number of drinks were served up on weekends. During the 1960s, the typical price for a mixed drink would cost anywhere from $1.25 to $2, while a beer might cost between 75¢ and $1.25. (Courtesy of Robert Perez.)

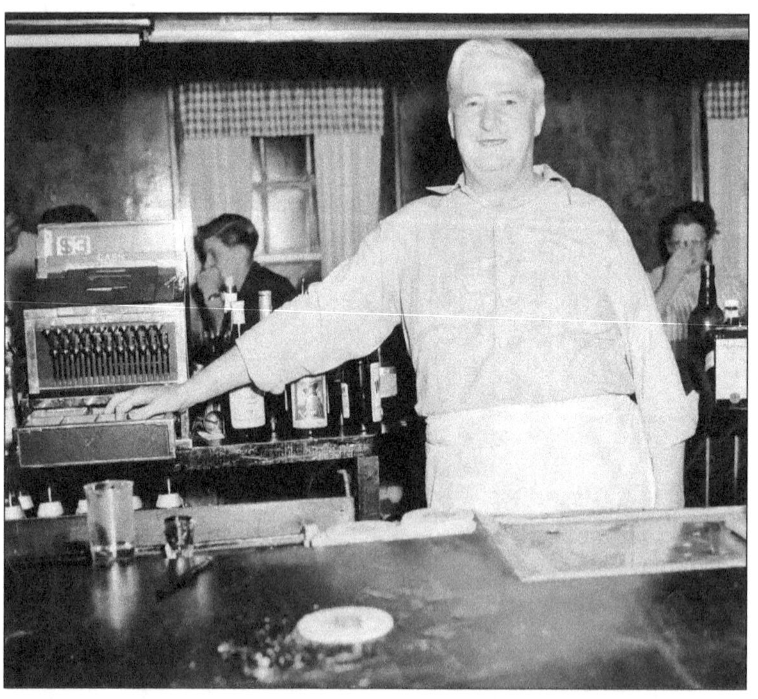

Ray Shea tends bar at his nightclub Club El Ray in the 1940s. The name was eventually changed to El Nilo. Ray Jr. would take over the business, and from the 1950s on, it catered mostly to the Hispanic weekenders who came to the villas in throngs. On weekends, more than a few pigs would be roasted outside on open spits for the large crowds. (Courtesy of Elizabeth Werlau.)

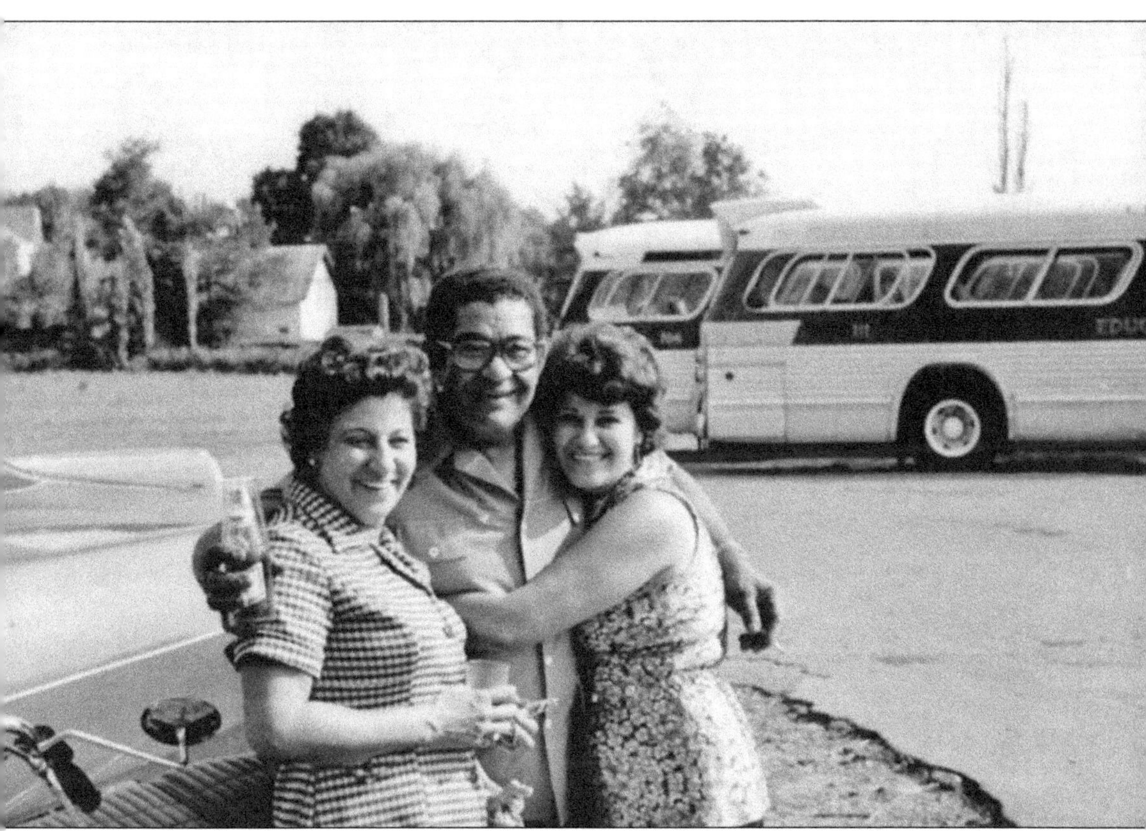

Sharing a lighthearted moment at the Villa Galicia are Ada and Miguel Quevedo, on the left, with their cousin and Plattekill resident Hilda Charriez. The buses (jiras) seen in the background were a common sight at some of the villas, as social clubs and other groups organized trips to the various villas through bus charters. (Courtesy of Roland Charriez.)

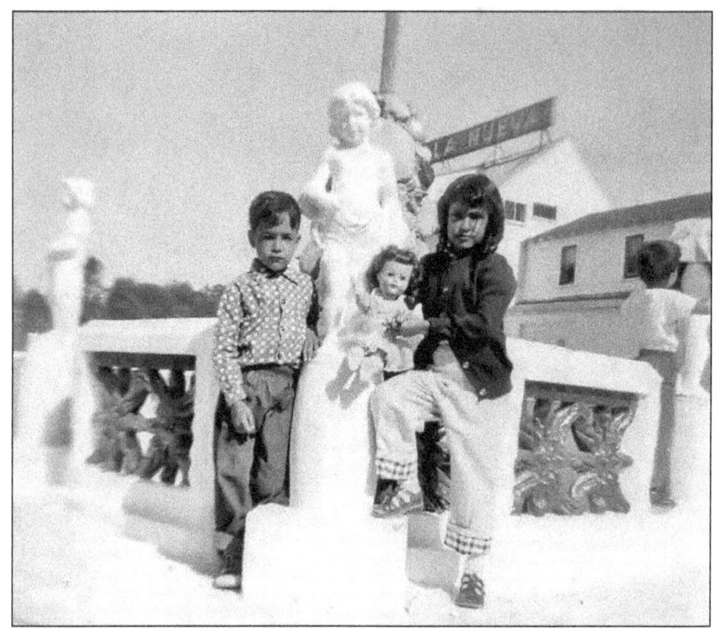

Robert Perez and his sister Linda are pictured at the Villa Nueva in the early 1950s. This villa was the favorite vacation destination for their parents, Roberto and Antonia Perez. The villa had a swimming pool, a playground, and other amenities that drew families with children to the resort. In general, Las Villas was very family oriented, so the sight of children in all areas of Las Villas was quite common. (Courtesy of Robert Perez.)

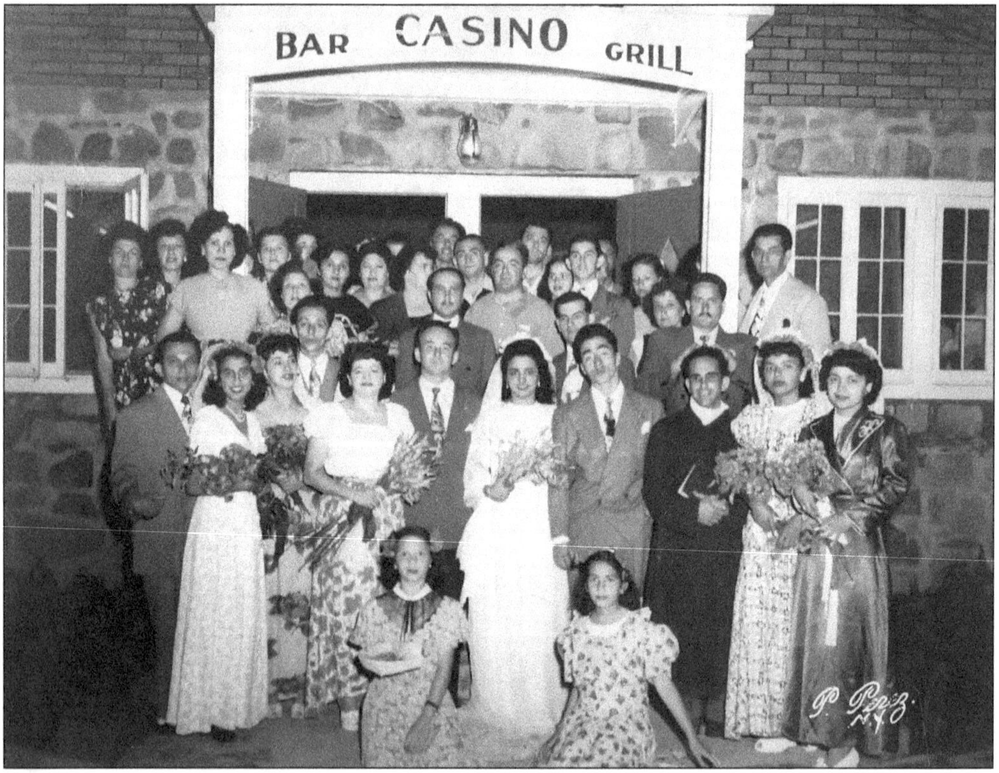

The Casa Perez was located on Unionville Road and was owned by Daniel Perez, a native of Spain. Not only were the villas a popular weekend getaway, but they were also popular venues for weddings. In this photograph, Daniel, standing at center and not wearing a suit jacket, poses with a wedding party in front of the entrance to the dance hall at the villa around 1950. (Courtesy of Roxy Santiago.)

This c. 1954 photograph shows Bill and Sue Rodriguez at the Villa Madrid. Sue's parents, Miguel and Carmen Baldassari, had been vacationing at the Villa Madrid since the 1930s and were among the first of the Puerto Rican families from New York City to discover this mecca of Spanish villas in the rural town of Plattekill. (Courtesy of Sue and Bill Rodriguez.)

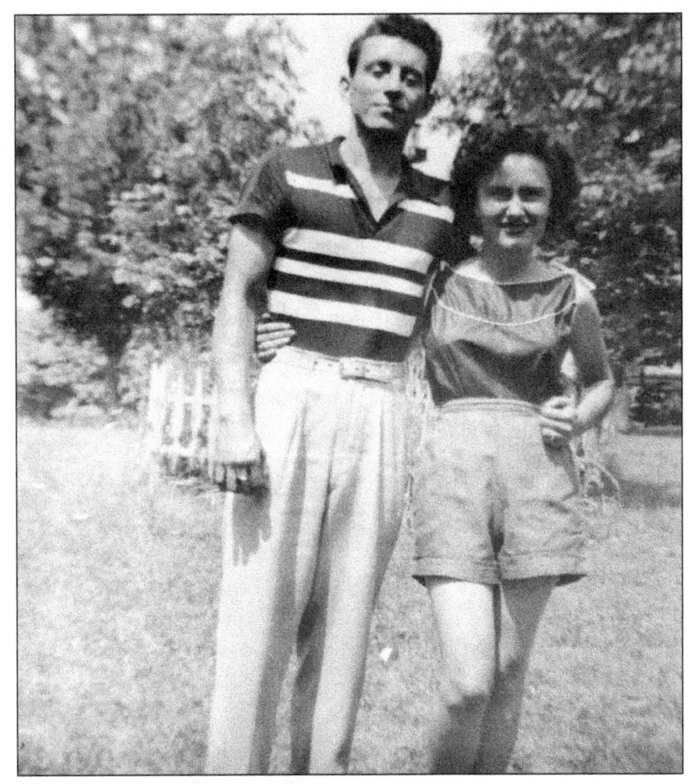

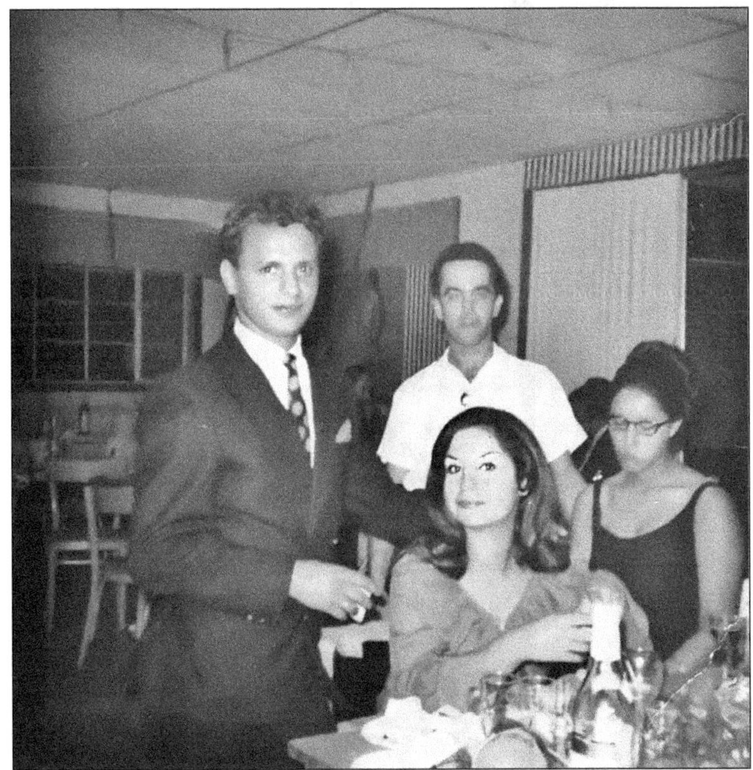

The busiest night for Las Villas was Saturday night. Music and dancing were in full swing, many drinks were sold, and a lot of food—especially sandwiches and side dishes—was ordered. Seen in the company of Victor Serrano and Norma Guardarramas, Larry and Frannie Martinez (in front) are enjoying a night out at Sunny Acres around 1967. (Courtesy of the Martinez family collection.)

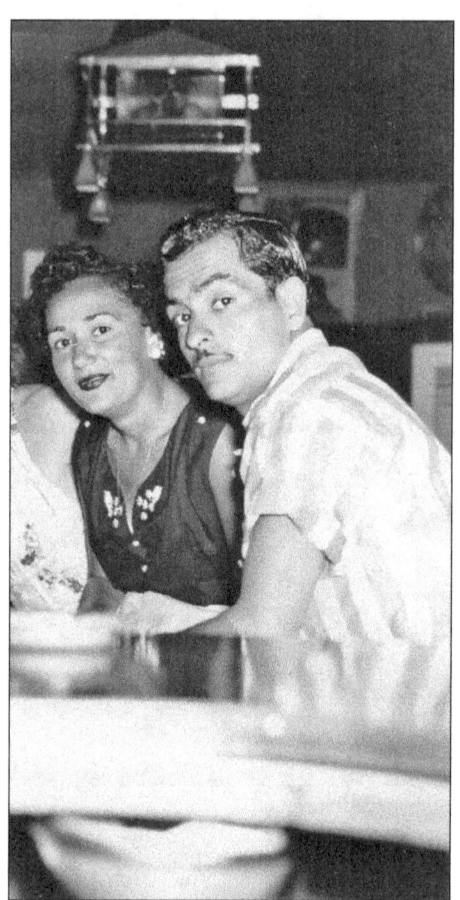

Antonia and Roberto Perez were frequent guests at the Villa Nueva during the 1950s. They had two small children and probably felt that it had a very family-friendly atmosphere, many amenities, and fun things for the kids to do. (Courtesy of Robert Perez.)

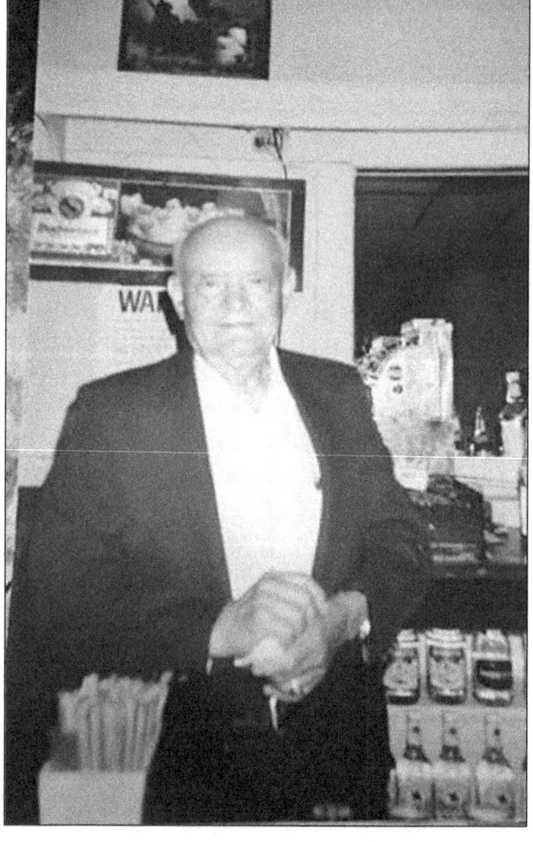

Pedro Guardarramas, co-owner of the Villa Guardarramas in Plattekill was the son of a sugarcane worker in Puerto Rico. As a young man, he worked as a dishwasher at the Commodore Hotel in New York City. Like most of the villa owners, he came from humble beginnings, but through hard work and perseverance, he ran a successful business for over 30 years. (Courtesy of Tara J. Quinones.)

Bob Perez sits atop a sawhorse while on an early-1950s vacation with his family at the Villa Nueva. Unlike the children of later generations, the kids of that era made do by playing with everyday objects. With imagination, an ordinary sawhorse could easily become a knight's great steed or Hopalong Cassidy's majestic white horse, Topper. (Courtesy of Bob Perez.)

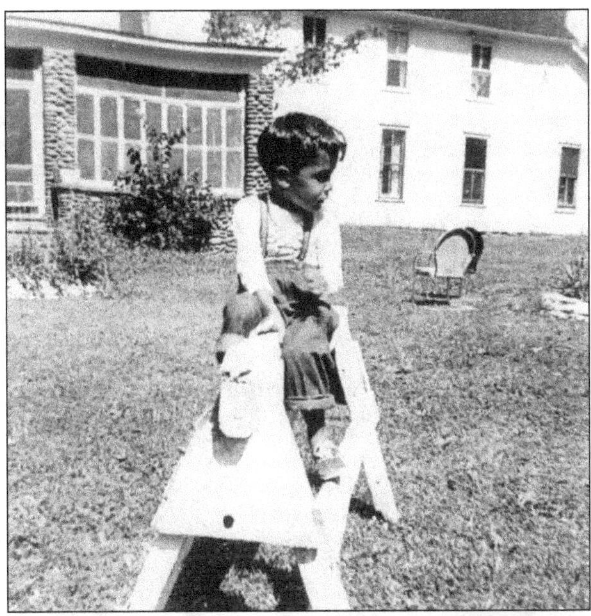

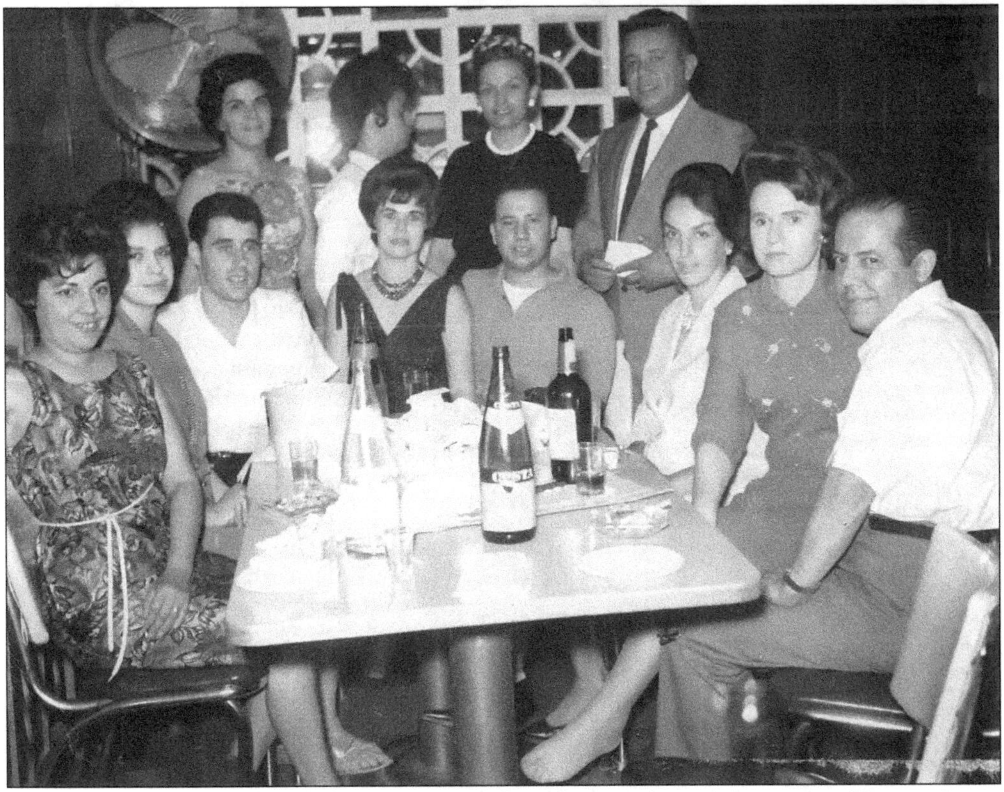

Lucy (sitting on the left) and Shorty Martinez (standing on the right), owners of Sunny Acres, gather with family and friends in the dance hall area of the villa around 1963. Others in the photograph are, from left to right, (sitting) Ilia Badillo, Manny Badillo, Carol Martinez, Ron Martinez, Toni Torrens, Lucy Candelario, and Joe Candelario; (standing) Marina Arzuaga, Irene Suarez, and Esther ?, the on-site beautician. (Courtesy of the Martinez family collection.)

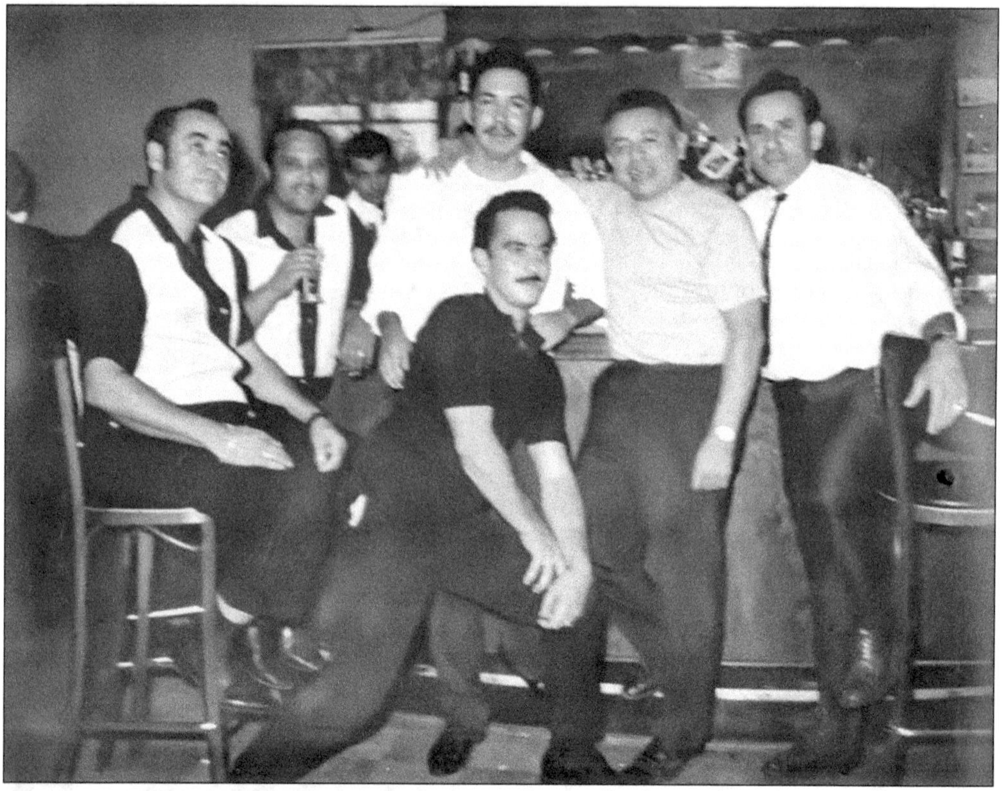

On September 13, 1969, villa musicians, employees, and owners found a few moments to socialize at the bar of the Villa Galicia. Seated on the far left is Carmelo Rosado, bandleader for the Trio Los Azores. In the center are a Villa Galicia waiter Luis Serret and Shorty Martinez. Kneeling down in front is Victor Serrano, head waiter at Sunny Acres. (Courtesy of the Martinez family collection.)

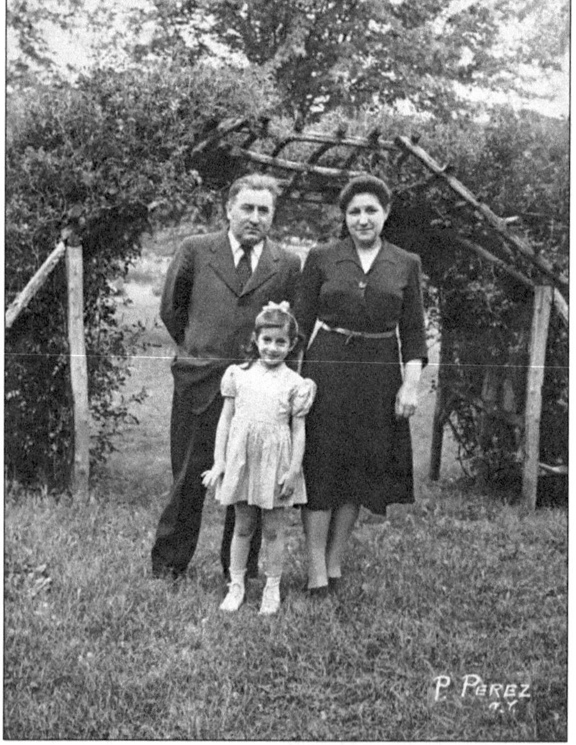

Alfredo Diaz, his wife, Pilar Montes, and their daughter Luz are pictured around 1945 on the beautiful grounds of the Rifton Hotel, their upstate resort. Alfredo passed away in 1949, but Pilar continued to run the business because she loved it and felt it was a great accomplishment for someone from a small town, such as the one she came from in Spain. (Photograph by Paul D. Perez, courtesy of Luz Diaz Damron.)

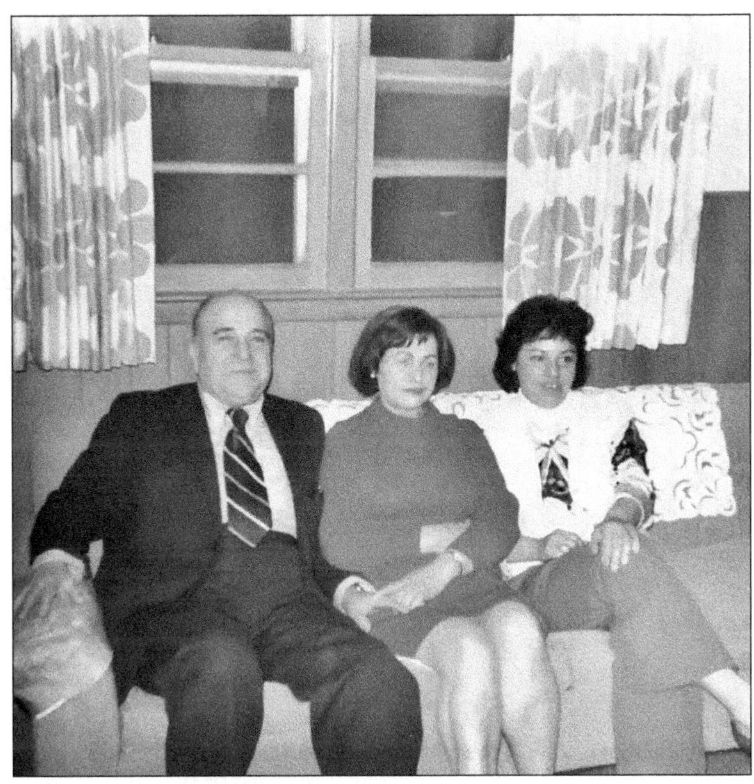

Brought together at a social gathering in Plattekill are, from left to right, Henry Cuney, Mercedes Cuney, and Lucy Martinez. Henry and Mercedes were the owners of Los Tres Argentinos, which was known for roasting pigs on outdoor spits and serving busloads of weekend villagoers. The couple was originally from Spain. (Courtesy of the Martinez family collection.)

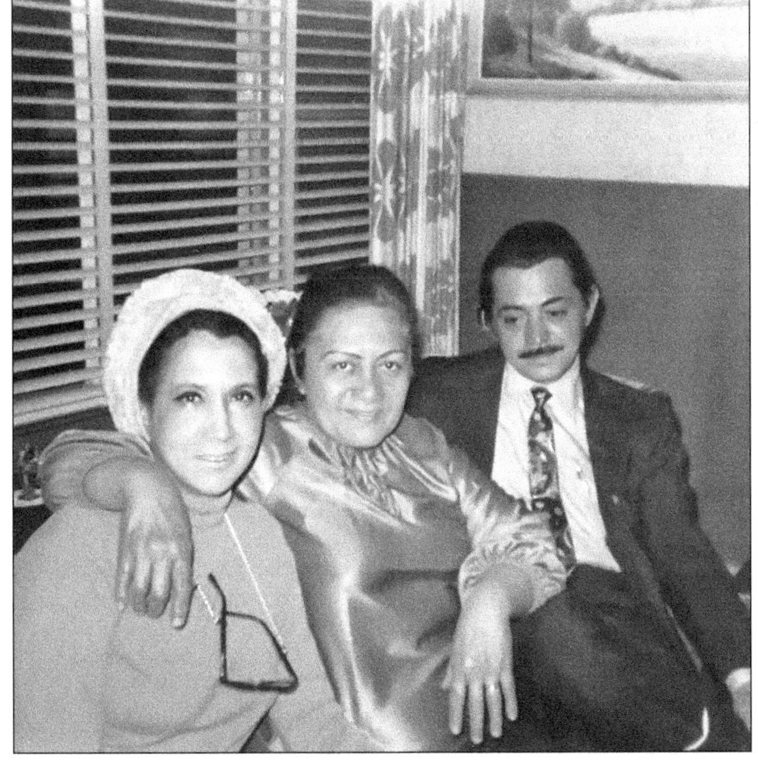

Fela Gomez of the Villa Galicia is depicted in a relaxed and friendly moment with Tula and Willie Ortiz, owners of the Villa San Juan. One might think that there was an intense competitive rivalry between the villa owners, but nothing could be further from the truth. Many were close friends and frequently socialized in the off-season at parties and other functions. (Courtesy of the Martinez family collection.)

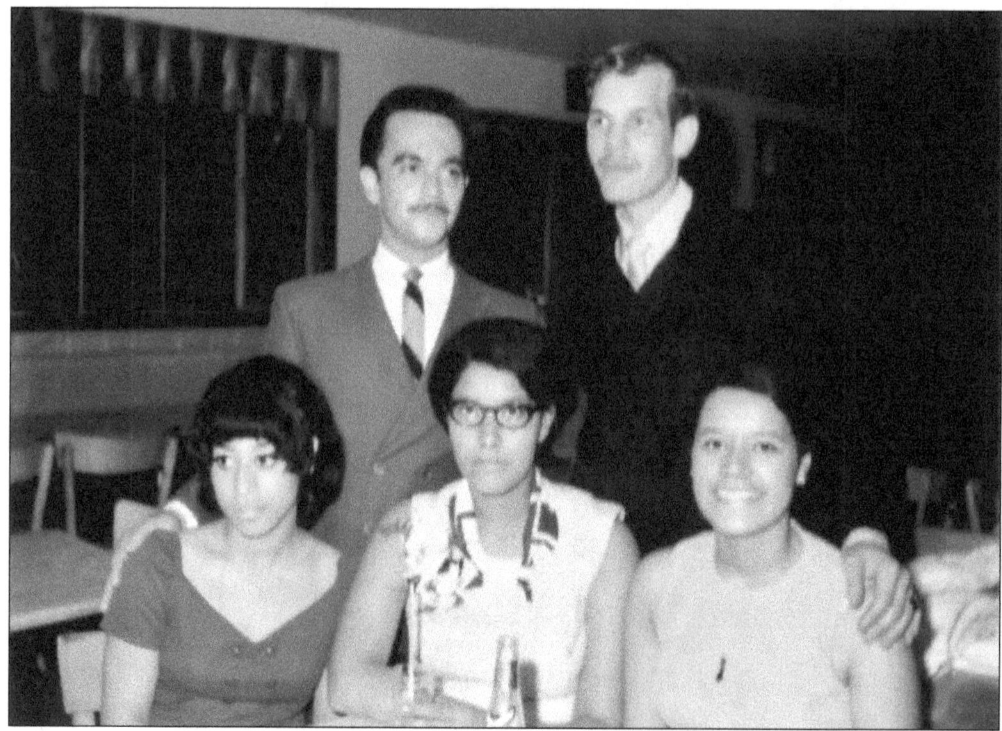

Aida Rivera, seated on the left, and Gladys Guardarramas, seated on the right, were members of the Wallkill Central High School graduating class of 1969. The class held its graduation party at Sunny Acres, as did the class of 1968. Standing are, from left to right, Victor Serrano and Eddie Artuz. Seated in the middle is Norma Guardarramas. (Courtesy of Henry Velazquez.)

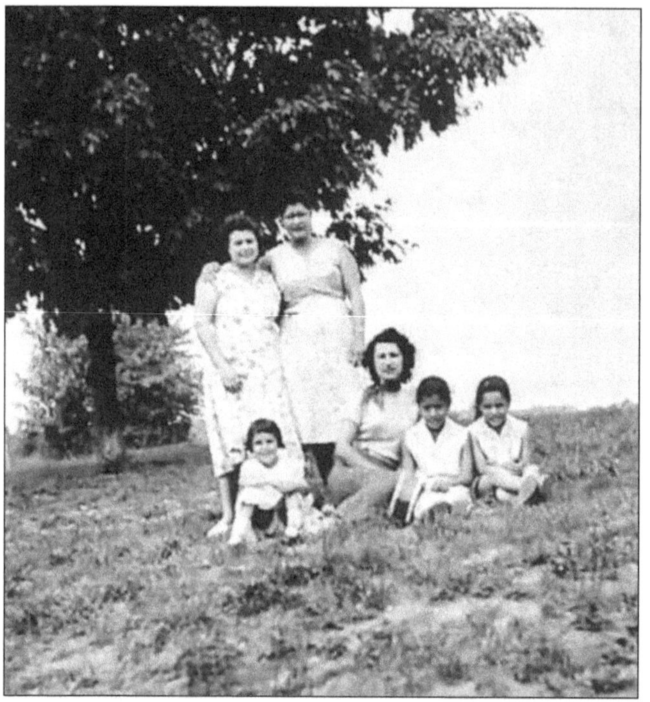

Luciano Diaz was the real estate agent in Plattekill involved in the sale of the Villa Rodriguez to the Guardarramas and Correa families in 1957. Luciano's wife, Tomasita, is standing on the left with Gonzala Guardarramas, the wife of Pedro Guardarramas. Sitting on the ground are, from left to right, Yvonne Correa, Carmen Aida Correa, Norma Guardarramas, and Gladys Guardarramas. Carmen's husband, Raul, was one of the other partners involved in the purchase of the villa. (Courtesy of Yvonne Correa Morales.)

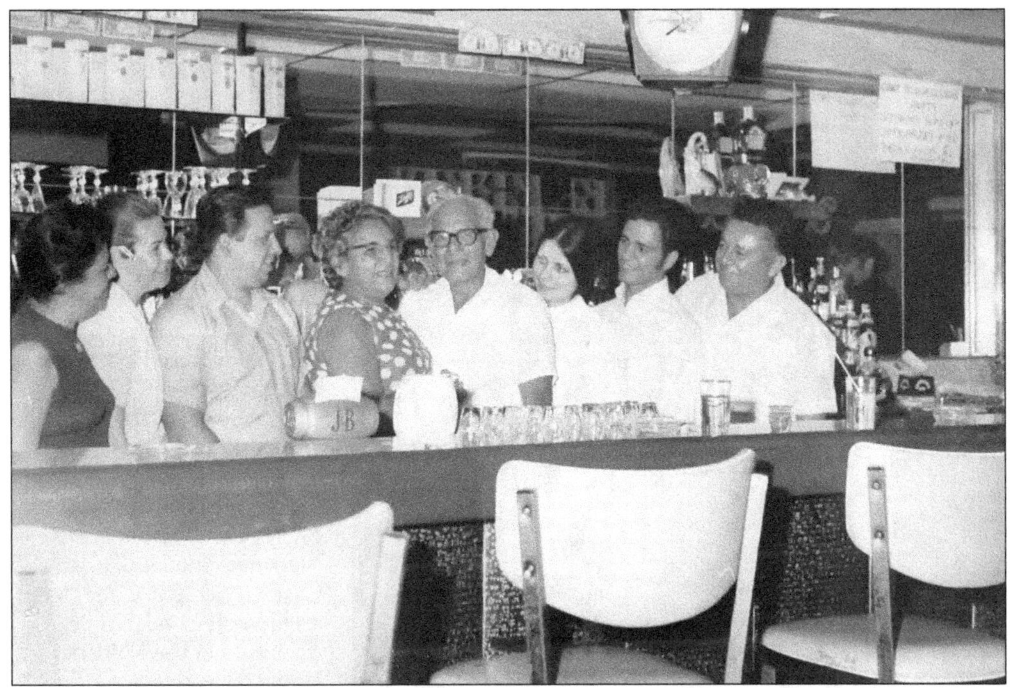

Sunny Acres, like most of the villas, was a family-run business, and no one worked harder than the matriarch of the family, Irene Martinez Anchundia, seen wearing the polka-dot dress. Her day would start at 5:00 a.m., and on weekends, she would not get to bed until 2:00 or 3:00 a.m. From left to right are Lucy Martinez, Carol Campbell Martinez, Ron Martinez, Irene Martinez Anchundia, Alfredo Anchundia, Maryann Vigorito, the author, and Shorty Martinez. (Courtesy of the Martinez family collection.)

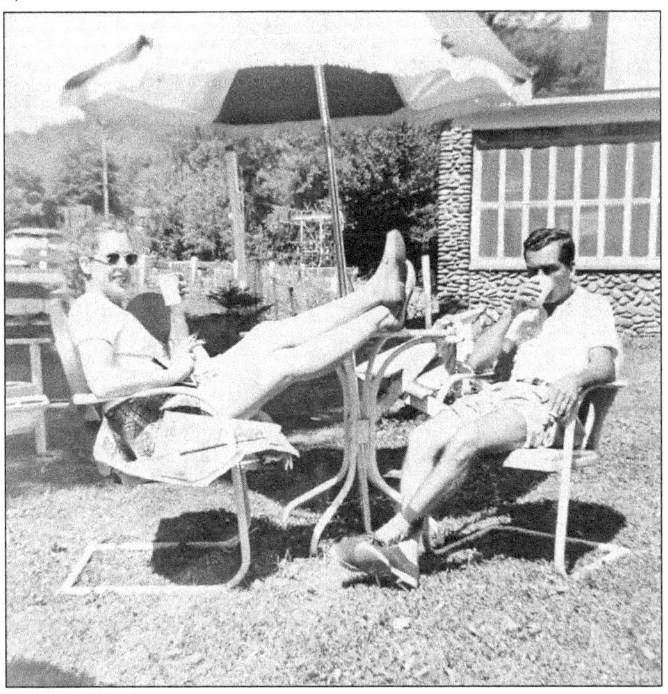

Roberto Perez and family friend Ann relax with refreshing drinks at the Villa Nueva on what would appear to be a weekday. Weekends at Las Villas were usually crowded and busy, with people coming and going all day long. Weekdays, on the other hand, were generally quiet, with fewer guests. (Courtesy of Robert Perez.)

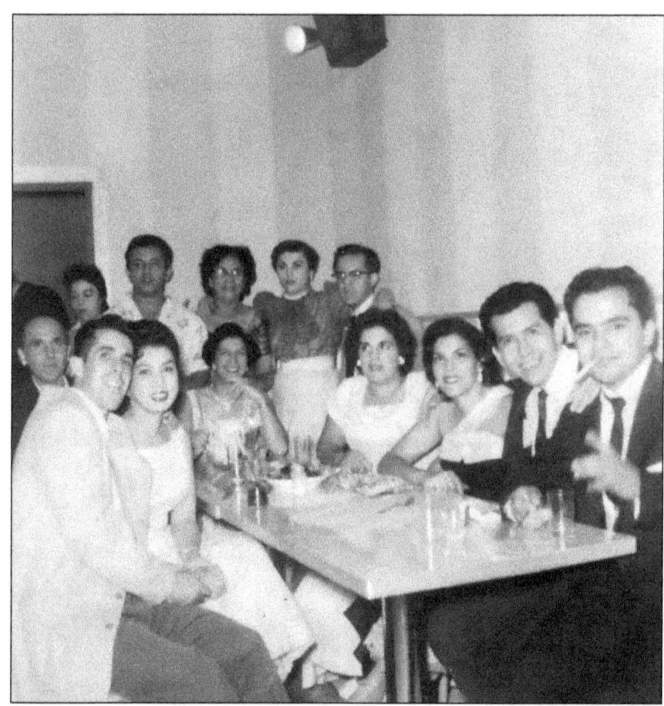

Summer weekend guests at Sunny Acres pose for a c. 1956 group shot with the owners on a Saturday or Sunday afternoon. Visitors to Las Villas could enjoy listening to live music starting on Friday night and ending on Sunday night around 9:00 p.m. Pictured are, from left to right, (sitting) George Rodriguez, Esther Rodriguez, Cardi Cardinelli, Bernie Cardinelli, unidentified, Gladys Velez, Tony Velez, and unidentified; (standing) Lucy Martinez, Shorty Martinez, Irene Martinez Anchundia, Carmen Sentena Candelario, and Joseph Candelario. (Courtesy of the Martinez family collection.)

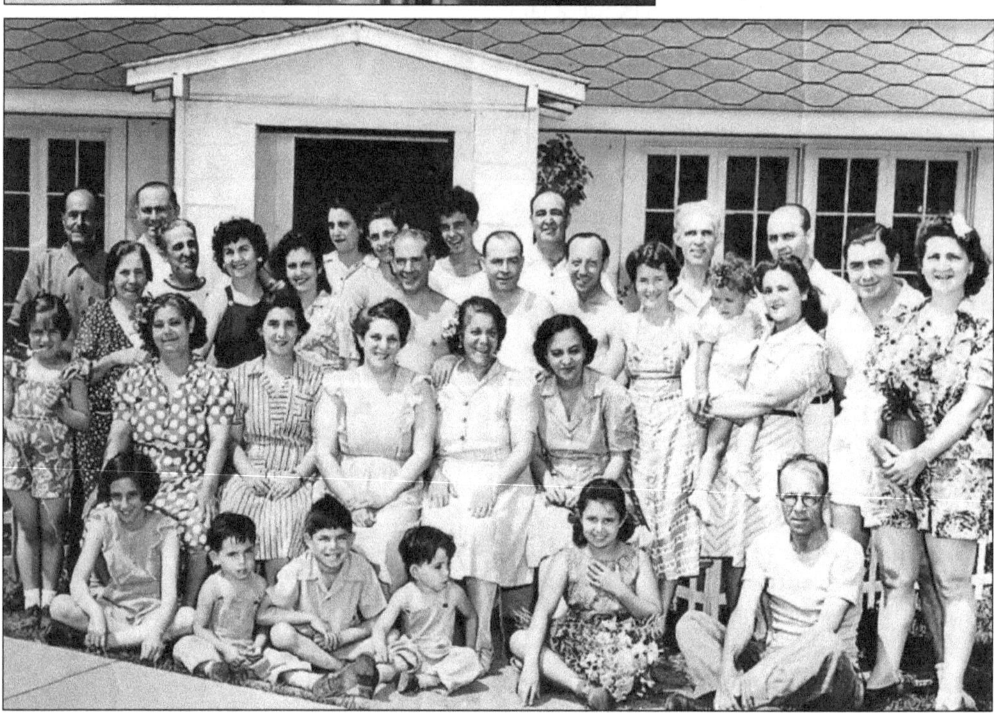

A group of customers gathers outside of the main building at El Cortijo. Juan Pliego, who started El Cortijo around 1941, was from Cadiz, Spain. Juan had previously been a cigar maker and a man of the theater. He was also one of the founders of an organization in New York City called Centro Andaluz. El Cortijo was located on Pressler Road in the town of Newburgh. (Courtesy of the Pliego family.)

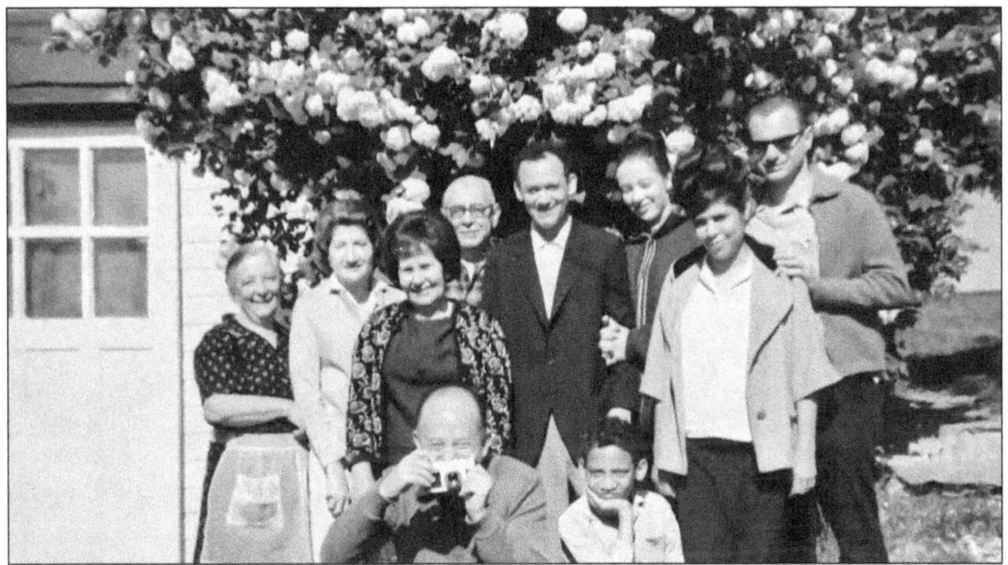

Dona Pilar Tafall, wearing the apron on the left, is pictured along with her guests at the Villa Madrid around 1961. Many of her guests returned to the villa year after year because they enjoyed the serenity and intimate atmosphere of the resort. Dona's husband, Manuel, was a serious and rather shy sort and never cared to be included in photographs. (Courtesy of Sue and Bill Rodriguez.)

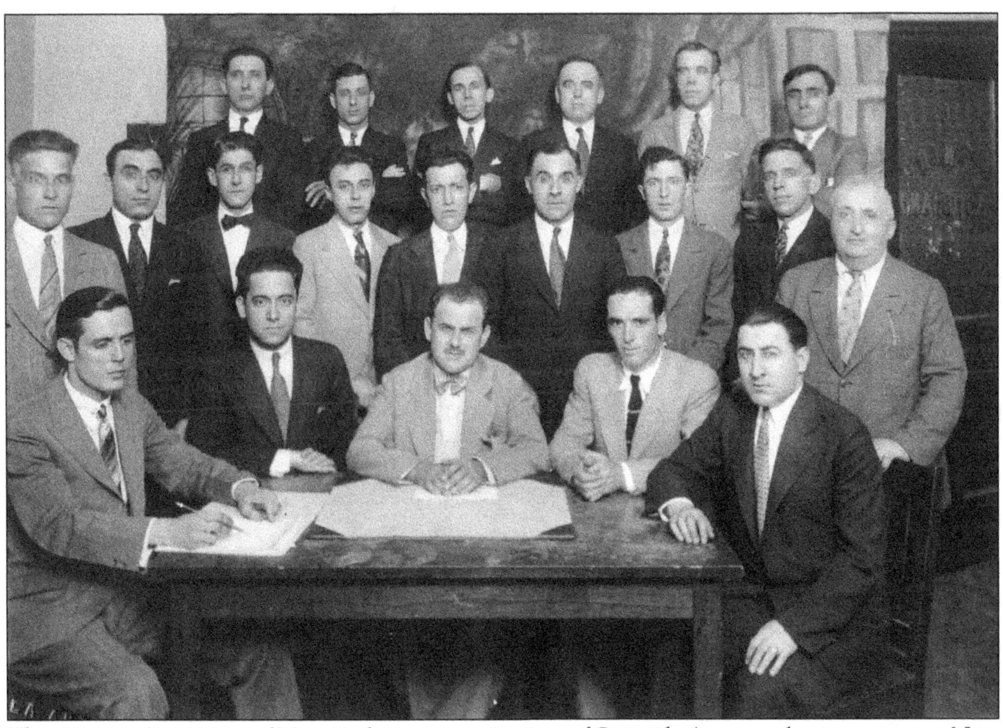

The Centro Asturiano of New York was organization of Spanish Asturian businessmen in New York City. Alfredo Diaz, seated to the far right, was one of the founders of the group. Alfredo also owned the Rifton Hotel, one of the villa-resorts of the Hudson Valley. (Photograph by Paul D. Perez, courtesy of Luz Diaz Damron.)

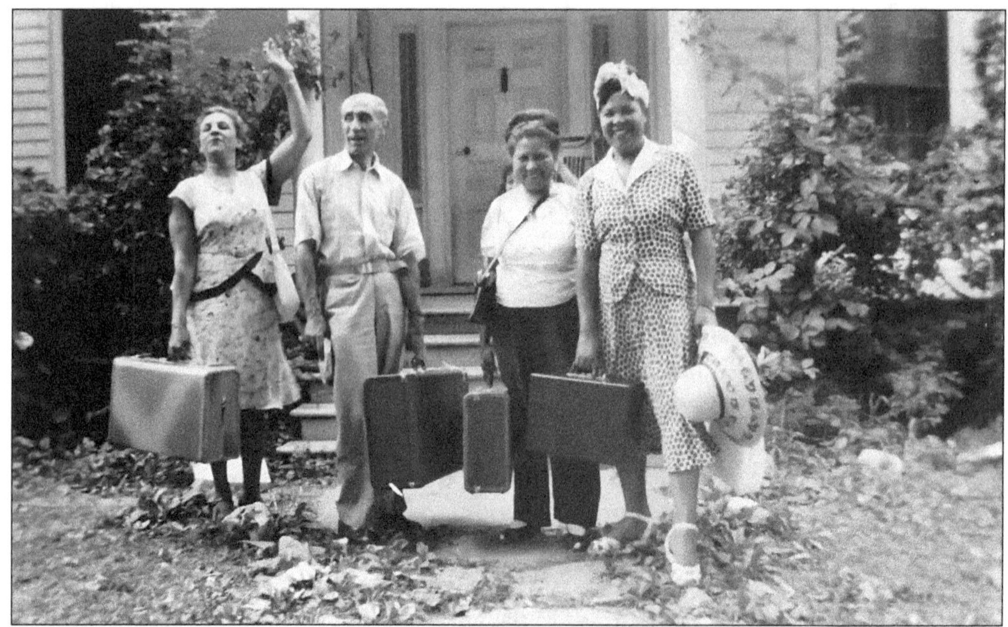

Guests carry their *maletas* (suitcases) as they arrive at the farm and boardinghouse of Cuban immigrants Nena and Juan Yanez around 1945. Located on Route 32 north of the village of Plattekill and just past Hunt Road, it was yet another farm-villa that took in boarders during the summer months. The guests are, from left to right, Irene Martinez, James Davoli, unidentified, and Juanna Davoli. (Courtesy of Nora Gallardo.)

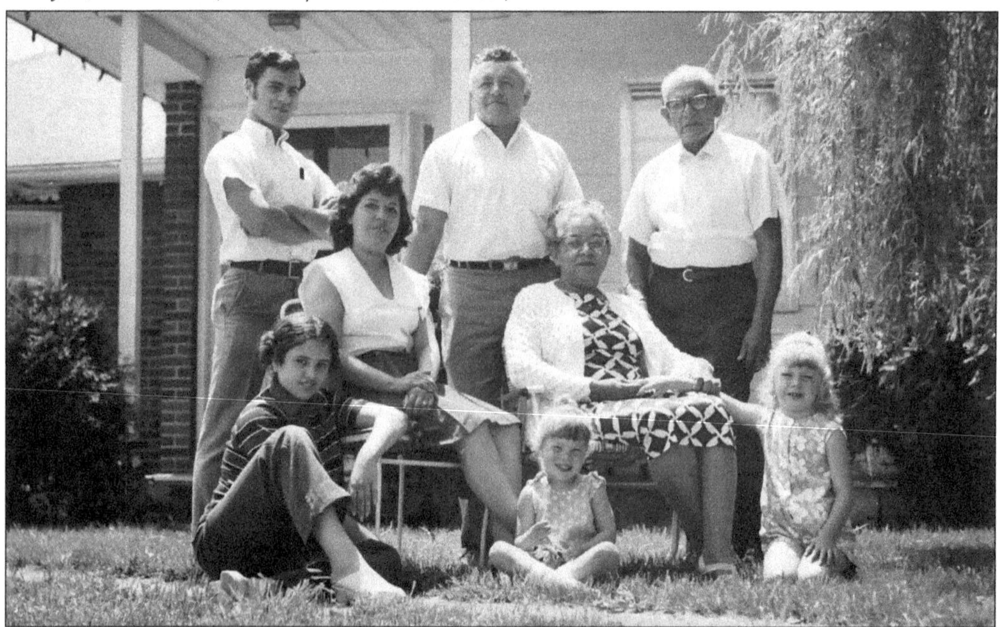

The author, standing at far left, is pictured with other members of the Martinez family around 1969 in front of their house on Sunny Acres Road. From left to right are (first row) Carla Martinez, Lucy Martinez, Denise Martinez, Irene Martinez Anchundia, and Darlene Martinez; (second row) the author, Shorty Martinez, and Alfredo Anchundia. (Courtesy of the Martinez family collection.)

Three

El Ritmo Latino
The Latin Rhythm

Musical entertainment was very much a central theme for the visitors to Las Villas, and as much as anything else, Las Villas was best known for the incredible performances of live music. The first villas started by the Spanish immigrants, hired musicians who played traditional Spanish music. As time went on, the music became ever more important to the villa experience. Some villa owners hired a singer or dancers, while others had either trios or larger orchestras. As a result of the increased influx of Latinos, especially Puerto Ricans, as both residents and tourists to the area, there emerged a new musical sound that would be heard at most of the villas. Traditional Spanish music, which had been the norm, could still be heard at some of the original Spanish resorts, but by the 1960s, it was mostly superseded by the latest sounds of the pachanga, the boogaloo, and salsa. This music was created by Puerto Rican and Cuban bands on the islands as well as by the Latin bands formed by New York City–born Puerto Ricans, or as they sometimes refer to themselves, "New Yoricans."

The best Latin music of the day by some of the most famous bands in the industry was heard at Las Villas. There were appearances by the greats like Tito Puente, Tito Rodriguez, Joe Cuba, and El Gran Combo, to name a few. At the same time, new, up-and-coming bands, like the New Swing Sextet, were starting to make their marks. Many of the bands played at clubs in various parts of New York City during the off-season months but took advantage of the opportunity to play at Las Villas for part or all the summer. It was typical for the bands to start performing early on Saturday afternoon at most of the villas and to continue playing with intermittent breaks until 2:00 a.m. Sunday morning.

Listening to the live music and dancing the night away were important reasons why so many people visited Las Villas. Free live music is what made Las Villas unique and very different from the clubs in New York City, where it was rare for the public to get in without being charged. Looking inside the dance halls of Las Villas, one would see an ocean of bobbing heads, as people danced to the sounds of mambos, merengues, and the latest dance crazes of the day.

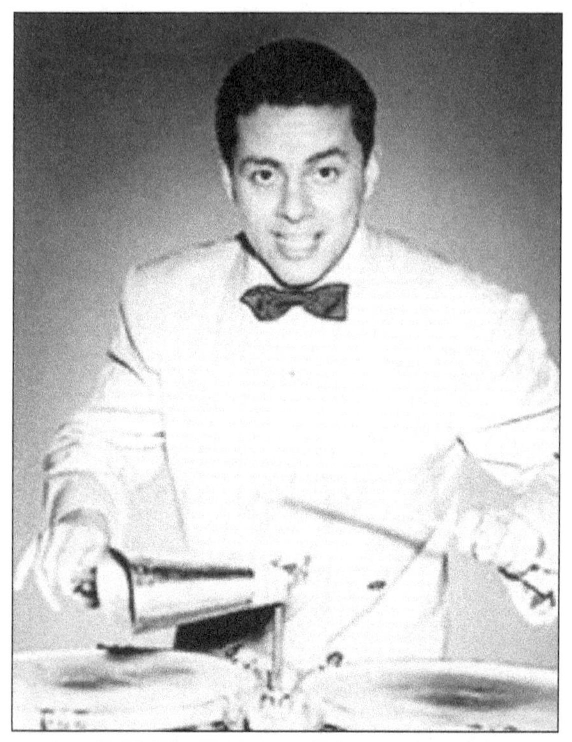

Collectively, the 1950s and 1960s have, at times, been called the golden era of Latin American music. In that industry, perhaps no two bands have had more of an impact on the spread and innovation of Latin music than the bands of two Puerto Ricans, Tito Puente (left) and Tito Rodriguez (below). (Left, courtesy of Tito Puente Jr.; below, courtesy of Hector Aviles.)

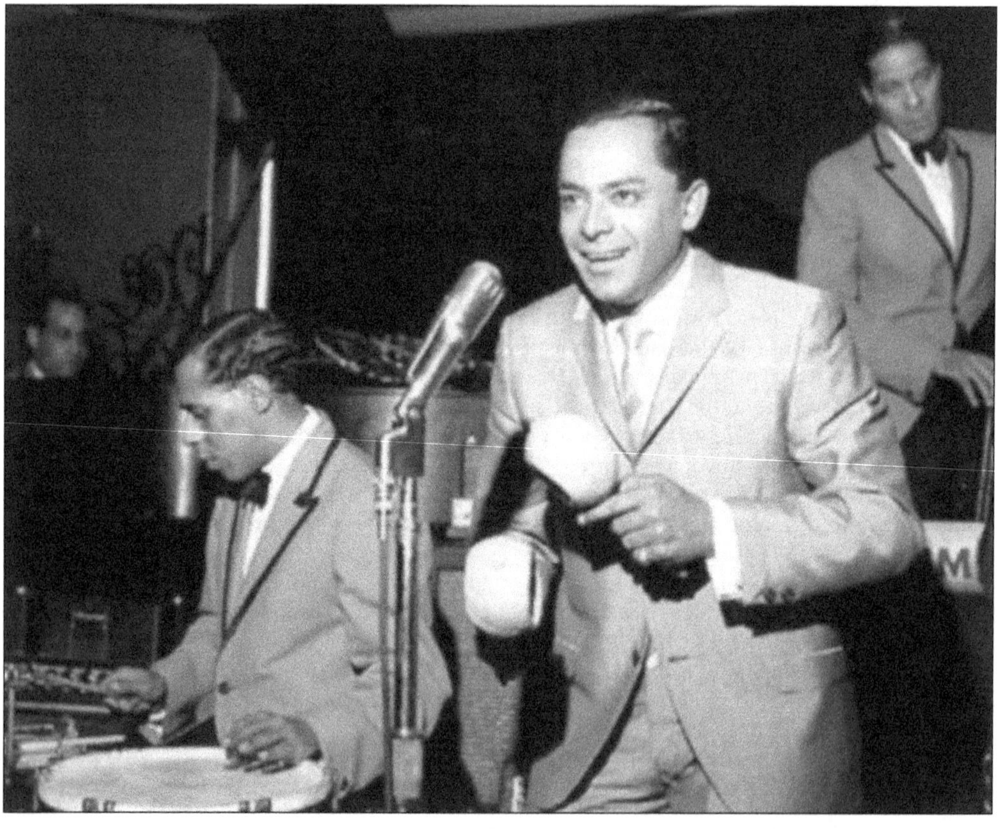

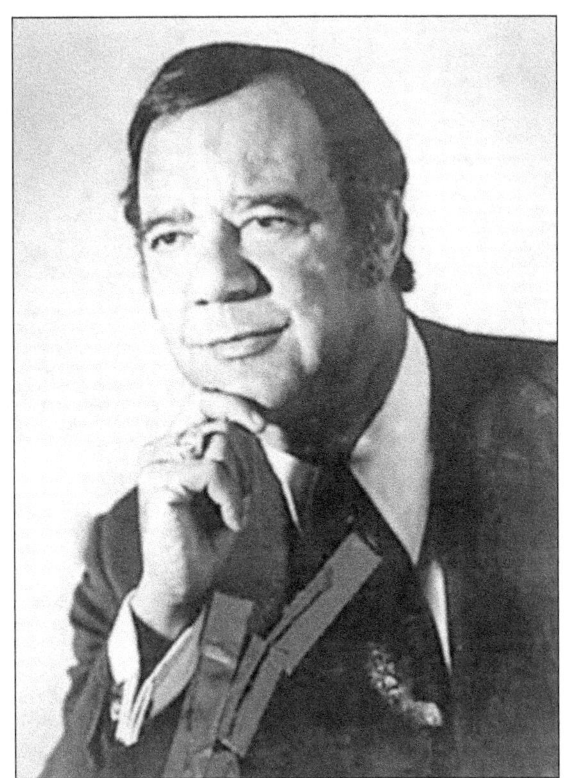

Two other Puerto Rican stars who set the standard for all the other singers that performed everywhere, including at Las Villas, were Bobby Capo (right) and Hector Lavoe (below). When it comes to naming the greatest singer-songwriters of their generation, their names immediately come to mind. (Both, courtesy of Wikimedia Commons.)

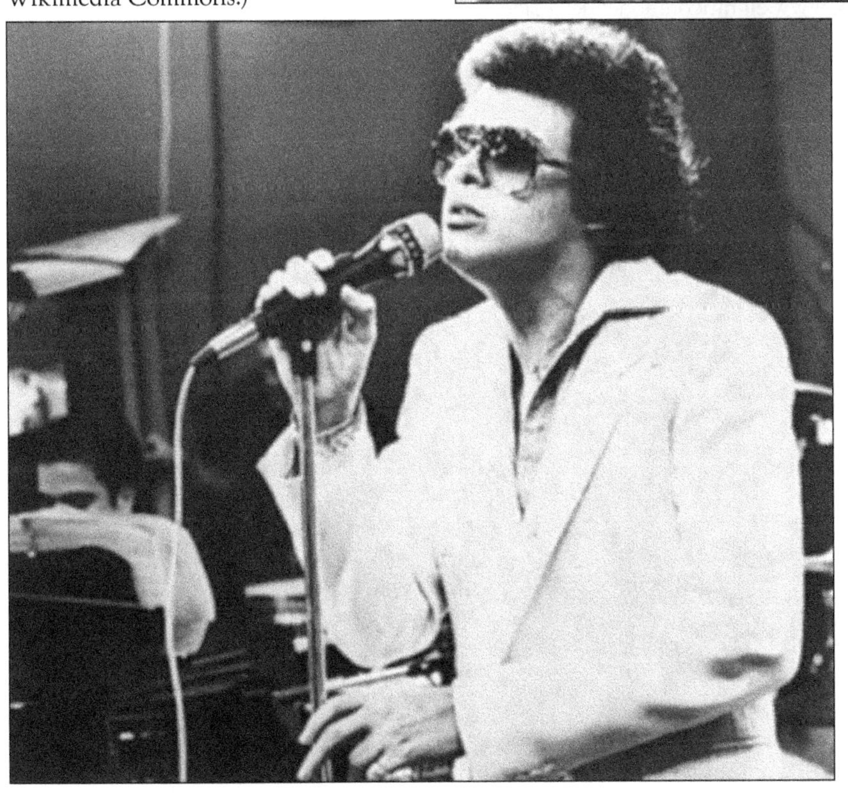

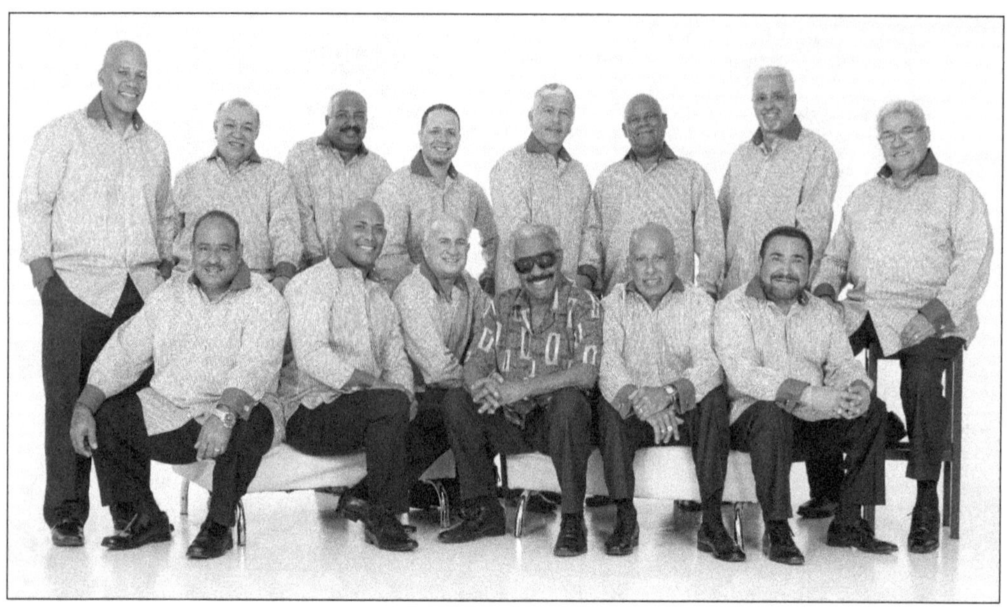

El Gran Combo de Puerto Rico is one of the most renowned Latin bands in the world. The band performed at Las Villas on several occasions when the popularity of the region was at its peak. El Gran Combo started performing in 1962 and has appeared all over the world. (Both, courtesy of Willie Sotelo, www.elgrancombodepuertorico.net.)

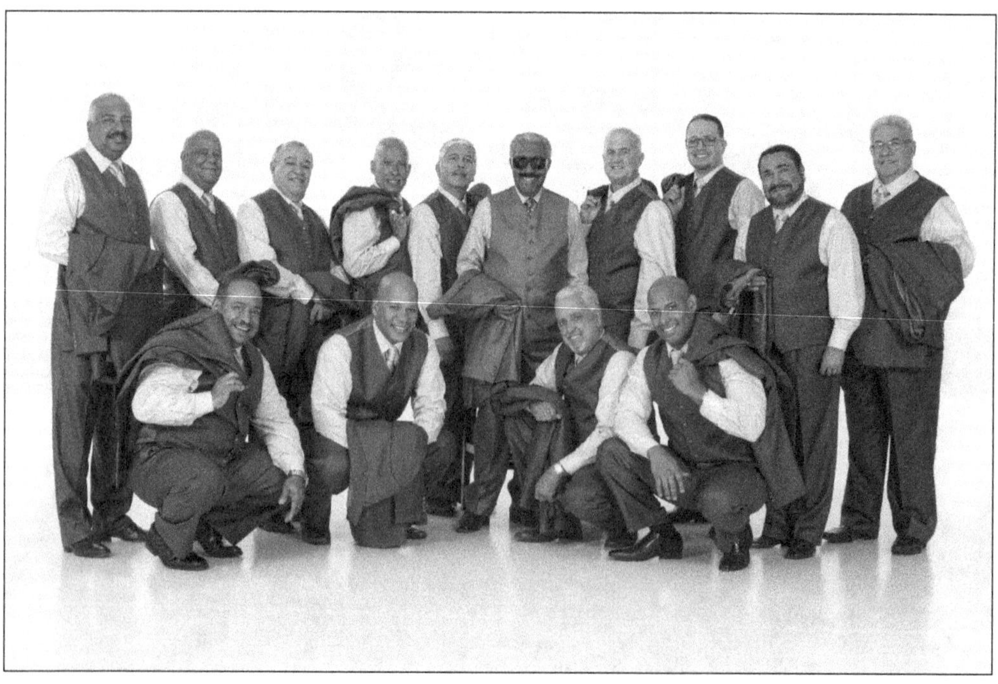

Roberto Ledesma was a Cuban-born Bolero singer of Spanish descent, who performed at the Villa Nueva during the 1960s. Some of the entertainers that performed at the villa were cabaret-style singers, but they also featured trios and larger bands as well. (Courtesy of the Martinez family collection.)

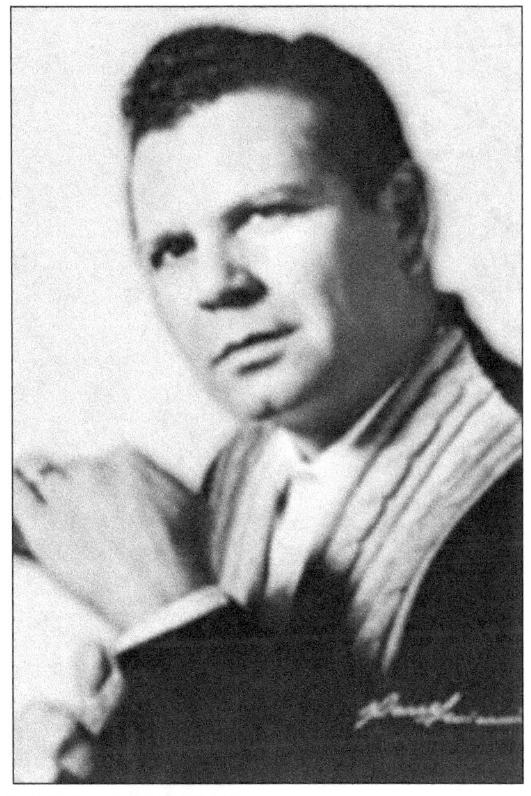

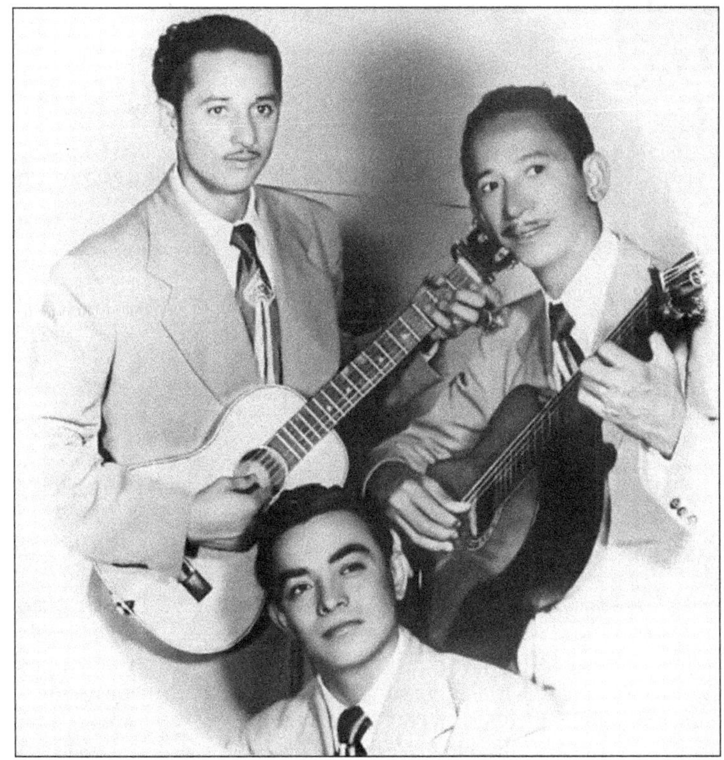

The Trio San Juan played at the Villa Victoria in the 1950s, which was when trios were very popular. Born in Yauco, Puerto Rico, Johnny Albino (bottom of photograph) was the lead singer of the group and became a world-renowned artist. He went on to play with Trio Los Panchos and performed as a solo artist as well. (Courtesy of Triomania.com.)

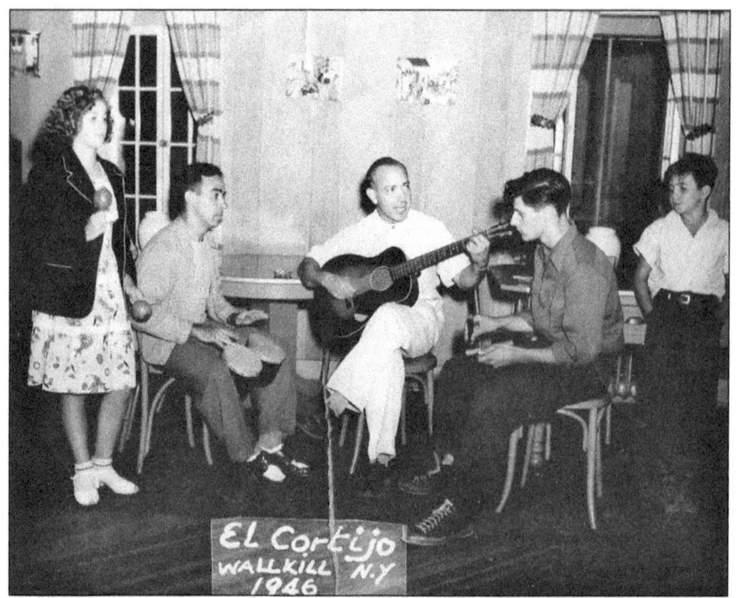

At Las Villas, there were a number of activities that a visitor could get involved in, but the most popular form of entertainment by far was the music. Whether it was a large orchestra, a trio, or a solo entertainer, the visitors expected and looked forward to the music, even if done in small, informal settings, such as seen here in 1946 at El Cortijo, near Plattekill, New York. (Courtesy of the Pliego family.)

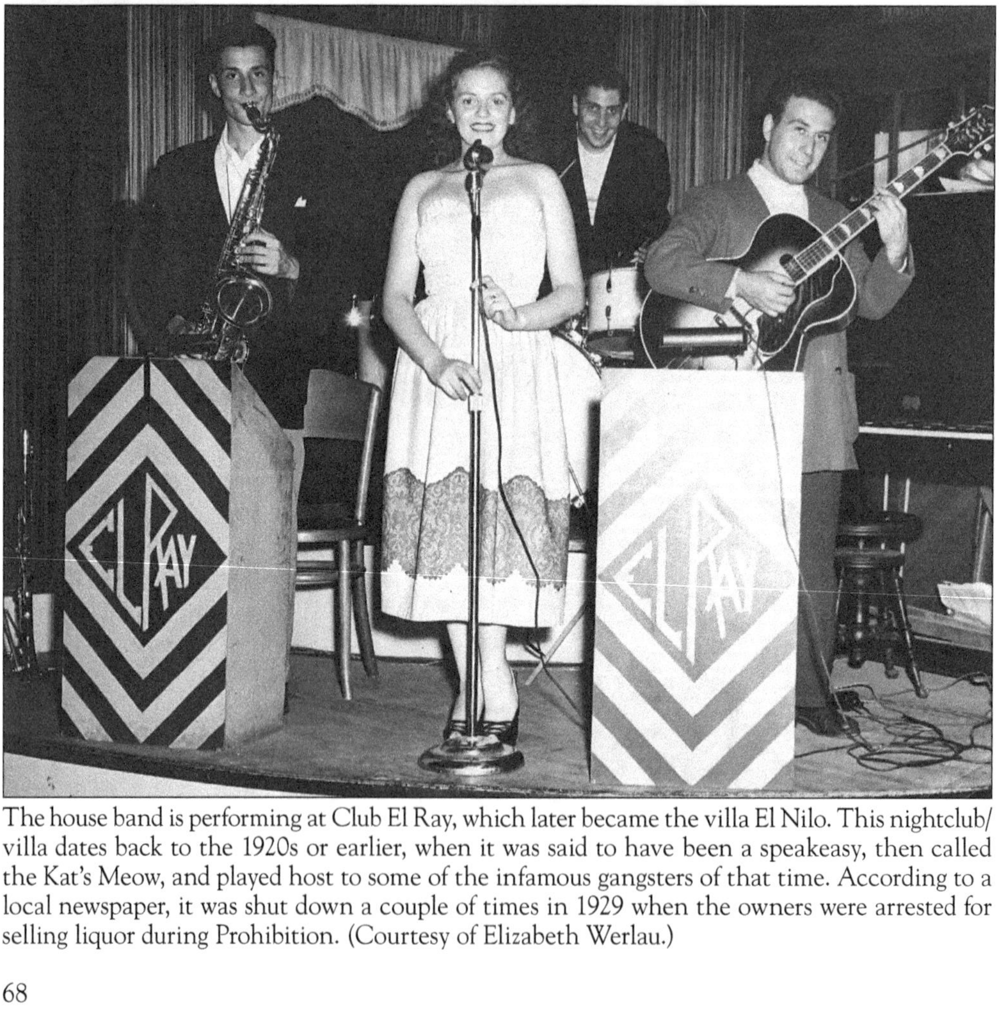

The house band is performing at Club El Ray, which later became the villa El Nilo. This nightclub/villa dates back to the 1920s or earlier, when it was said to have been a speakeasy, then called the Kat's Meow, and played host to some of the infamous gangsters of that time. According to a local newspaper, it was shut down a couple of times in 1929 when the owners were arrested for selling liquor during Prohibition. (Courtesy of Elizabeth Werlau.)

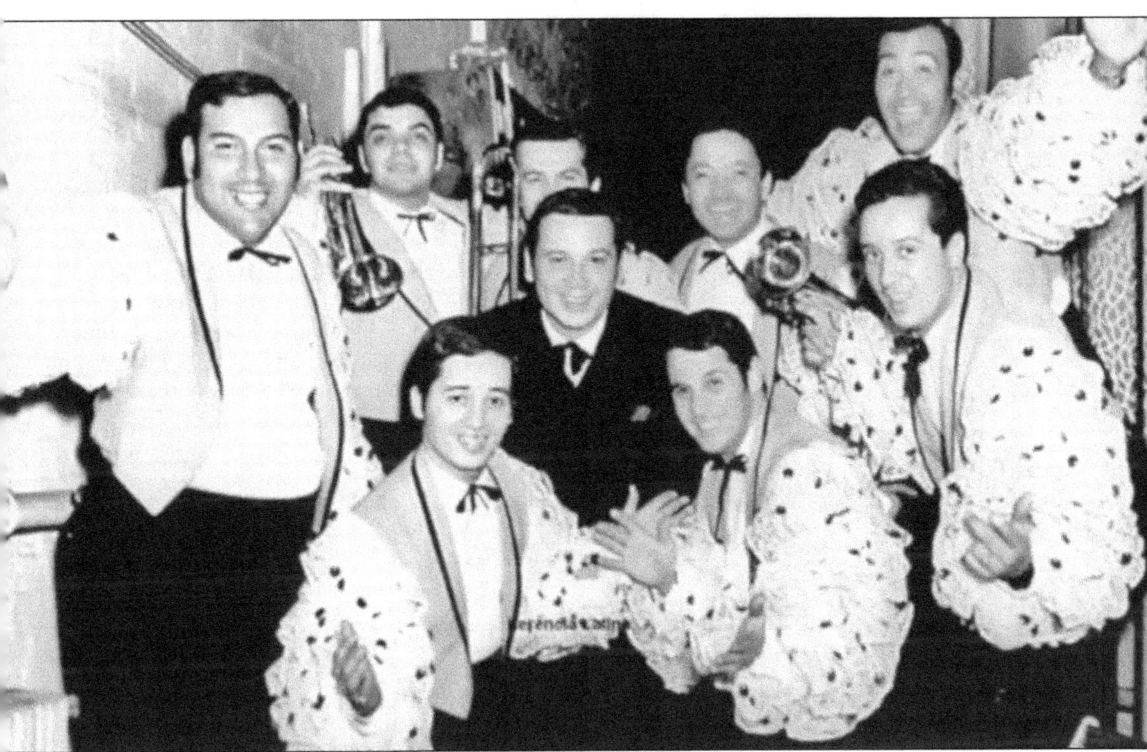

The Pete Rodriguez Orchestra, or Conjunto as they were sometimes billed, played at both Sunny Acres and the Villa Guardarramas for several summers in the early to mid-1960s. The group was at the forefront of the creation of a new Latin sound and dance called the boogaloo. Pete, in the center, was often promoted and recognized by many in the Latin music industry as the "King of the Boogaloo." (Photograph by Hiram Mercado, courtesy of Benny Bonilla.)

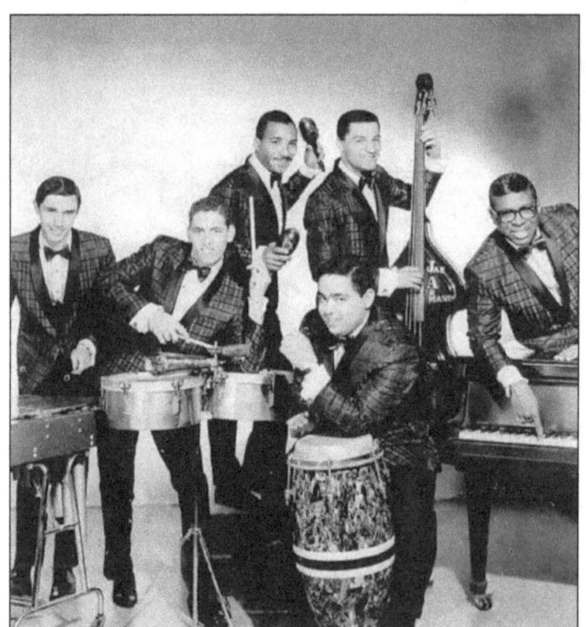

The Grammy-nominated New Swing Sextet is a very popular salsa band that performed at the villa, Sunny Acres during the 1960s. Now over 40 years later, they are still in high demand and play regularly all over the United States. Henry "Pachi" Algain, at the conga drum, is pictured with fellow band members, from left to right, George Rodriguez, Eddie Muniz, Pete Ortiz, Jae Armando, and Aurelio "Yeyo" Salgado. (Courtesy of Richie Blondet.)

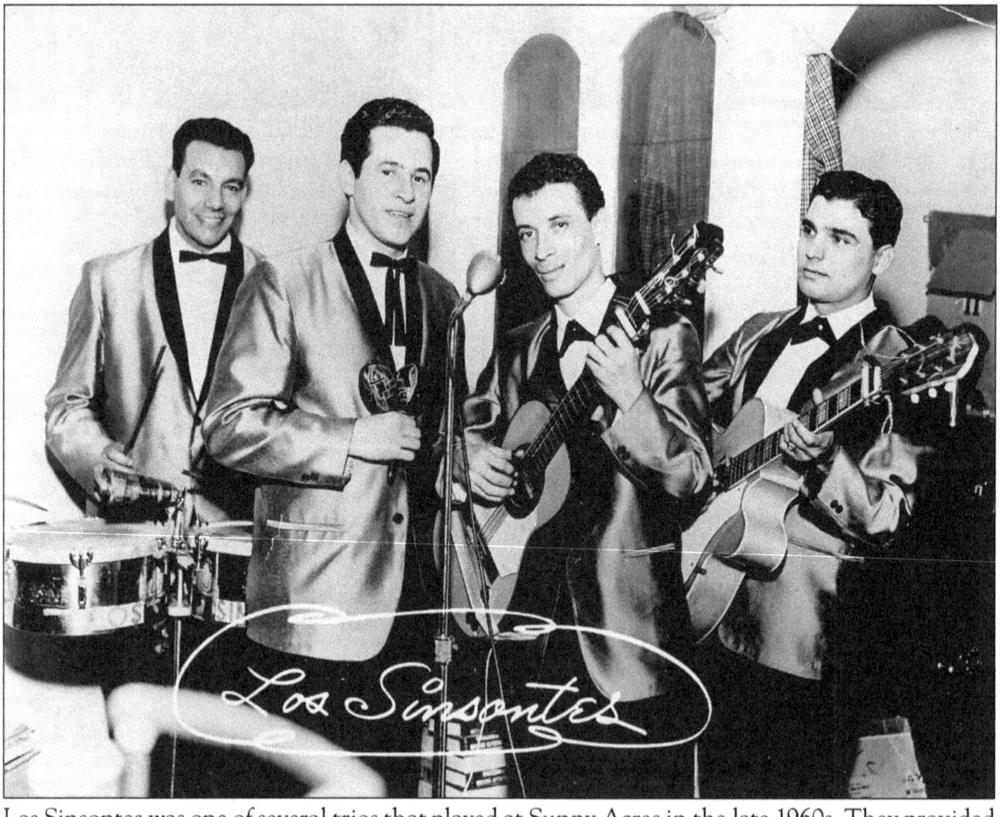

Los Sinsontes was one of several trios that played at Sunny Acres in the late 1960s. They provided their audiences with the traditional music of Puerto Rico, while the larger bands and orchestras were playing mambos and introducing their followers to the new and exciting sounds of the pachanga, the boogaloo, and the salsa. (Courtesy of the Martinez family collection.)

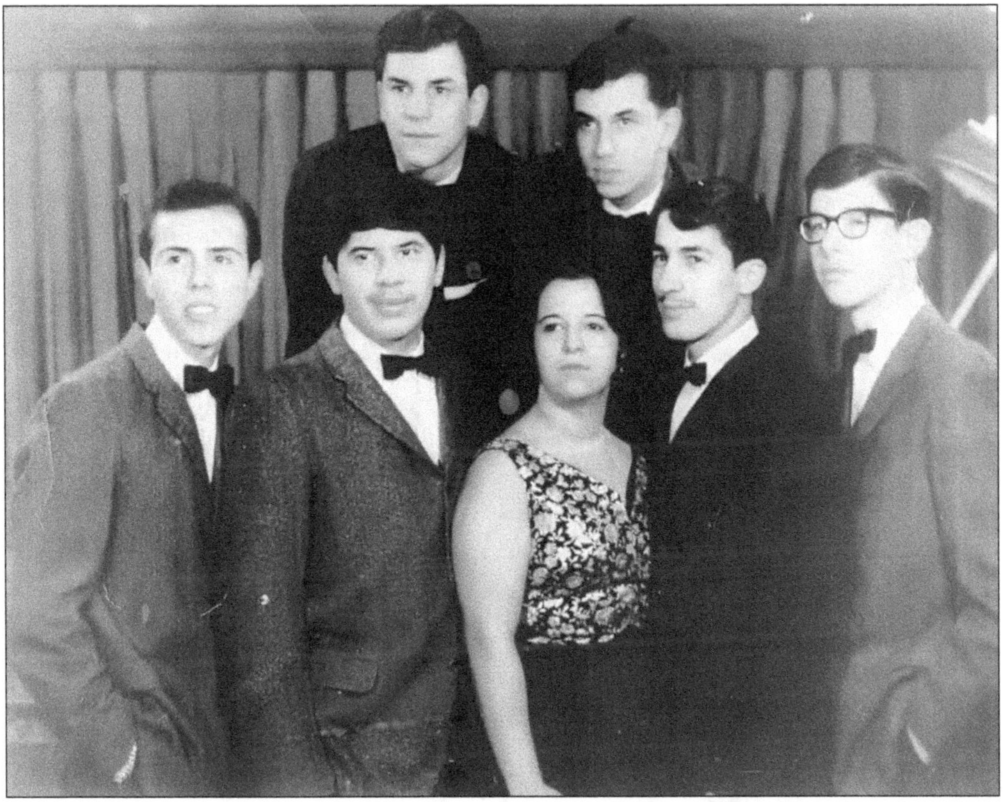

The incredible music heard at the villas inspired some of the local Plattekill youth to form their own bands. Shown here is the group Irene and Her Latin Sextet; it performed at many local venues including Las Villas. From left to right are (first row) George Charriez, Eddie Alicia, Irene Suarez, Willie Vargas, and Henry Velazquez; (second row) Alfred Arzuaga and Angelo Velazquez. (Courtesy of the Martinez family collection.)

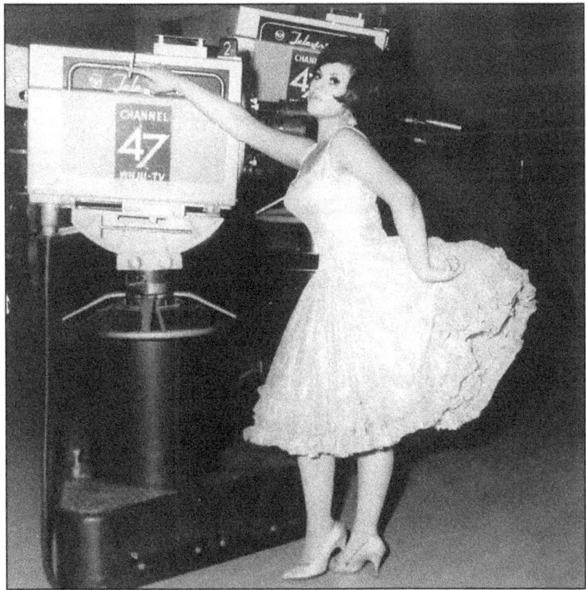

Daisy Guzman was a singer and dancer who performed on weekends during the summer at Sunny Acres in the mid-1960s. Most of the entertainers were booked out of New York City, where they performed on a regular basis, but some solo entertainers and bands were brought in from Spain, Puerto Rico, and other Latin American countries as well. (Courtesy of the Martinez family collection.)

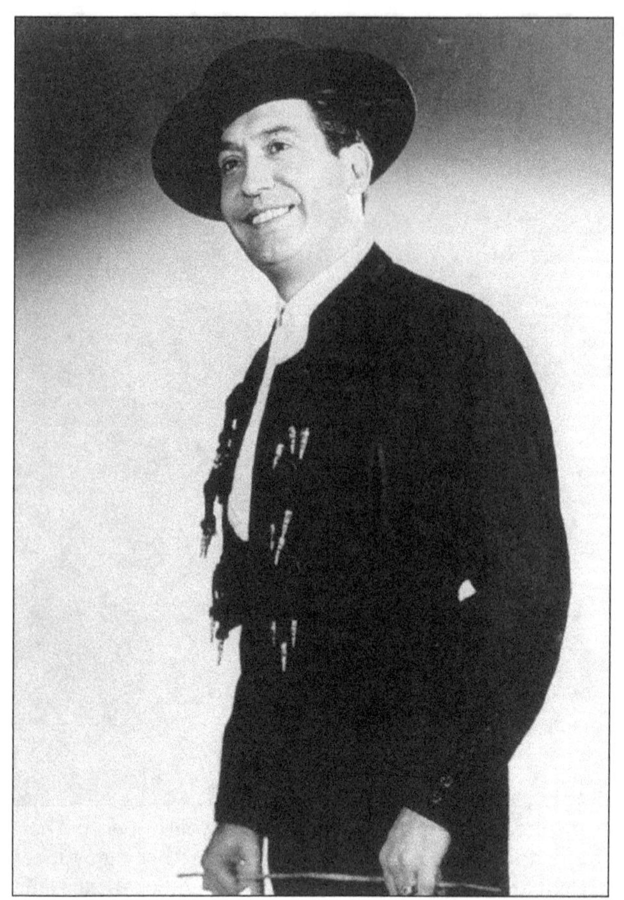

Juan Legido, a famous classical Spanish singer and entertainer known as "El Gitano Senoron" ("Big Shot"), performed at the Villa Nueva in the mid-1960s. His career had started in Spain as the lead singer of the band Los Churumbeles de Espana, but he had his biggest success in Latin America, where he wrote his music and performed his act most of the time. (Courtesy of Juan Legido Jr.)

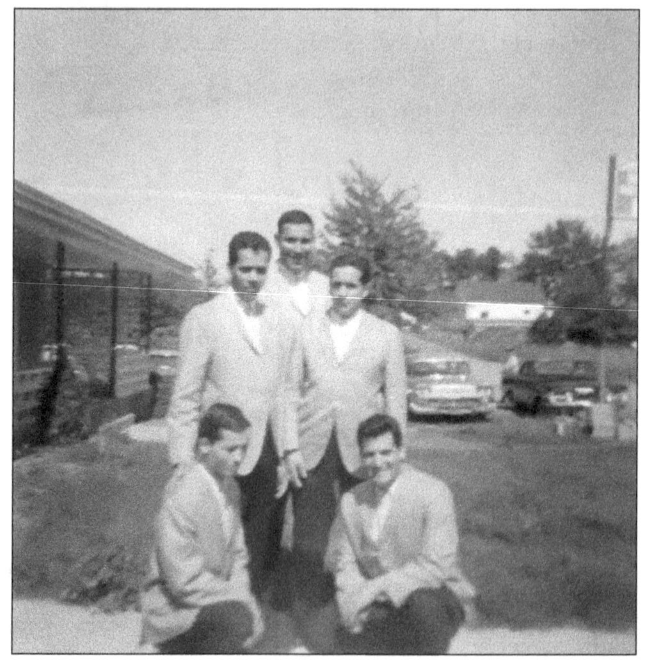

Band members of the Pete Rodriguez Orchestra are pictured at Villa Sunny Acres in 1963. Of the nine band members, the five pictured here are, from left to right, (kneeling) Manny ? and Albert ?; (standing) Ritchie ?, Angelo ?, and Gilbert ? With all the activities and music that were available, it has been stated on a number of occasions that the experience people had at the villas was like a Latin version of the movie *Dirty Dancing.* (Courtesy of Wilfredo Castillo Jr.)

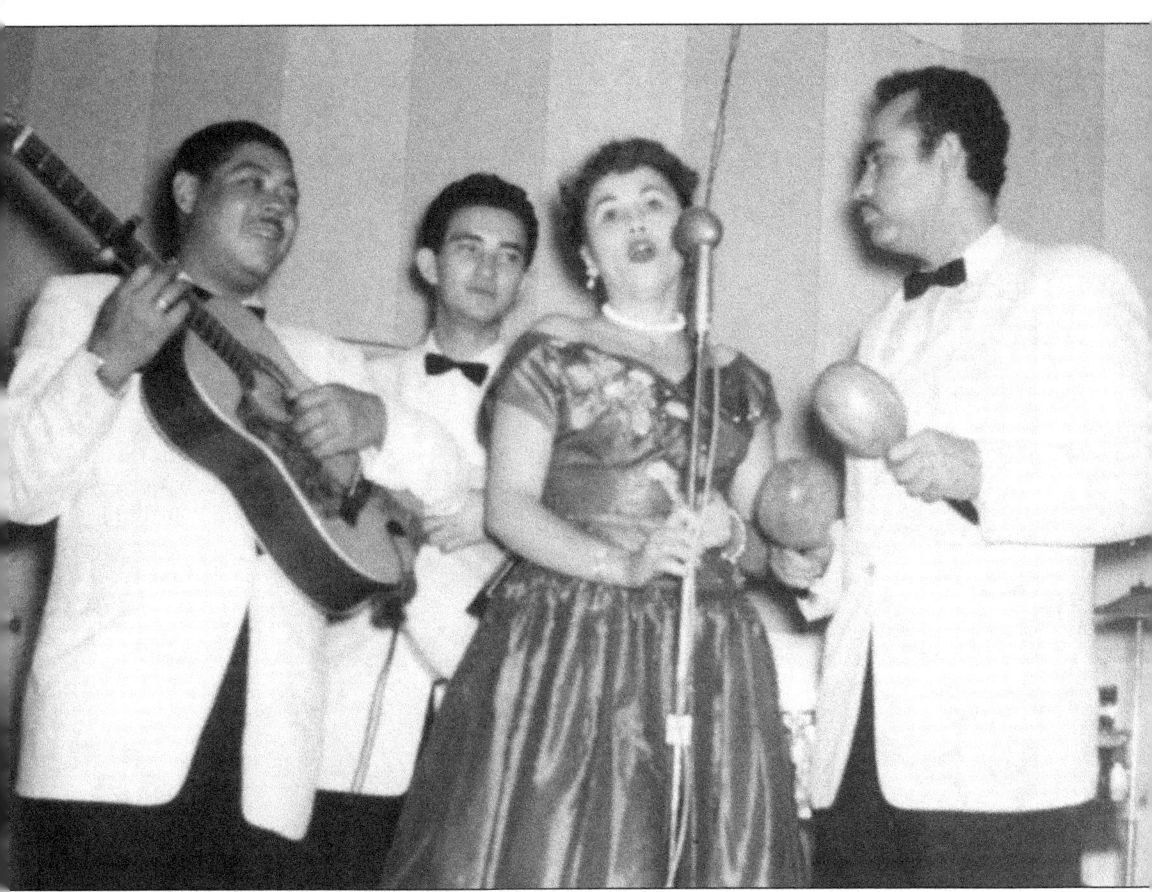

Carmelo Rosado, playing the maracas, belonged to one of the house bands at the villa Sunny Acres during the mid-1950s. Carmen Sentena Candelario, performing as a guest singer with the trio, had performed on Spanish radio on a several occasions. Besides the trio, Sunny Acres also employed a large band, or orchestra, that performed on weekends throughout the summer. (Courtesy of Nisa Dawn Ramirez.)

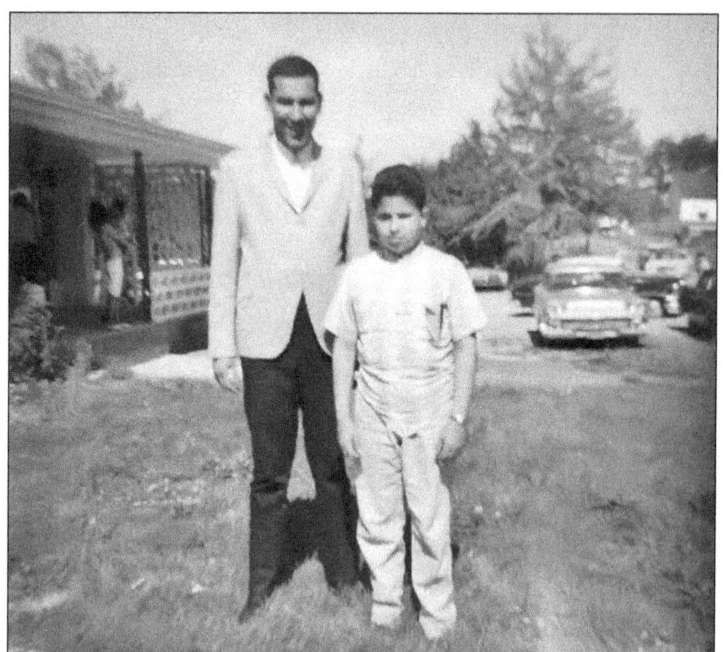

Gilbert Archiball (left), the bass player for the Pete Rodriguez Orchestra, takes the time to pose with starstruck young guest Wilfredo Castillo Jr. at Sunny Acres. Bands that played at the same villa for an entire season, and in some cases for multiple seasons, would oftentimes get to know individuals in their audience. (Courtesy of Wilfredo Castillo Jr.)

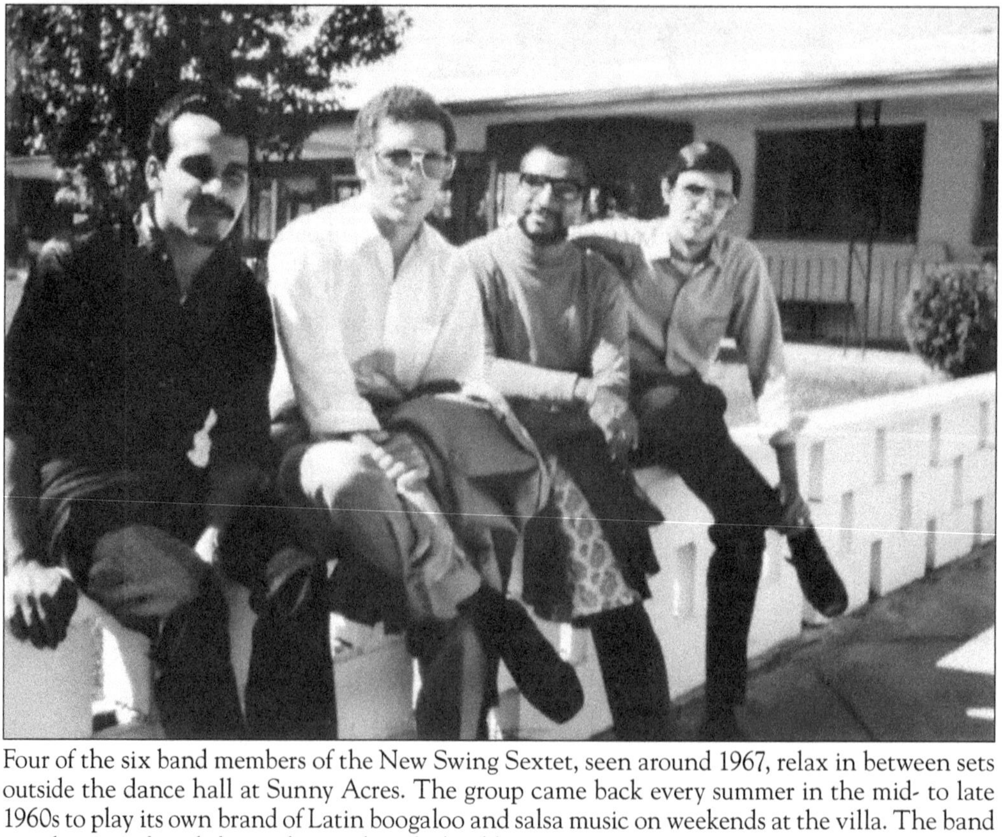

Four of the six band members of the New Swing Sextet, seen around 1967, relax in between sets outside the dance hall at Sunny Acres. The group came back every summer in the mid- to late 1960s to play its own brand of Latin boogaloo and salsa music on weekends at the villa. The band members are, from left to right, unidentified, Eddie Muniz, Pete Ortiz, and George Rodriguez (the band leader). (Courtesy of Henry Velazquez.)

An informal gathering of musicians entertains other villa guests at El Cortijo in this c. 1942 photograph. Playing the maracas is Carmelo "Frank" Cerro, with his wife, Marie Haire Cerra, standing behind him. Their daughter Alma Cerra is the young costumed dancing girl. El Cortijo was owned by Juan Pliego from Andalucia, Spain. (Courtesy of the Pliego family.)

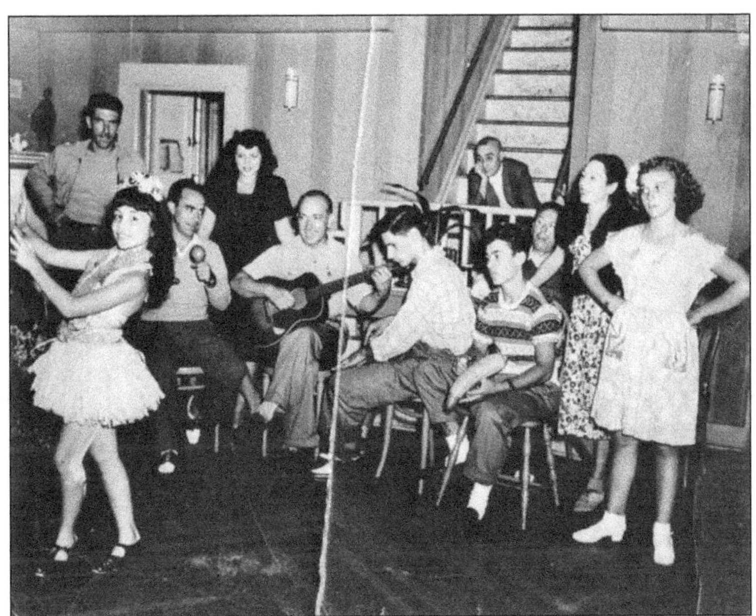

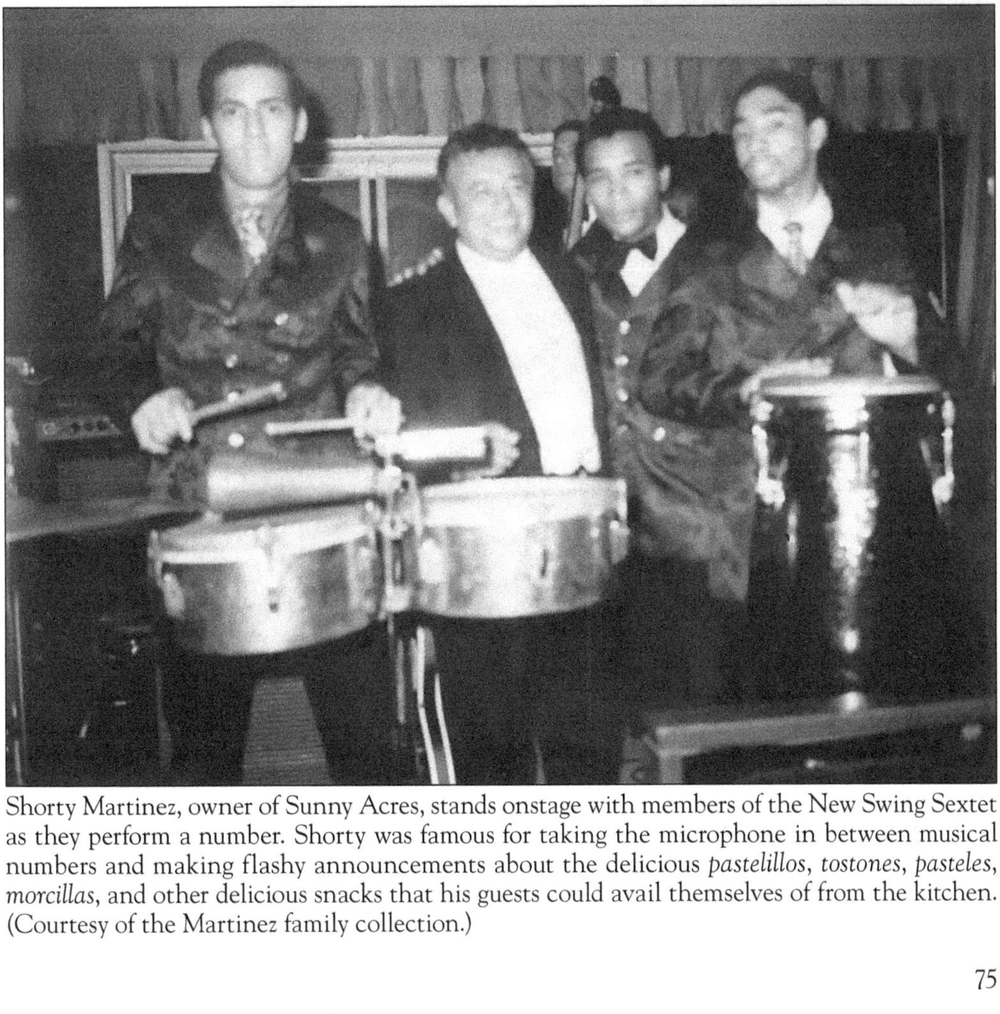

Shorty Martinez, owner of Sunny Acres, stands onstage with members of the New Swing Sextet as they perform a number. Shorty was famous for taking the microphone in between musical numbers and making flashy announcements about the delicious *pastelillos*, *tostones*, *pasteles*, *morcillas*, and other delicious snacks that his guests could avail themselves of from the kitchen. (Courtesy of the Martinez family collection.)

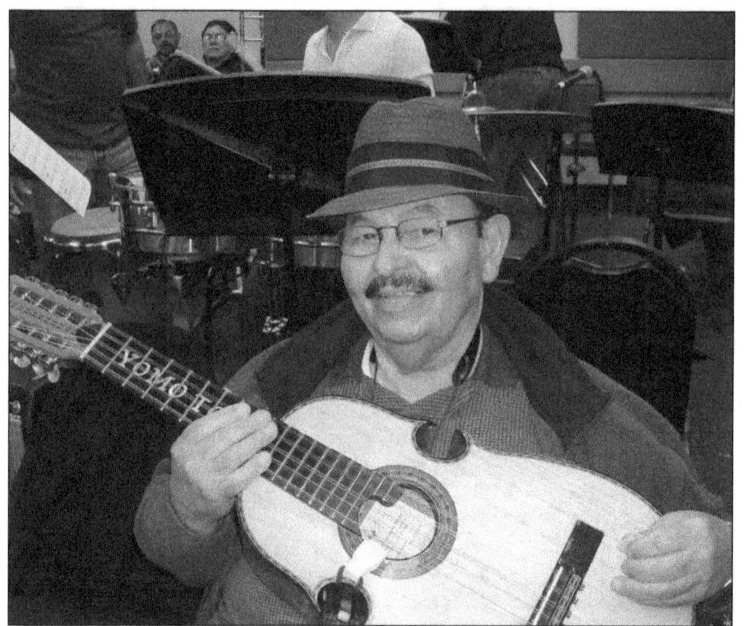

Victor Guillermo Toro, or Yomo Toro as he was commonly known, was an international guitarist who specialized in a Puerto Rican guitar called the cuatro. Though he started out with the traditional Puerto Rican jibaro (country) music, in his studio work, he crossed over to many other genres of music. Yomo played at several of the villas, most notably at the Villa Guardarramas. (Courtesy of Denise Toro.)

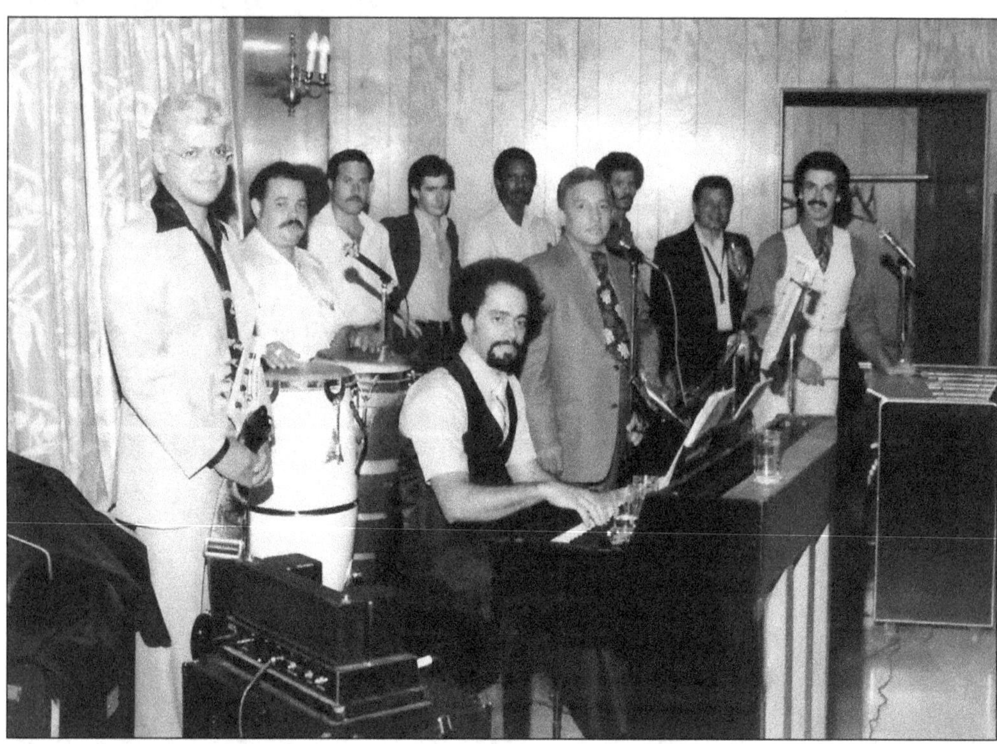

The Orchestra Soul performed at a number of the Plattekill villas as well as at other venues outside the area. Most of the members of the band had previously performed with other musical groups throughout their careers. From left to right are (first row) Hector Martinez, Felix Huertas, and Angelo Velazquez (leader); (second row) Walter Oyola, Johnny Rivera, Ralph Fernandez, Chris Santos, John Fudgy Torres, Sammy Dandrade, and Julio "Julito" Rodriguez. (Courtesy of Angelo Velazquez.)

Lily Yuen sits on the front steps of the Club El Ray, which was eventually renamed El Nilo. Yuen performed under the stage name Hoy Hoy and was publicized as a singer, dancer, emcee, and comedienne. At times, she also performed with her sister Libo "Oliva" Yuen in an annual touring review called the "Brown-Skin Models." (Courtesy of Shirley Anson.)

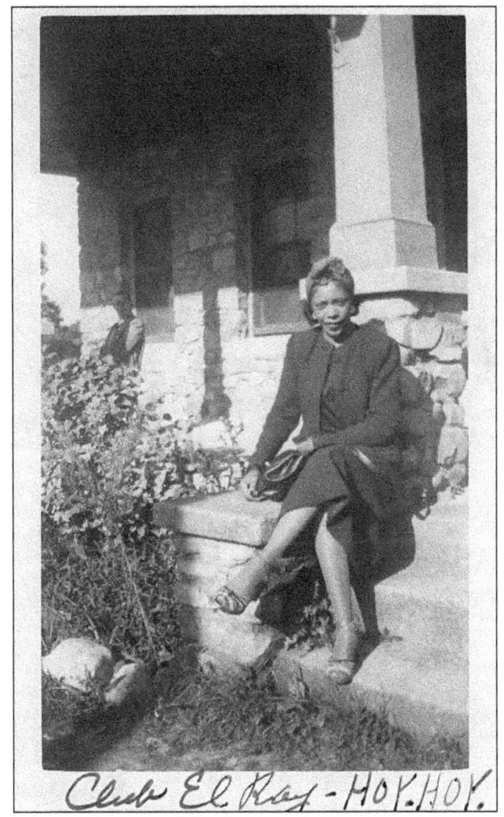

The Latin Soul Sextet was performing at Villa Calderon when this photograph was taken around 1967. Most of the members of the band were also residents of the town who had grown up hearing Latin music being performed at the nearby villas. Band member seated at the table are, from left to right, Ralph Fernandez, Reggie Marks, Louie Guzman (band leader), Hector Torres, Angelo Velazquez, and standing on the left is Henry Velazquez. (Courtesy of Henry Velazquez.)

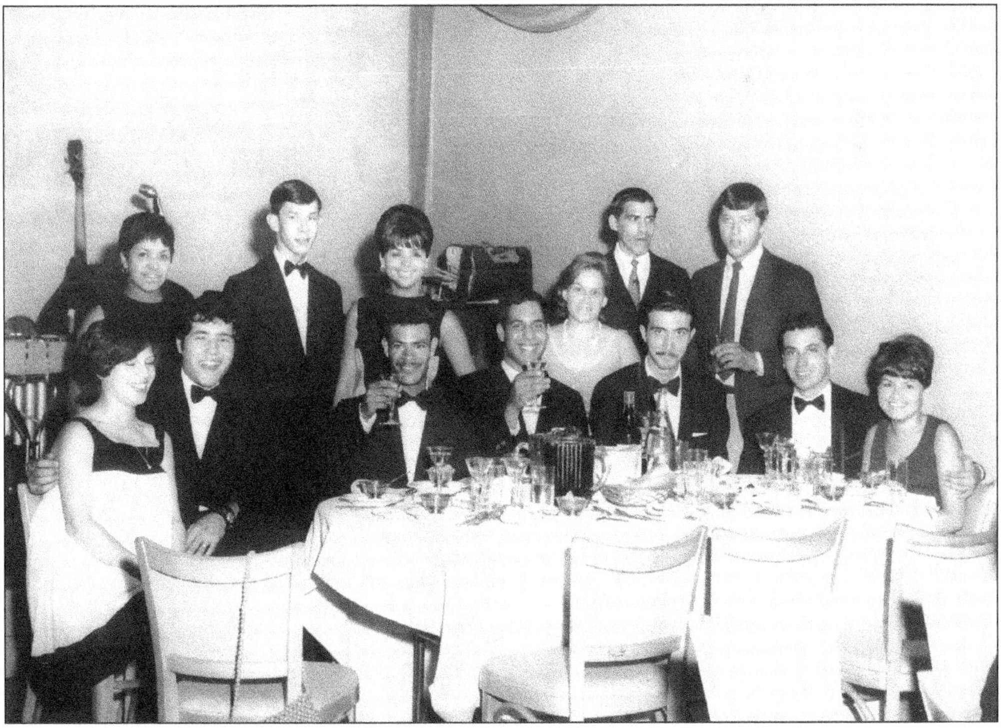

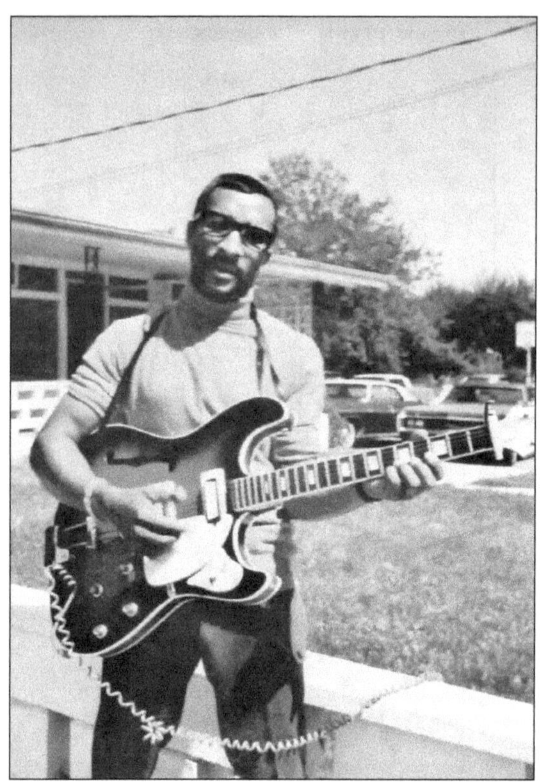

Pete Ortiz, pictured around 1969, was the singer for the New Swing Sextet, but no doubt his musical talents went beyond singing. Pete was probably just having some fun with the electric guitar since they were typically not used in Latin sextets, which generally employed percussion-style instruments in the group to create the sound and style of music they wished to produce. (Courtesy of Henry Velazquez.)

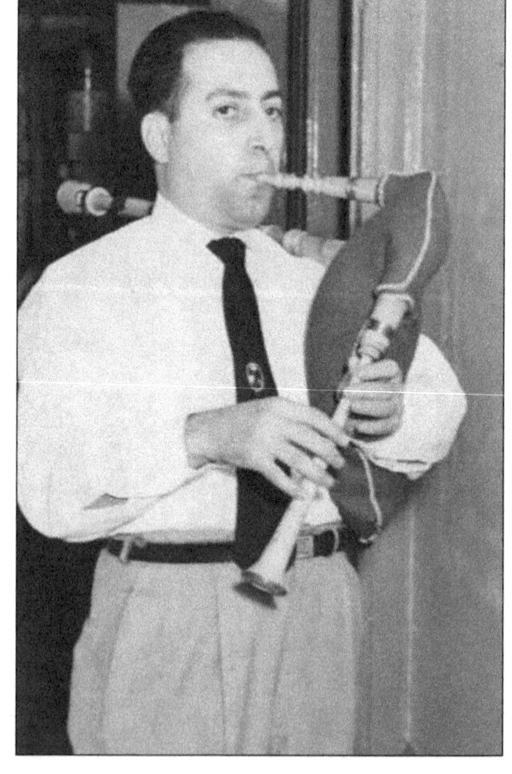

The gaita is an ancient instrument similar to the Celtic bagpipes that has been a traditional instrument of Galicia, Spain, for hundreds of years. Carlos Rodriguez, a member of the Casa Galicia social club in New York City, was known to have played with a gaita group at excursions to Villa Nueva in the 1950s. (Courtesy of Xoan Vazquez and James Fernandez.)

Four

La Comida
The Food

In all ethnic groups, food plays a very important role in identifying the culture, and in the case of Las Villas, the same principle applies, except that instead of one ethnic group, there are multiple groups from various culturally Hispanic backgrounds. The first villa owners were Spanish, which reflected the types of food they served their guests, but the food also differed based on the region of Spain the owners had emigrated from. Asturians were famous for *fabada*, Galicians for *caldo gallego*, Andalusians for gazpacho, and all Spaniards for paella and chorizo.

As Puerto Ricans and other Hispanic groups began to discover and move into the region of Las Villas, the food being served changed to meet their tastes. The foods of the Caribbean and South America were both based on the cooking style of the Spanish, especially when it came to rice and pork dishes. The older Spanish villas also began to cater to the increased influx of the other groups, and most villa menus included *comida criolla*—in other words, dishes from Spanish Caribbean islands and South America.

Visitors to Las Villas could find more intimate restaurants to have a meal if they made their way to places like the Casa Roxana and Casa Lydia, where dining tended to be more leisurely. Other villas with a high volume of customers, like the Rifton or Glenbrook Hotels, or those that catered to jiras, like the Villa Guardarramas or El Nilo, could expect to serve hundreds of dinners from their hectic kitchen facilities. But regardless of the size of the villa, all those who were responsible for the cooking had years of experience and rarely disappointed their customers. The preparation of delicious meals was absolutely essential at Las Villas because the business could not survive if the food was not first-rate.

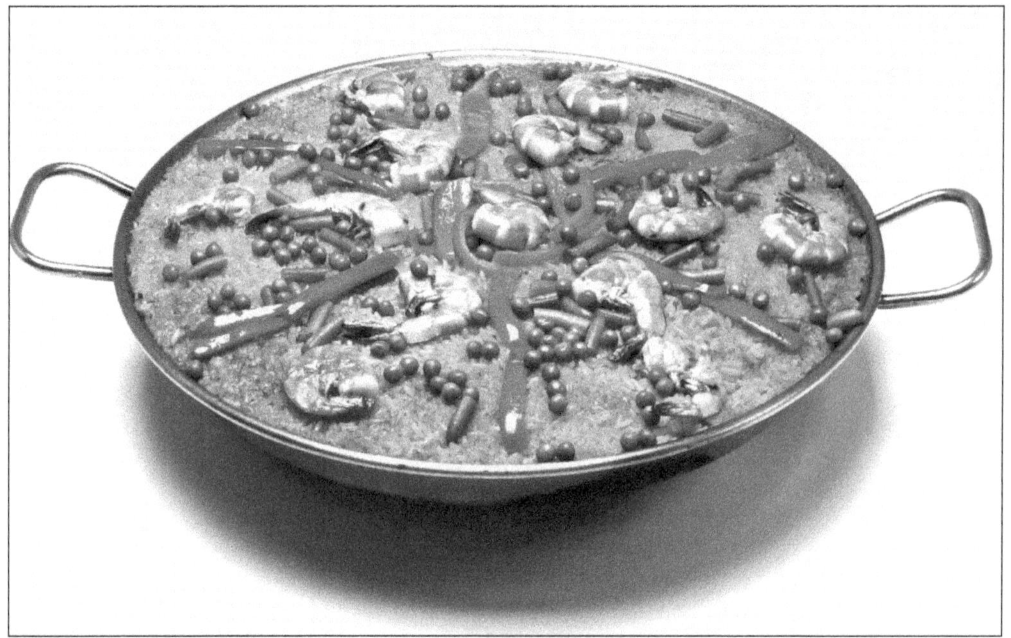

Traditional Spanish dishes like paella (above) or *fabada asturiana* (below) might be on the menu of those villas owned by Spaniards who were immigrants or still had strong ties to Spanish traditions. The paella was sometimes made with just seafood, and at other times, it also contained chicken. *Fabada* is a heavy stew containing white beans, pork or bacon, *morcilla* (blood sausage), chorizo, and saffron. (Both, courtesy of freestockimages.com.)

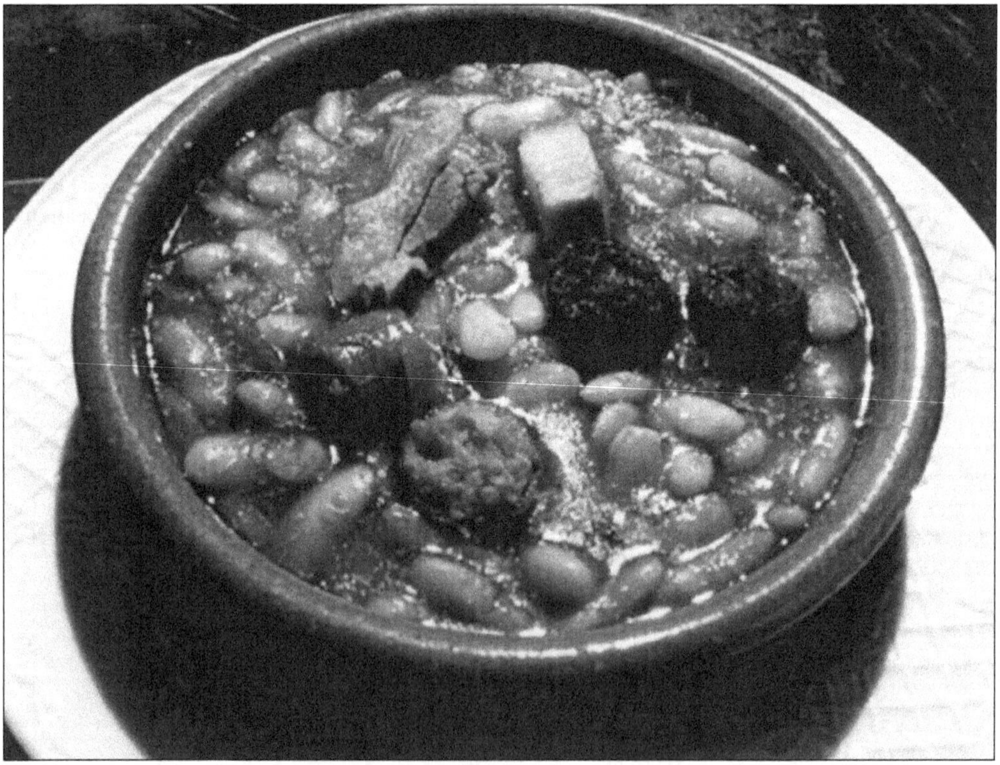

Villa Madrid guest Carmen Dilia Baldassari, pictured on the left, visits with one of the owners, Dona Pilar Tafall, in the dining room of the villa around 1946. Dona Pilar, as she was known, was said to be very sweet and kept a neat and tidy boardinghouse. (Courtesy of Sue and Bill Rodriguez.)

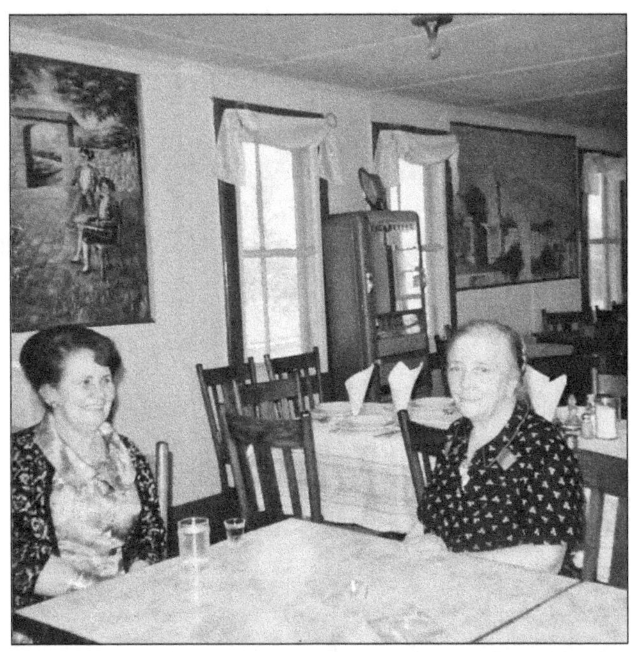

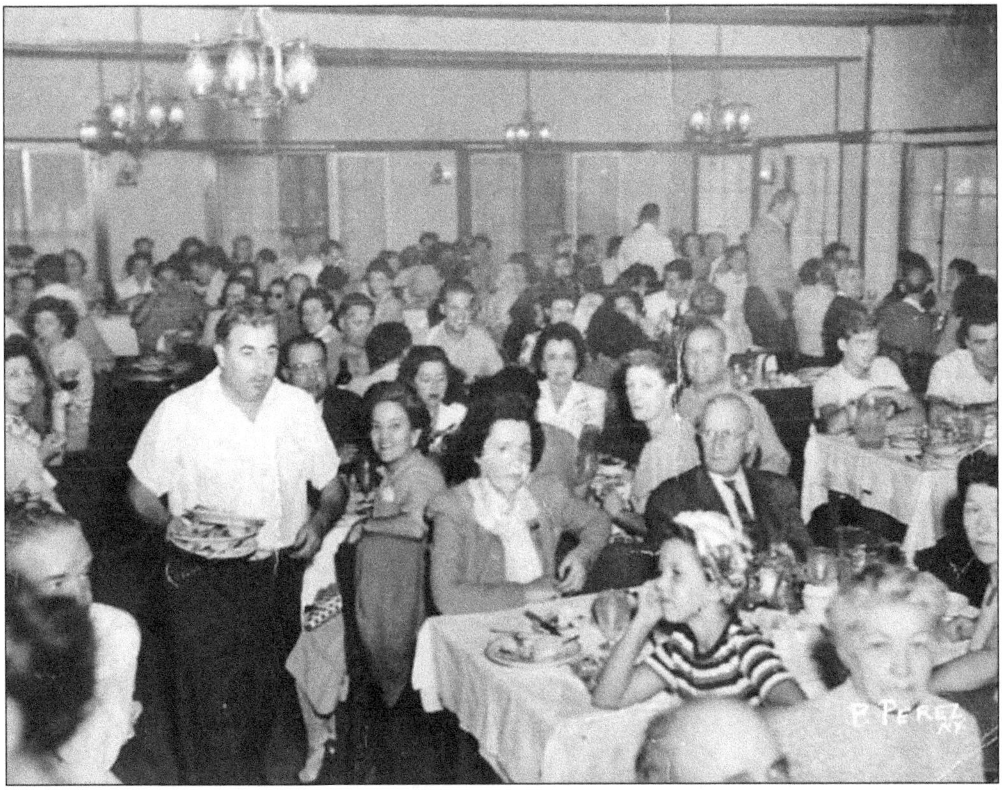

This c. 1945 photograph depicts a busy dining room at the Rifton Hotel. The gentleman carrying the dishes is Alfredo Diaz, the owner of the hotel, and the woman sitting at the table and facing the camera with her elbow on the table is Nina Perez. She is the wife of this picture's photographer. (Photograph by Paul D. Perez, courtesy of Luz Damron.)

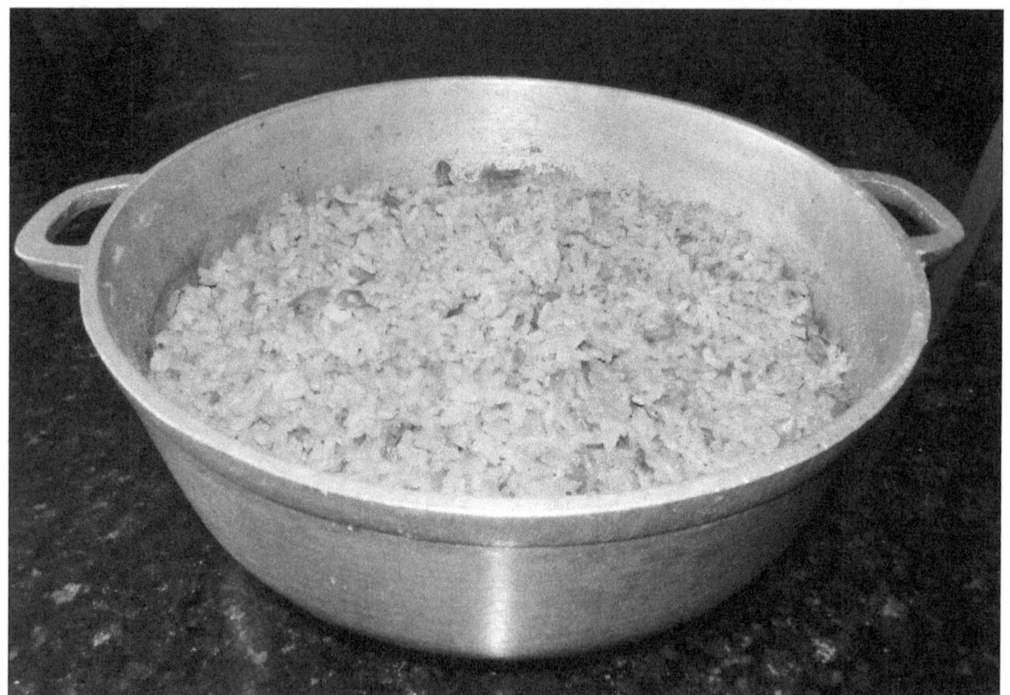

Rice and pigeon peas (*arroz con gandules*) was one the most popular dishes to be served throughout Las Villas. At some of the villas, it was the standard meal to be served for dinner on Sunday. This rice dish was usually served with roast pork (*lechon asado*), a side of fried plantains (*tostones*), a salad, and oftentimes with avocado and bread and butter. (Courtesy of the Martinez family collection.)

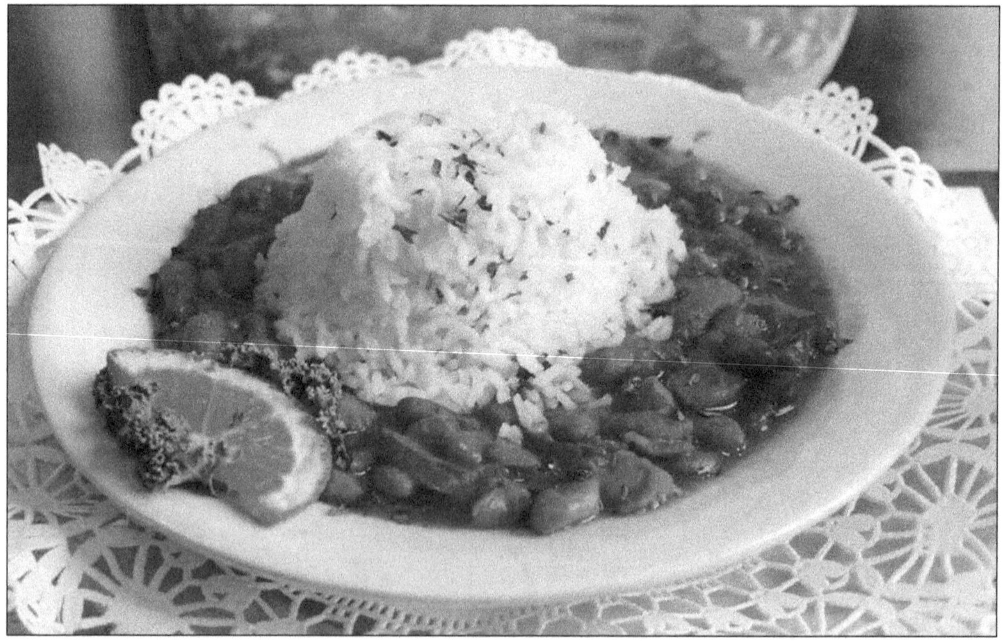

Rice and beans (*arroz con habichuelas*) was another dish that was in high demand at Las Villas. Red beans are most often used, but white, black, and pink beans can also be used instead. They are frequently served with roasted chicken (*pollo asado*). (Courtesy of freestockimages.com.)

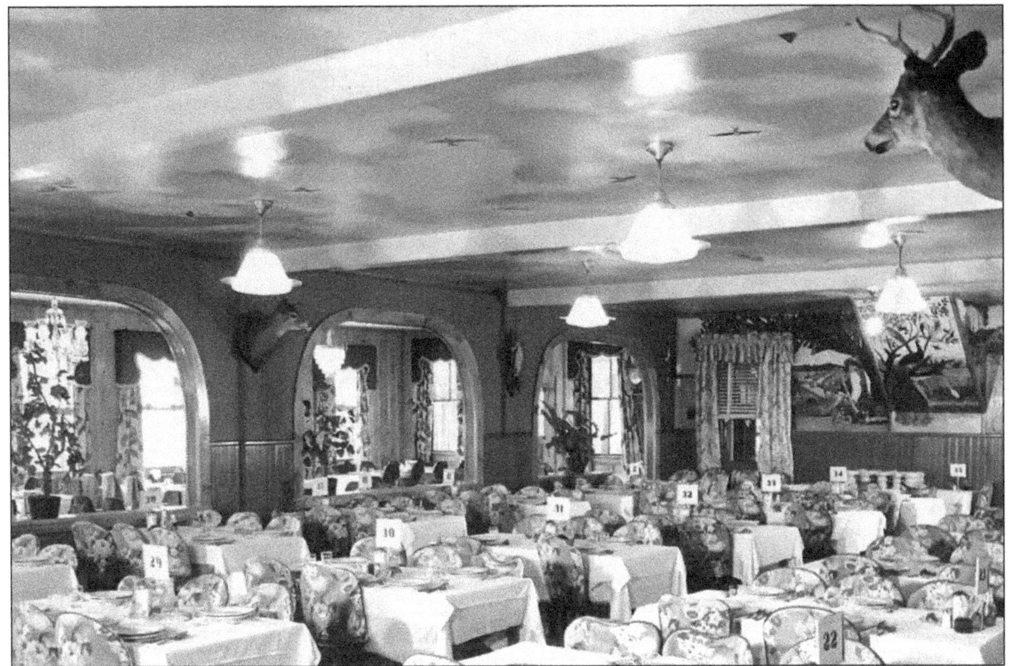

Seen around 1955, the banquet room at the Villa Nueva was made available for weddings and other formal occasions. The mural on the far wall depicts a scene from the owners' country of origin (in this case, Spain), which was typically found at many of the villas. Villa Nueva was one of the few villas whose dining room, bar, and banquet facilities were open to the public year-round. (Courtesy of Shirley Anson.)

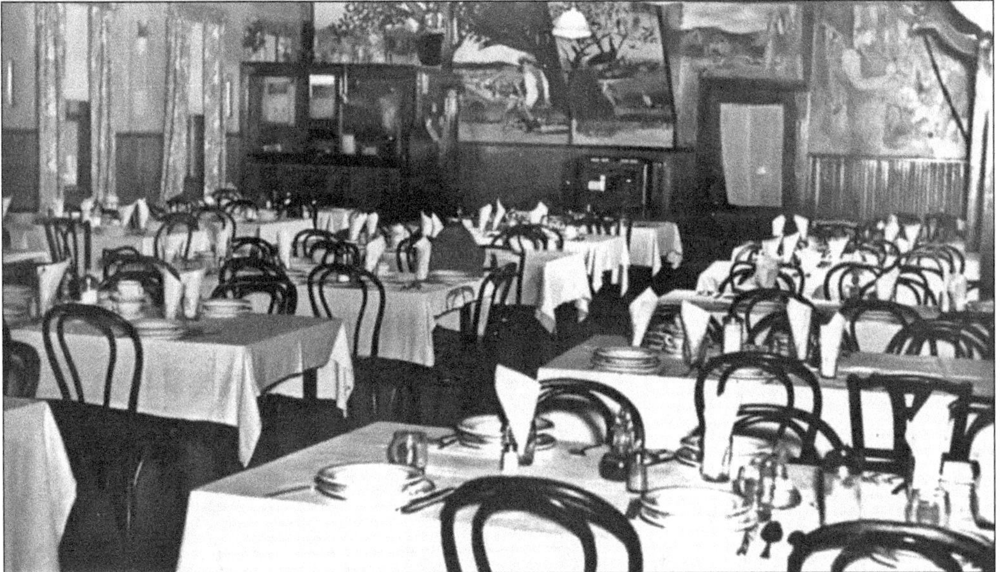

The c. 1950 dining room at the Villa Nueva has a scene from Spain painted on the far wall. Murals on the walls of restaurants in Spain and throughout Europe are very common. The owner of the villa, Severino Garcia, was from the Asturias region of Spain. He did a lot of promotions for the villa and often advertised that the villa was famous for their traditional Spanish dishes. (Courtesy of Shirley Anson.)

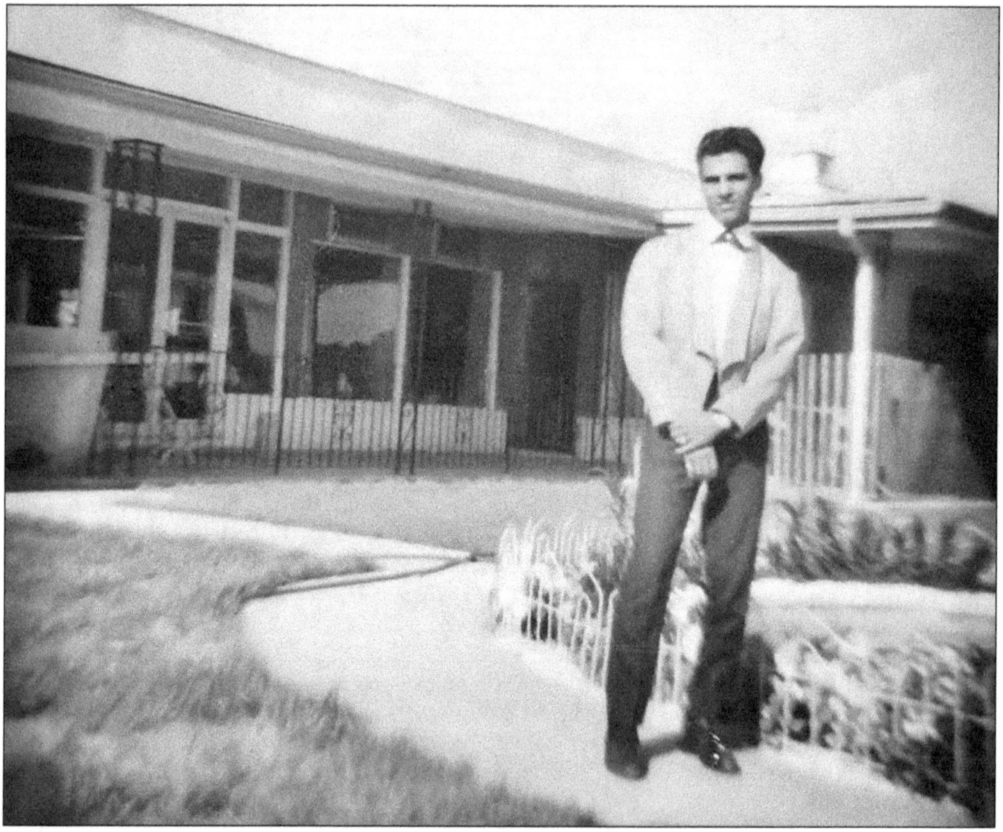

The author, pictured around 1967, worked as a waiter at Sunny Acres; the villa was owned by his parents. The children of villa owners were expected to help out in the business wherever they could, even if in a small way. Although it might not seem like it at the time, the benefit of having those obligations taught them some very important life lessons. (Courtesy of the Martinez family collection.)

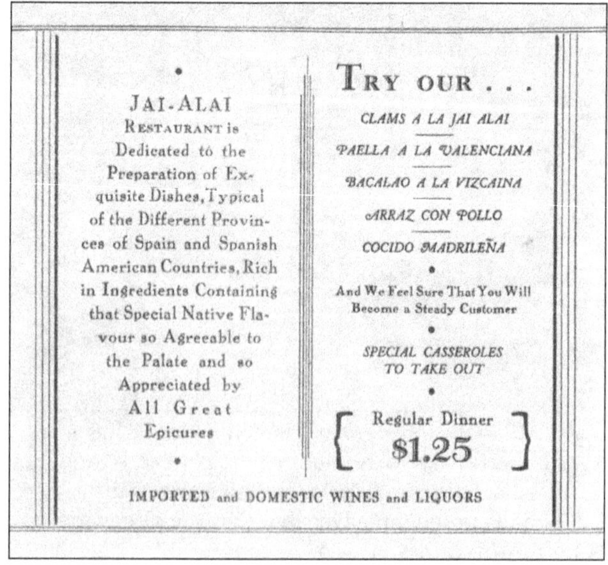

Pictured is a 1930s or 1940s villa menu with many of the traditional Spanish foods that were being offered for what seem today to be very modest prices. In general, the food prices were very reasonable, especially when compared to what one would pay at a New York City restaurant. (Courtesy of James Fernandez.)

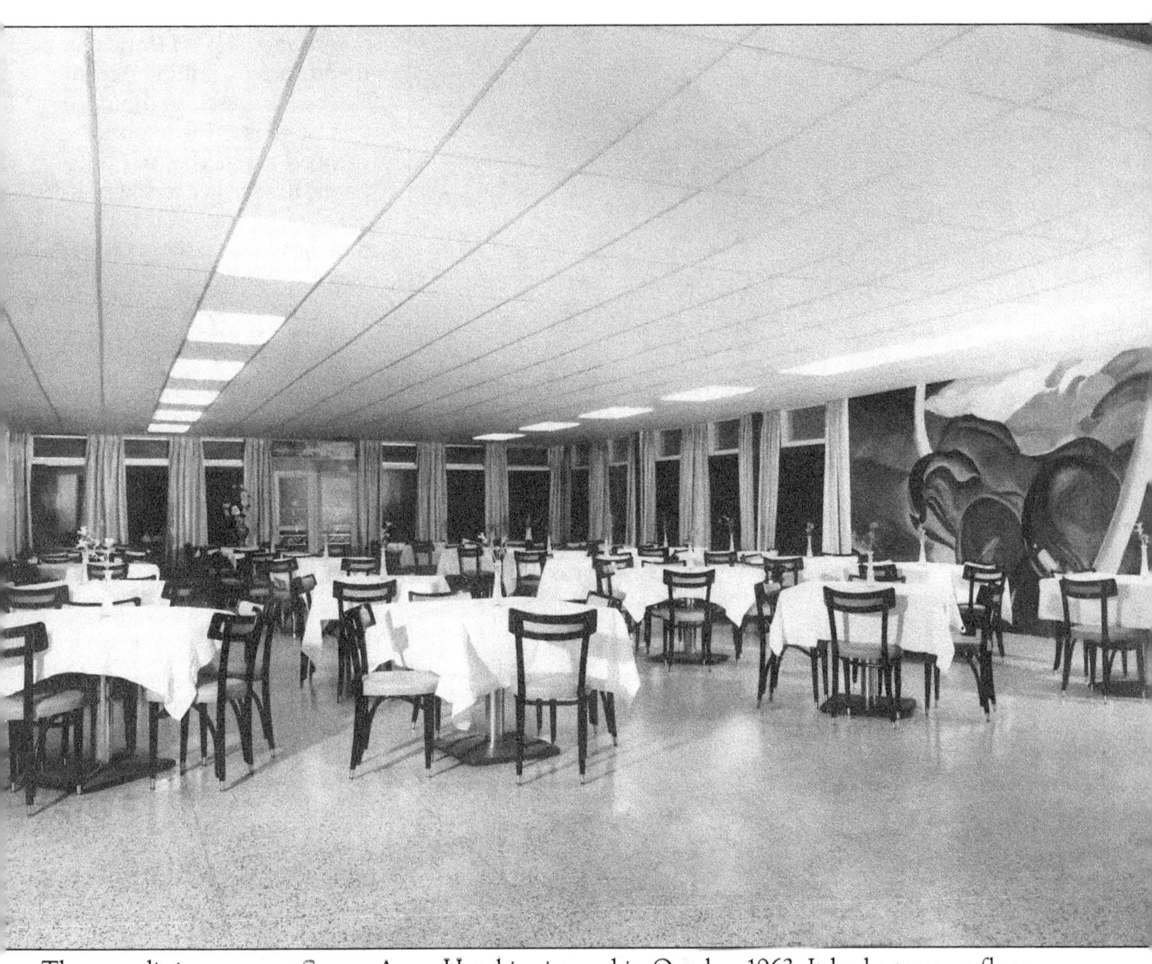

The new dining room at Sunny Acres Hotel is pictured in October 1963. It had a terrazzo floor, which was a new flooring trend at the time and was said to be very durable. The mural on the right is a reproduction of a 1911 painting by German painter Franz Marc called *The Large Blue Horses*. (Photograph by Frank V. Zadroga, courtesy of the Martinez family collection.)

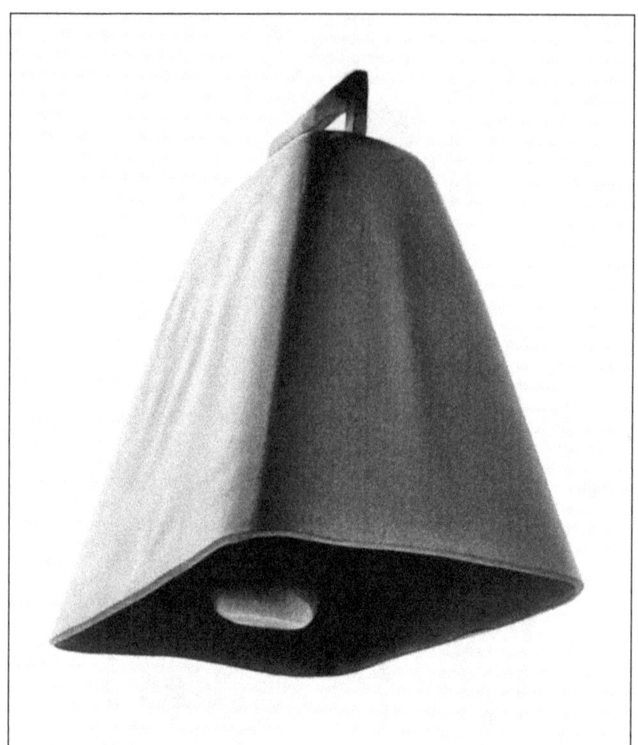

This dinner bell is identical to the one used at Sunny Acres. The bell was used by dining room staff as a way to notify the hotel guests that one of the meals—either breakfast, lunch, or supper—was ready to be served. (Courtesy of the Martinez family collection.)

Just as rice was likely the most common entrée served at Las Villas, there is no question that more roasted pork was consumed than any other type of meat. Even as late as the 1970s or 1980s, some of the villas still retained the old tradition of roasting pigs on an outdoor spit. (Courtesy of freestockimages.com.)

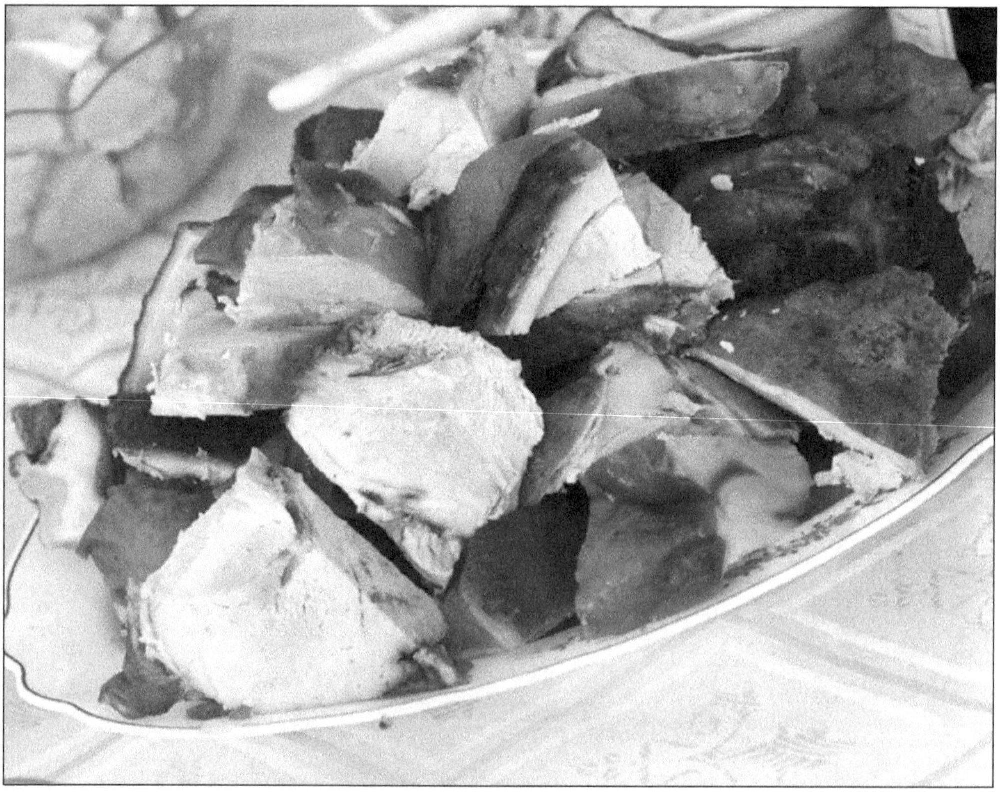

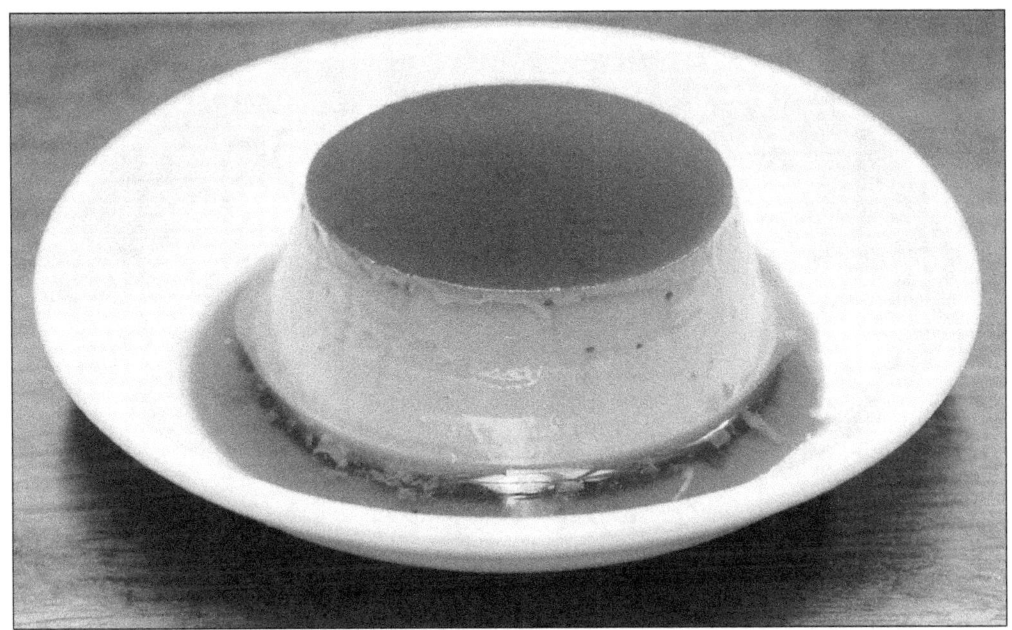

A variety of desserts were served at Las Villas, including fruit, ice cream, Jell-O, pudding, guava, and goat cheese, but the one most often served and requested was flan. This is a Spanish egg custard that is traditional in all countries of Latin America. (Courtesy of freestockimages.com.)

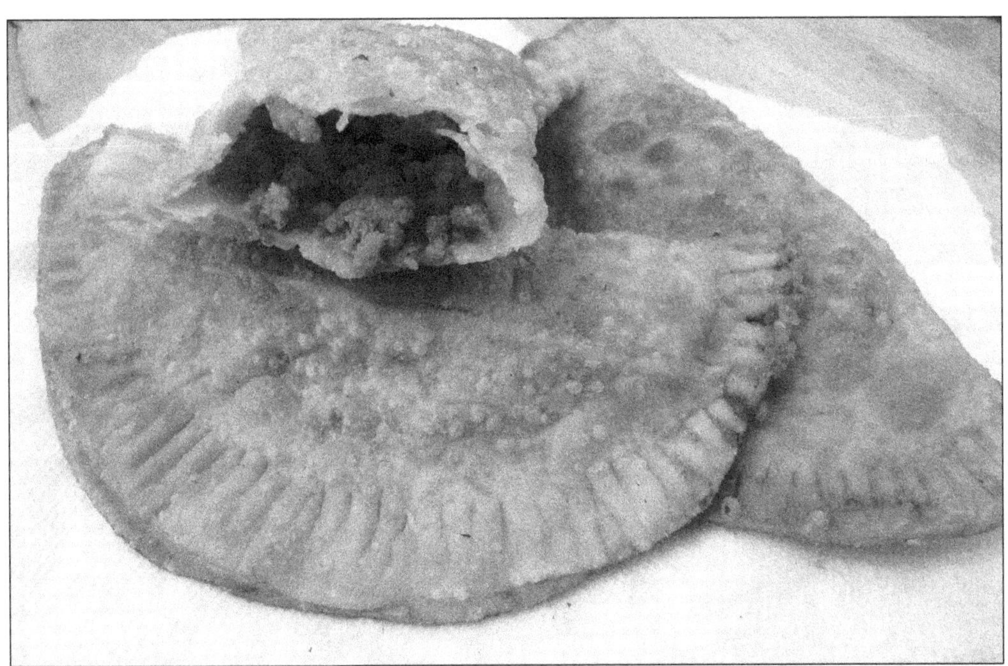

Empanada (*pastelillo*) (pictured) was one of the favorite side dishes at Las Villas that could be ordered with a meal or just by itself. Many *pastelillos* were sold as snacks in the dance hall while customers were drinking, dancing, and listening to afternoon or nighttime performances of music. (Courtesy of freestockimages.com.)

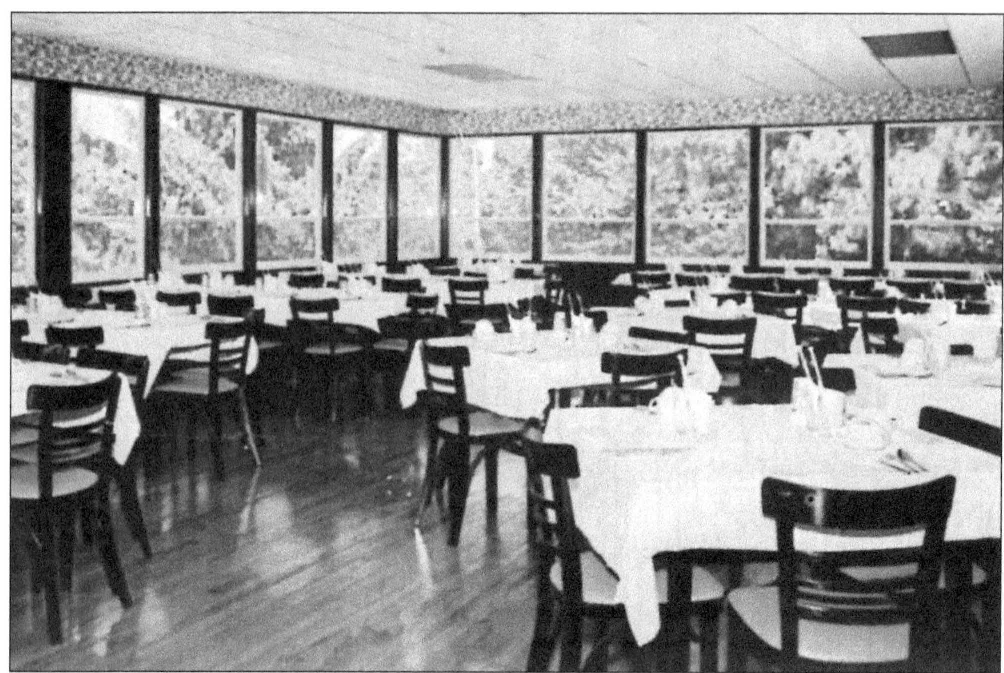

These two distinct dining rooms (above and below) at the Villa Guardarramas, pictured in the 1960s, could easily accommodate the very large groups of guests that the villa frequently catered to when the jiras were invited to visit. All members of the Guardarramas family pitched in to help Pedro and Gonzala when it came time to prepare for the arrival of the jiras. Glass tumblers, ceramic plates, and standard flatware were always used for the place settings. As in many of the villas, a generous portion of rice and pigeon peas and pork was the basic meal being served. (Both, courtesy of the Guardarramas family collection.)

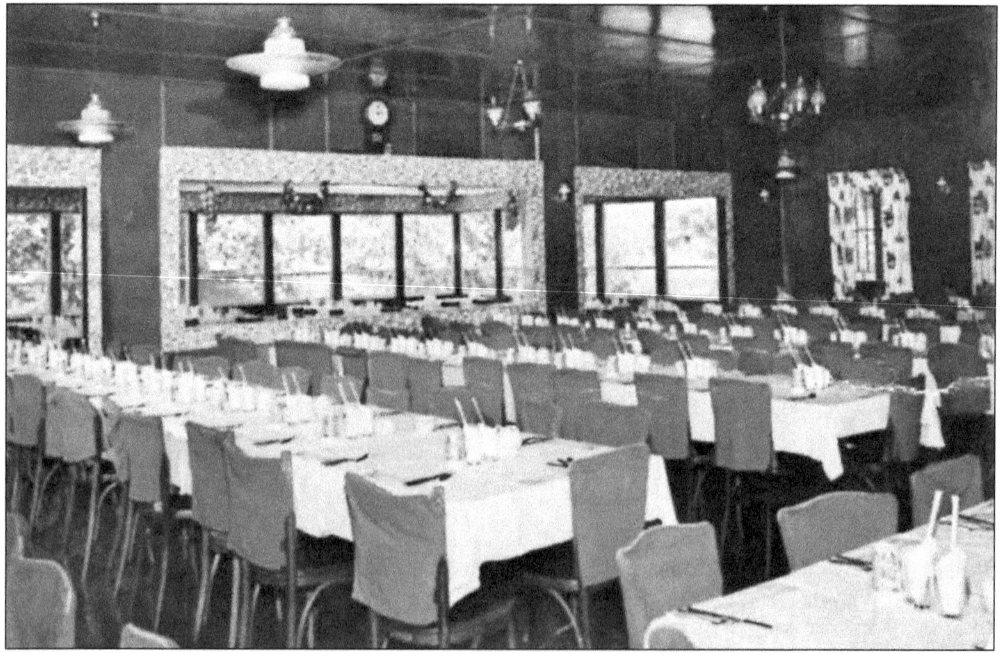

Fried plantains (*tostones*) were also enjoyed by patrons as a snack or as a side dish. Not all villas offered the same food, since it might differ based on who their customer base was, but one could be certain that somewhere in Las Villas, he or she could get every possible type of Puerto Rican food. (Courtesy of freestockimages.com.)

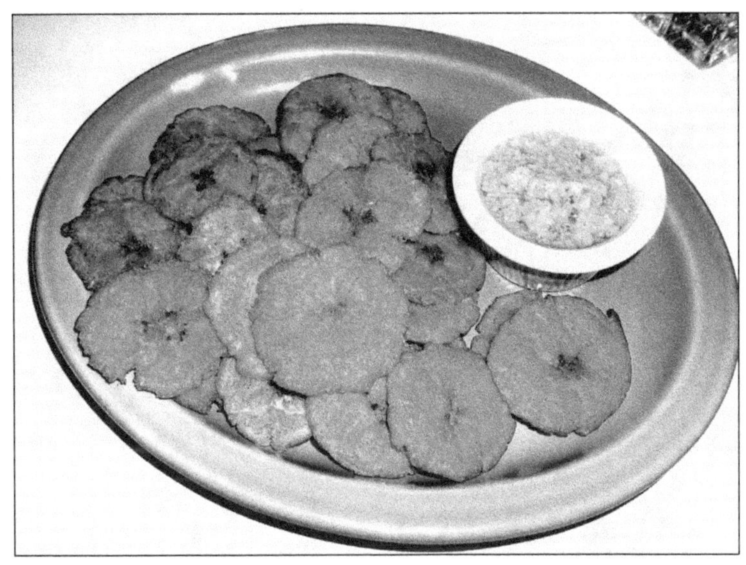

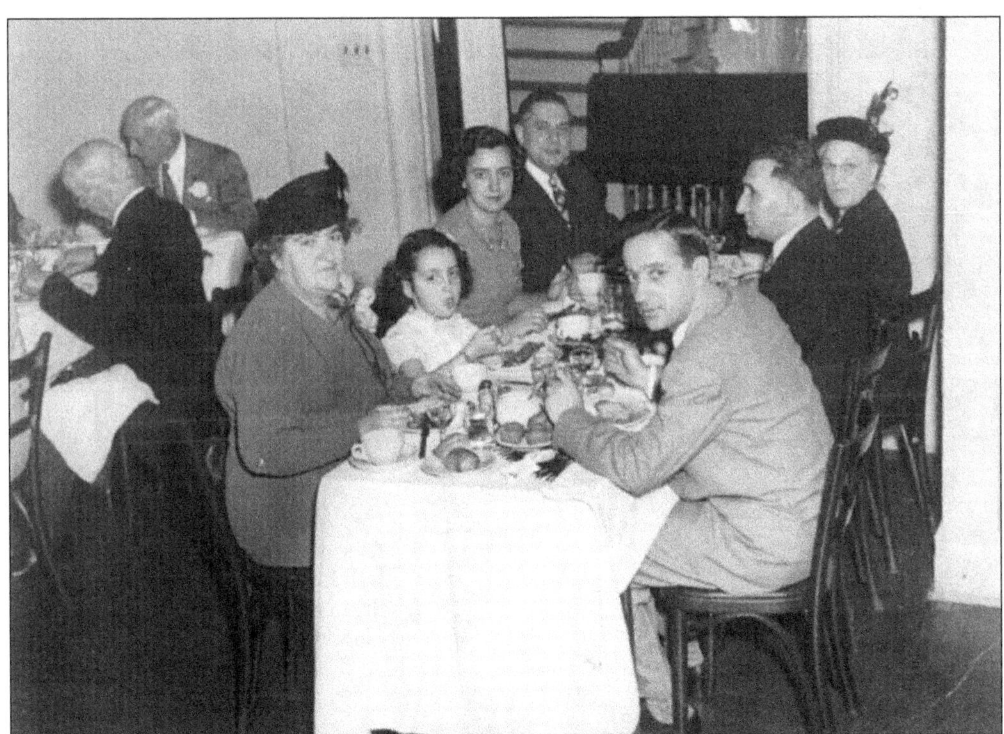

Guests at the Rifton Hotel, pictured around 1945, sit at a table apparently set up in a doorway, which might indicate that the sizable Rifton dining room was at capacity. With 100 rooms in the hotel, the Rifton was one of the largest and also one of the most popular of the Spanish resorts in Ulster County. The Rifton Hotel was an outlier resort, being about 30 minutes from the other two main villa resort regions. (Courtesy of Luz Damron.)

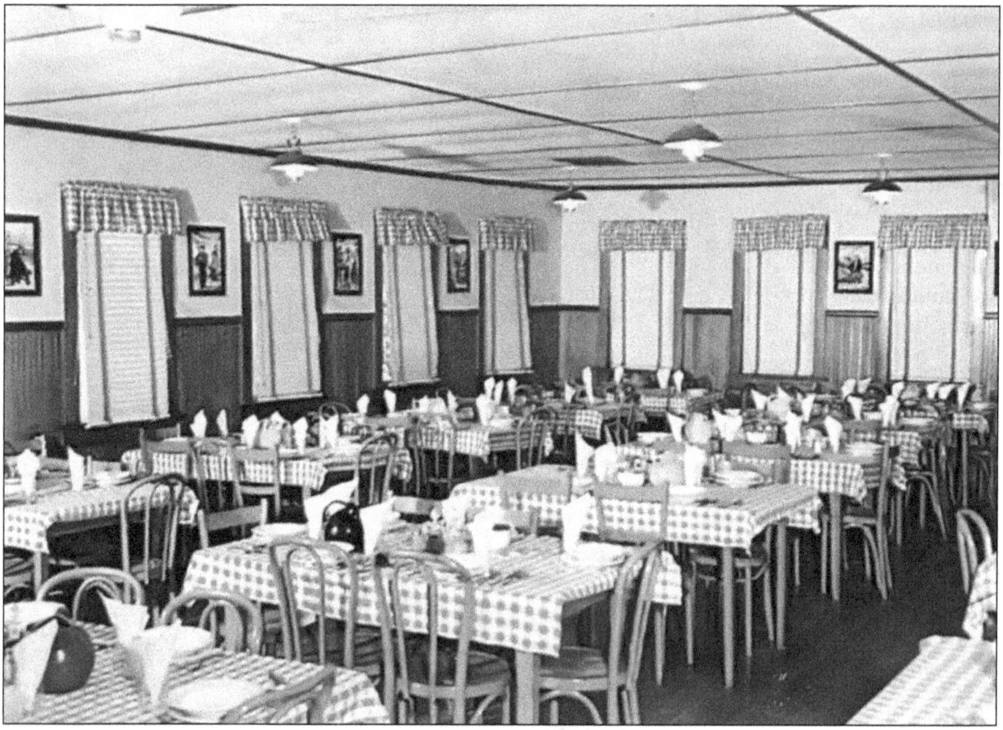

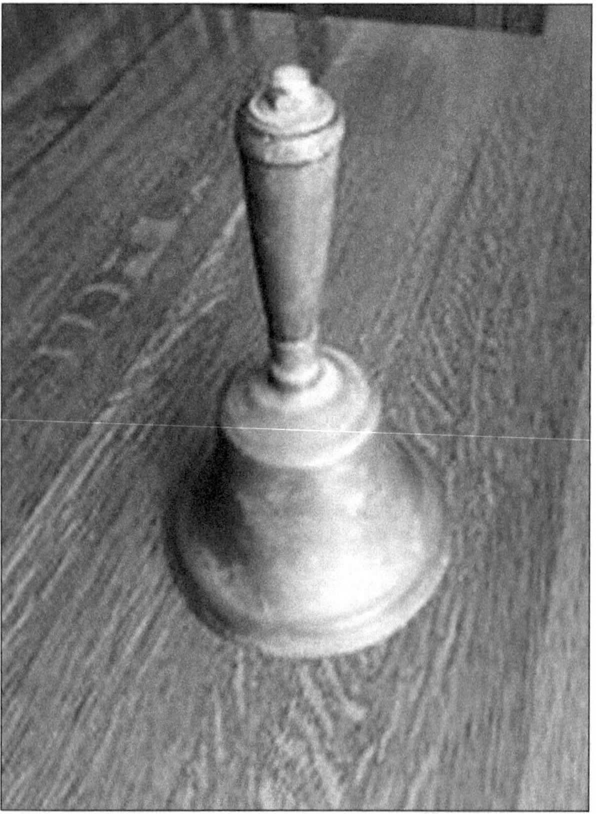

The quaint dining room (above), complete with checkered tablecloths, at the Villa Garcia was typical of many of the 1950s villa dining rooms. Staff members set up simple place settings and placed water pitchers, sugar shakers, and the classic oil and vinegar cruet sets on the tables. At the villas, family-style dining was usually the case with one or sometimes two families per table. Meals were set out in bowls or platters from which everyone was served. This is the actual dinner bell (left) from the Villa Garcia that was used to summon guests to the dining hall for breakfast, lunch, and dinner. (Both, courtesy of Denise Garcia-Cornog.)

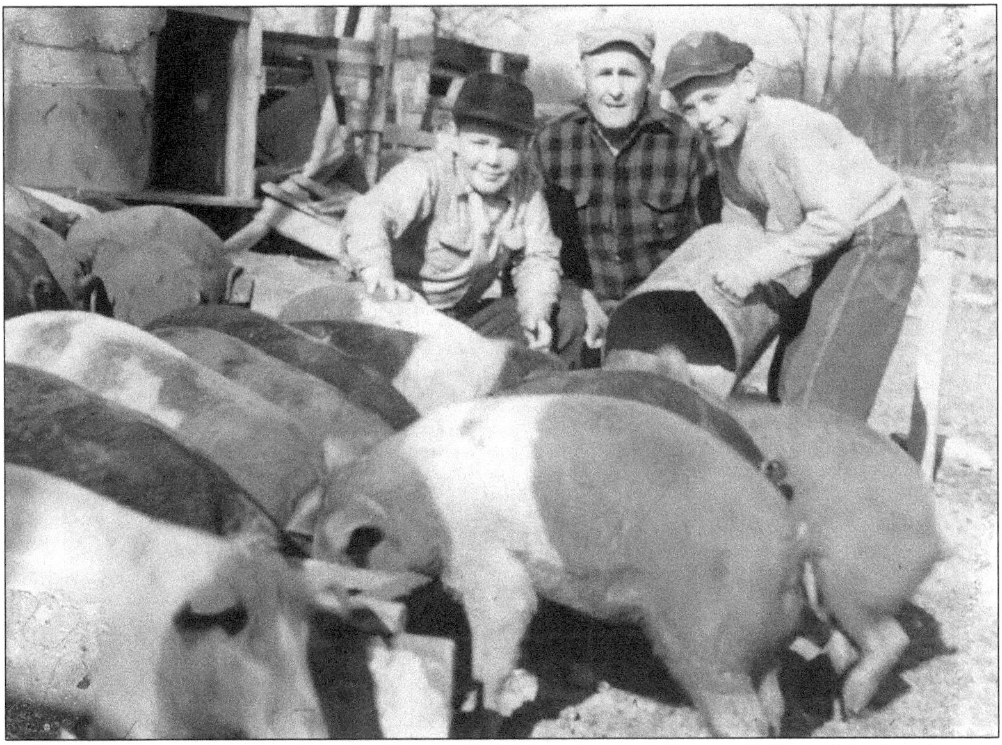

Isidoro Romero tends to his hogs with some help from his sons Henry (left) and Richard at the Casa Los Andes resort. Isidoro raised chickens and hogs for the sole purpose of feeding his guests. The chickens provided eggs for breakfast and as an ingredient for other foods while the hogs were slaughtered to provide guests with fresh ham, bacon, pork chops, and a Spanish sausage called chorizo. (Courtesy of Henry "Hank" Romero.)

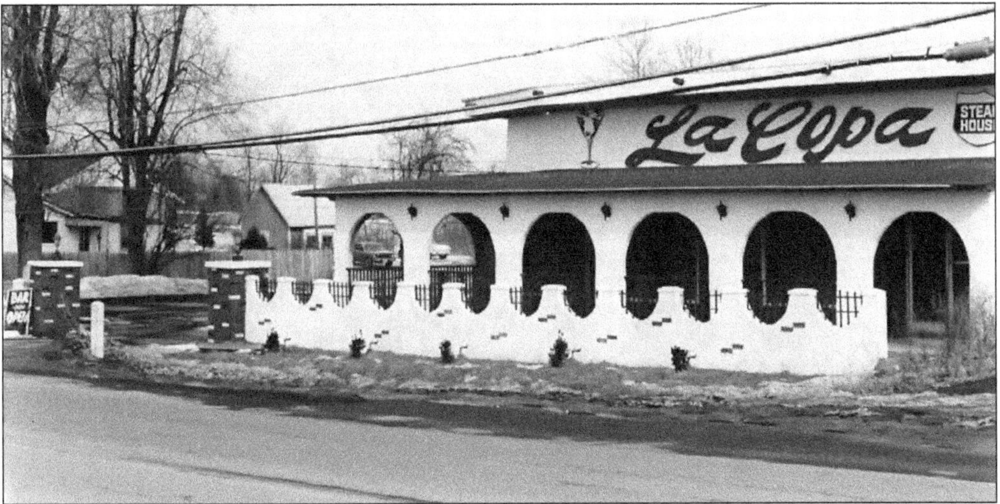

La Copa, seen in 1977, was one of just a few restaurants in town that were open year-round and, for the most part, limited its operations to food service alone. The menu at La Copa featured traditional American cuisine but also included a number of Spanish dishes. The establishment was operated by Shorty and Lucy Martinez, the previous owners of the Villa Sunny Acres. (Courtesy of the Martinez family collection.)

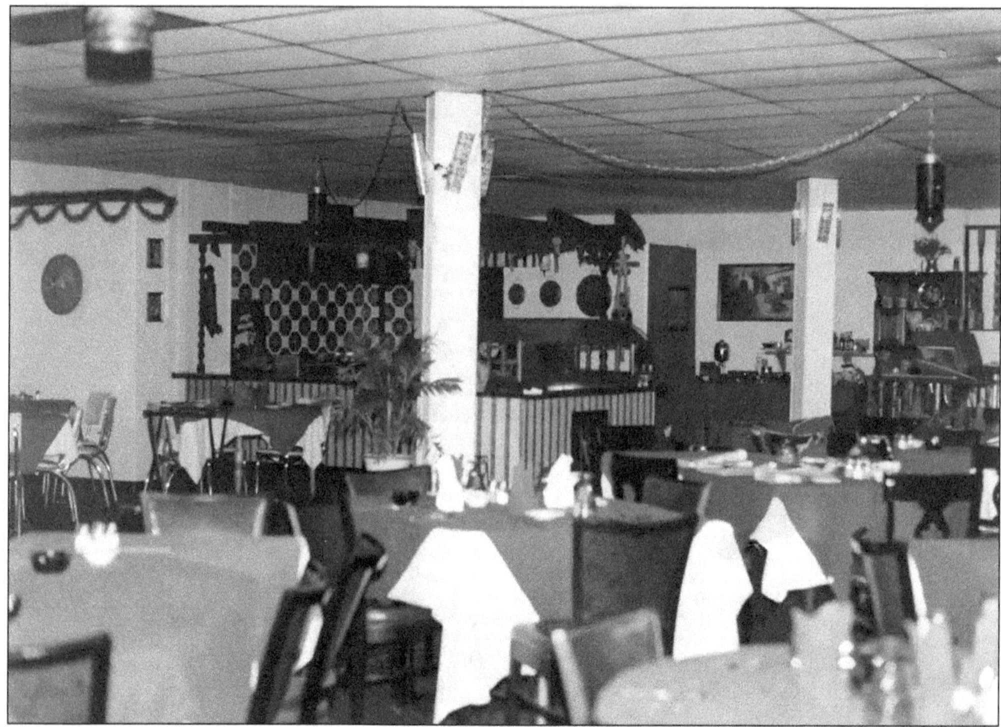

This photograph shows the dining room at La Copa, as seen from the bar at the restaurant. The customer base of the restaurant was primarily from the towns of Plattekill and Newburgh, but it also drew customers from the villas during the summer months. The restaurant was in operation during the 1970s and did have live music at times. (Courtesy of the Martinez family collection.)

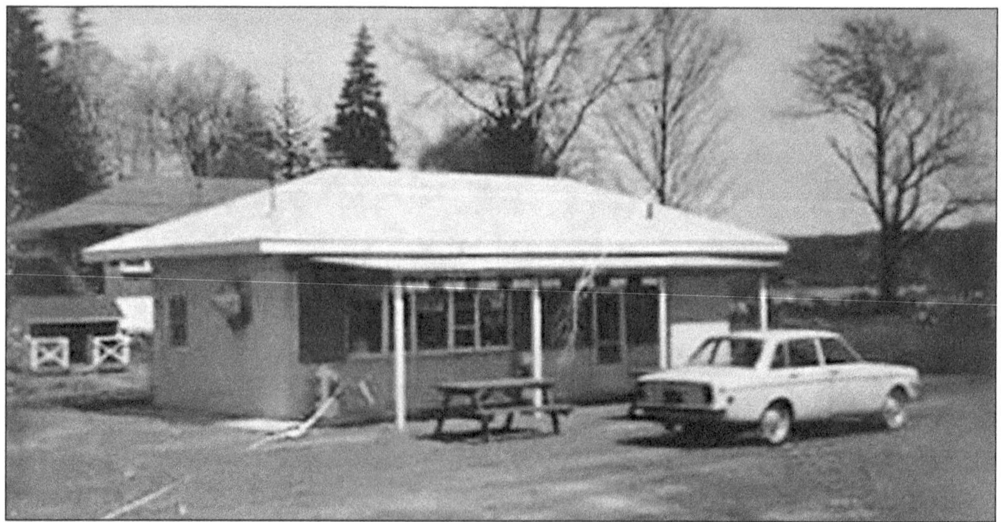

The R&C Drive-In was owned by Raul and Carmen Correa and was located on the corner of Plattekill Ardonia Road and Unionville Road. Though it was technically not a villa in the traditional sense, many of the visitors to the villas found their way here to catch a quick bite to eat. Customers would drive in and walk up to a window to order from a large selection of Puerto Rican foods. (Courtesy of Yvonne Correa Morales.)

Five

Actividades y Deportes
Activities and Sports

During the era of Las Villas, the way people vacationed and sought diversions from their daily routines evolved and followed the trends taking shape in the rest of the United States. When the first villas appeared during the 1920s, traveling to the mountains or into the countryside was already a very popular recreational activity. This was especially true for people whose desires were to simply spend their time in a place where they could enjoy the peacefulness and beauty of their surroundings. This form of recreation had been going on since the mid-19th century in New York State's Catskill and Adirondack Mountains as well as in the rolling hills of the Hudson Valley. These regions had hundreds of small farms and dozens of hotels, lodges, camps, and boardinghouses, some of which the first villa owners looked to buy.

Spanish families and their friends found pleasure in vacationing together, not only because they enjoyed each other's company but also to get back in touch with nature. At that time, the main incentive for traveling to Las Villas was to escape the noisy, crowded, and gritty conditions of New York City and seek out those places that offered a relaxing atmosphere with quiet, restful surroundings. As time went on and leisure activities became more diverse within American society, they also became more diverse for those who vacationed at Las Villas. By the 1940s and 1950s, there were already many more activities for people to enjoy at Las Villas. Softball fields, handball, basketball, and even tennis courts might be available in some places that had the room and money to build them. Of course, music and dancing would always remain the most popular form of entertainment for the majority of villa tourists, but there were now many other distractions to fall back on. On more than a few occasions, people discovered that Las Villas was the ideal place to celebrate a wedding reception or to make a honeymoon destination. Without a doubt, for many years, Las Villas was the most popular vacation and getaway destination for Hispanic families in the entire Northeast.

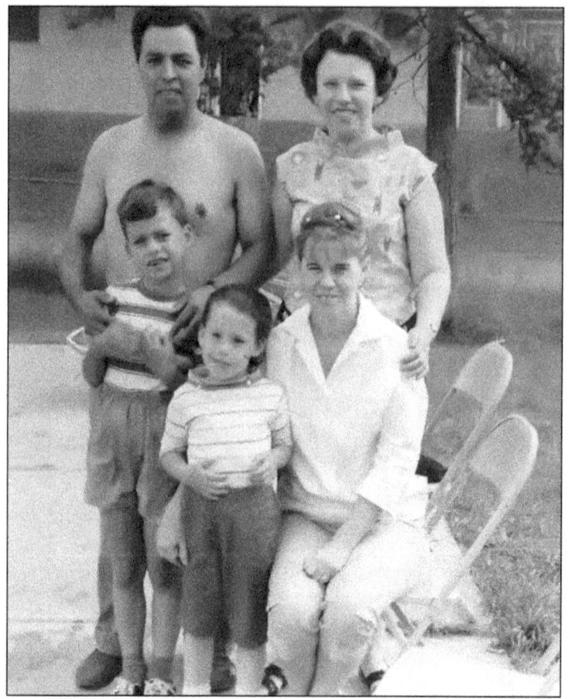

The Nietos share a moment at Sunny Acres swimming pool on July 9, 1963, with a couple of other family members. The swimming pool was one of only two in all of the villas that was made out of steel, the other being at Villa Galicia. Family members are, from left to right, (first row) Keith Nieto, Lynn Cruz, and Carol Campbell Martinez, (second row) Armando Nieto and Veronica "Ronnie" Campbell Nieto. (Courtesy of Keith Nieto.)

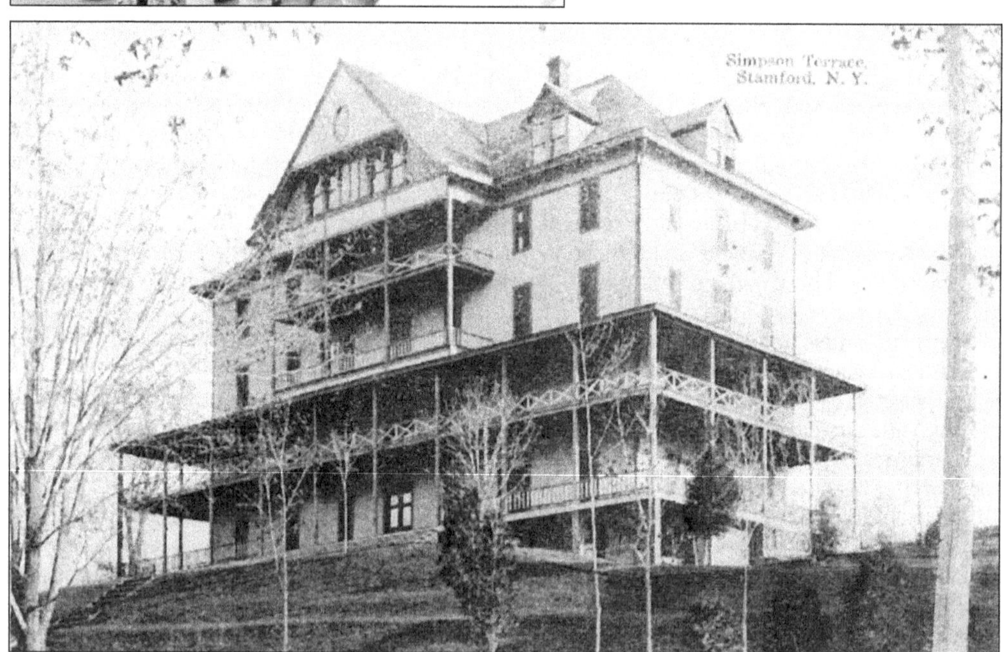

The Habana Hotel shown here was actually in the Delaware County town of Stamford, New York. The Habana was one of several hotels owned by Emmanuel M. Barros in the town. It is believed that Emmanuel was either a Cuban citizen or a Spanish immigrant who had lived in Cuba before setting up several businesses in Stamford. The other hotels that catered to Cubans or Spaniards in Stamford were La Perla de Cuba, the Tea Time Inn, and the Hotel Alcazar. La Perla de Cuba might very well be the earliest of all the Hispanic villas to established in New York State, as records of its existence date back to 1912. (Courtesy of Karen Cuccinello.)

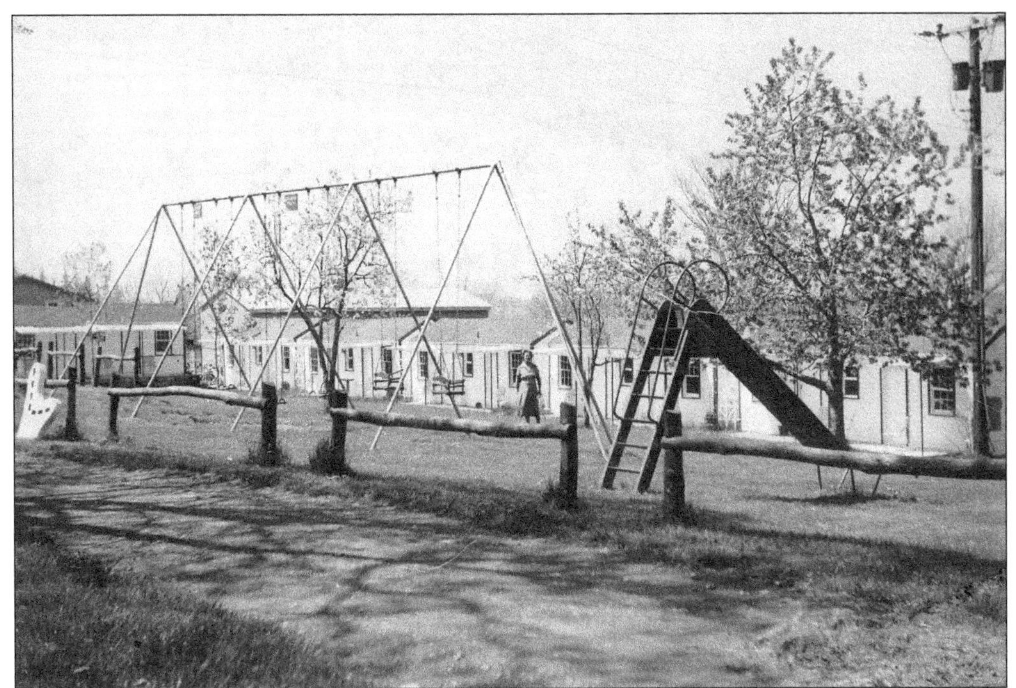

The playground area with swings and a slide was located behind the main house at the Villa Garcia. In the background of this c. 1960 photograph are the bungalows, just one of several guest accommodations at the villa. Standing in the center of the photograph is Hattie Ferraiuolo, a Plattekill resident and one of the villa's employees. (Courtesy of the Martinez family collection.)

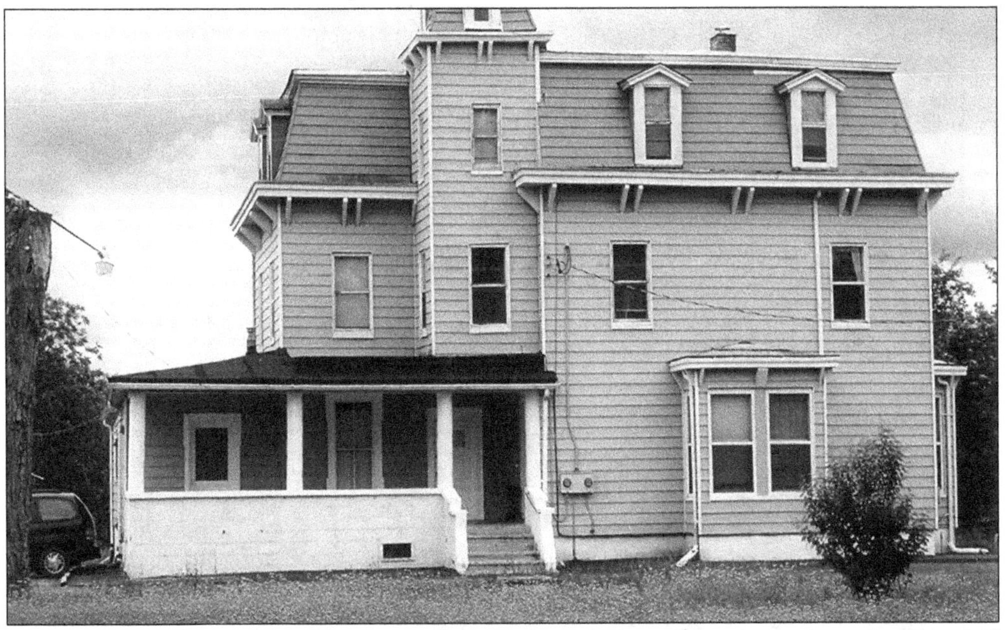

Spanish Bits dude ranch and bar opened in the late 1960s and was located on the Plattekill Ardonia Road. Horseback riding was made available to both local residents and villa tourists alike. The terrain and the scenic surroundings of the area made for the most interesting of trail rides. (Courtesy of the Martinez family collection.)

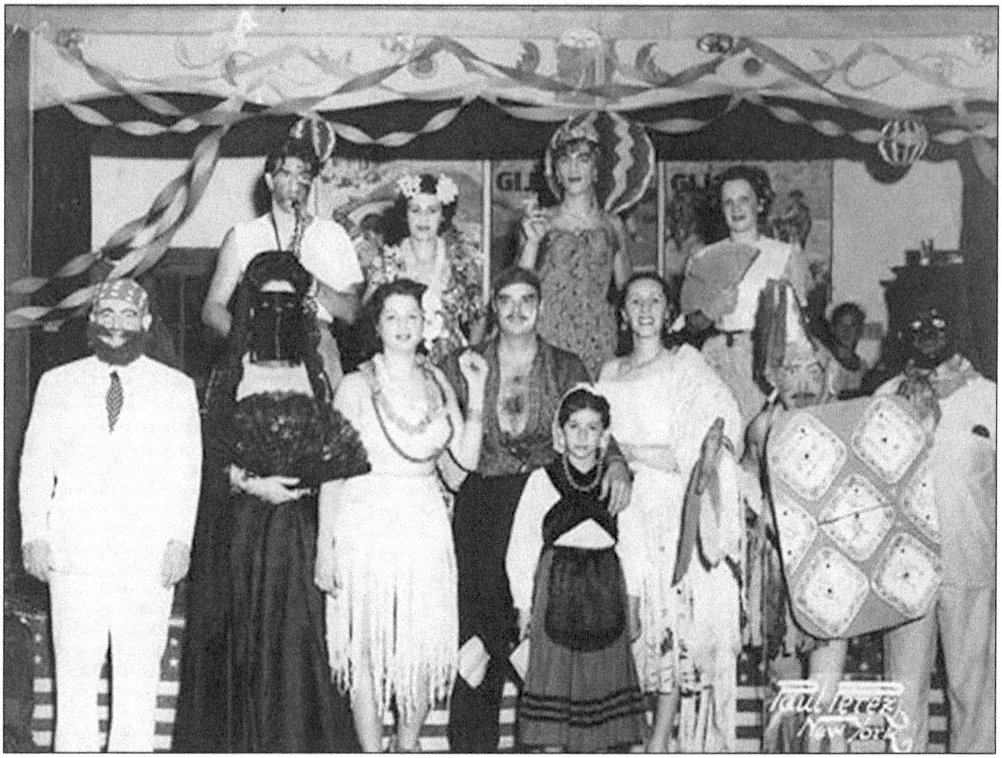

A group of young Spanish guests at the Rifton Hotel, dressed in elaborate costumes, takes part in a masquerade ball of sorts. The event also included children and even a dog (below) who pose proudly for the camera. (Both, courtesy of Luz Damron; photographs by Paul D. Perez.)

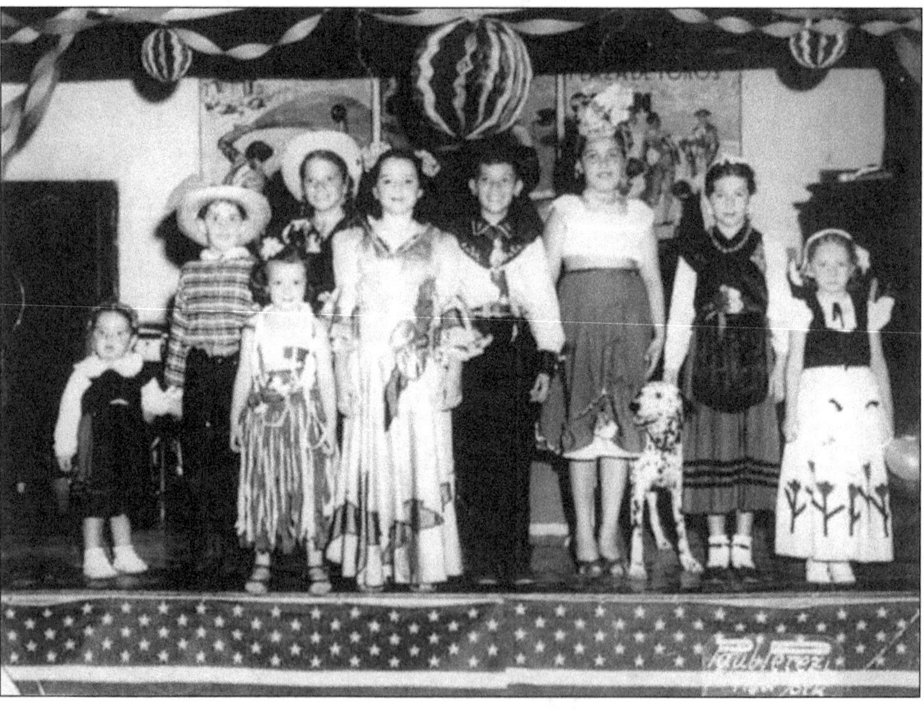

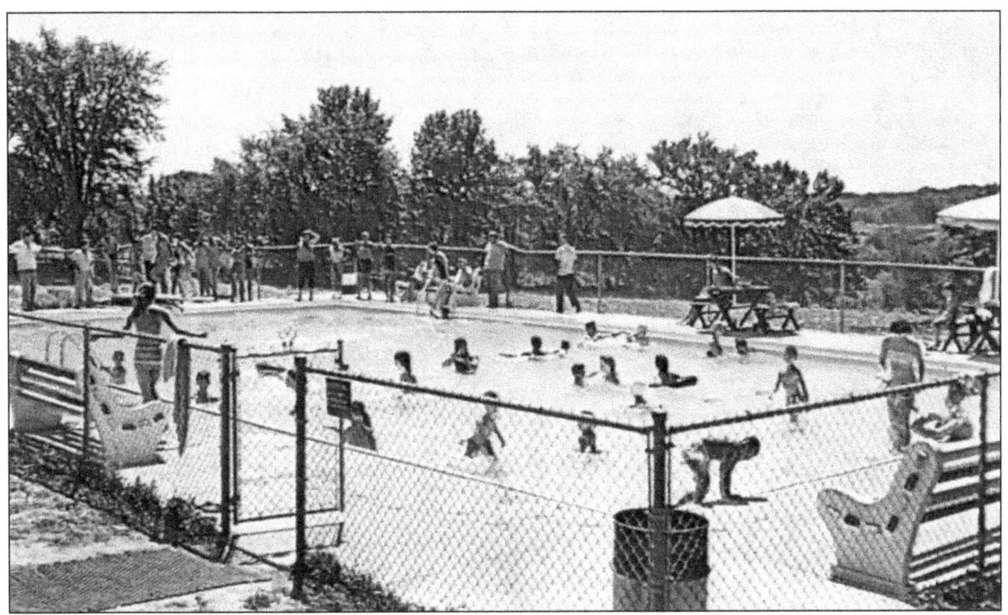

The pool at the Villa Garcia was located behind the main house and adjacent to the playground. Though heavily used at times, most villa pools did not have lifeguards on duty. Most of the owners posted signs that usually read, "Swim at your own risk," so it was up to the parents to keep a close eye on their children. (Courtesy of Elizabeth Werlau.)

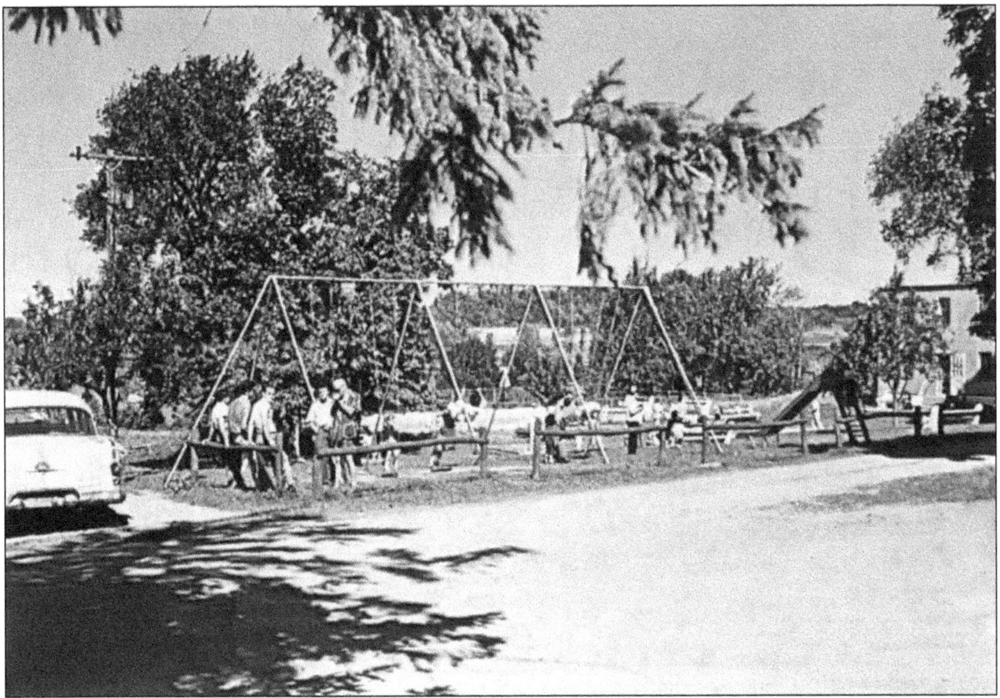

Pictured around 1959, the playground at the Villa Garcia had a set of swings, a seesaw, and a slide for children to enjoy. , Having been established by Celestino and Flora Garcia in the late 1920s, the Villa Garcia was one of the earliest of the villas. The mature shade trees throughout the property gave the villa a very peaceful and relaxing quality. (Courtesy of Elizabeth Werlau.)

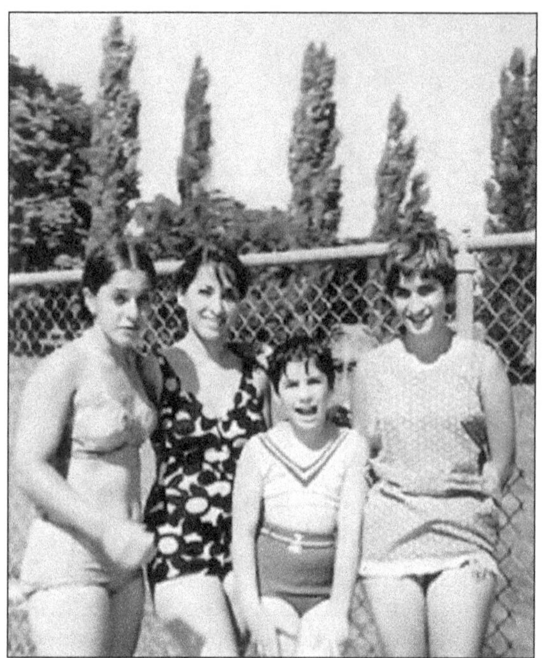

The Pagan sisters are pictured—from left to right, Nilda, Rosa, Diane, and Pauline—at the Villa Galicia swimming pool around 1967. Though the villas could be a source of loud music, large crowds, and heavy traffic that the locals had to put up with, the owners tried very hard to be good neighbors and good community members. Most of them would frequently allow access to their facilities (pools, courts, and so on) for use by the locals. (Courtesy of Carlos and Pauline Santiago.)

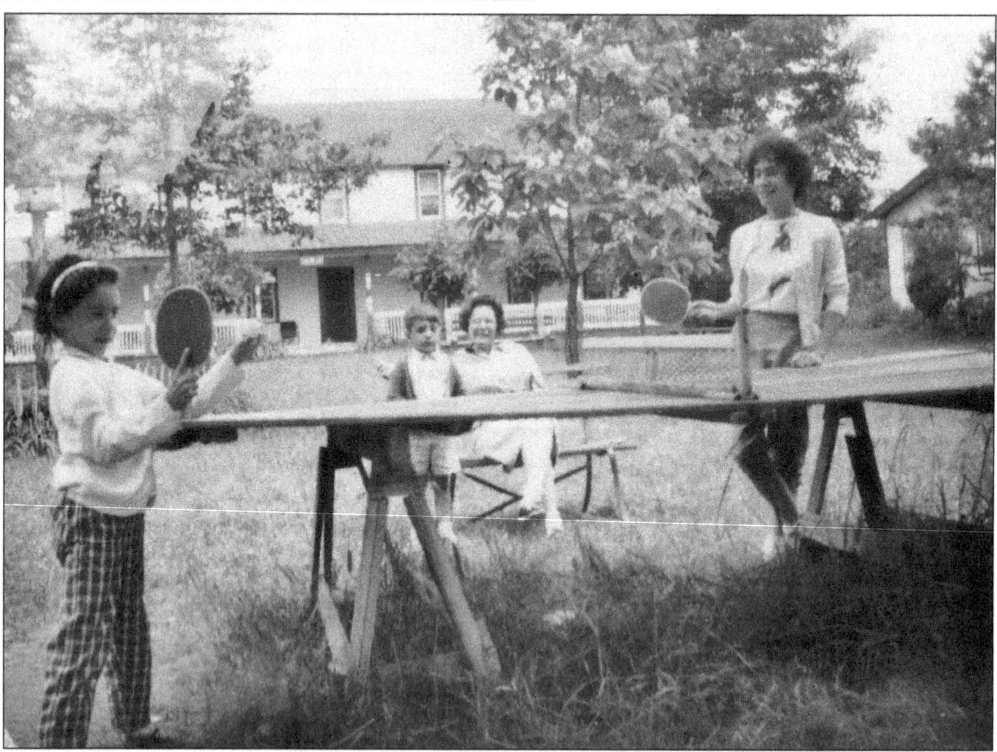

At the Villa Madrid, Sue Rodriguez plays a game of Ping-Pong with her daughter Dee while her younger daughter Cookie and her mother, Carmen Baldassari, look on. Unlike most Ping-Pong tables, this one was situated outside, so, at times, breezes became a factor in the serves and volleys of the game. The boardinghouse, which accommodated most of the guests at the villa, can be seen in the background. (Courtesy of Sue and Bill Rodriguez.)

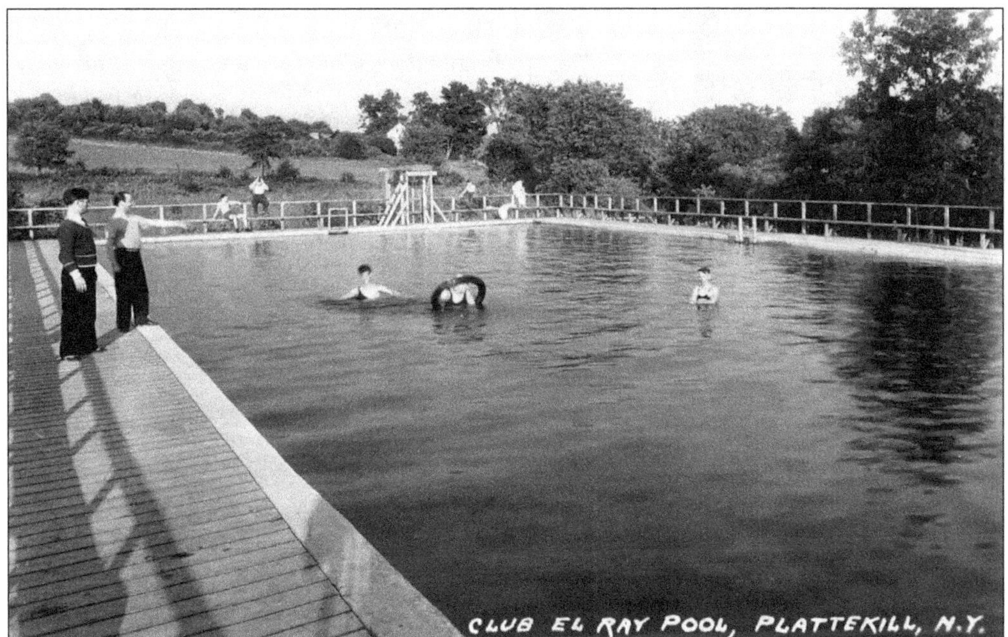

The swimming pool at Club El Ray, later renamed El Nilo, was one of the largest in the area. At one point, in the 1940s or 1950s, the pool was permanently closed down. Rumor has it that the pool was closed down permanently because of a drowning that occurred, and yet another rumor was that several children had contracted polio from swimming in the stream-fed pool. (Courtesy of Shirley Anson.)

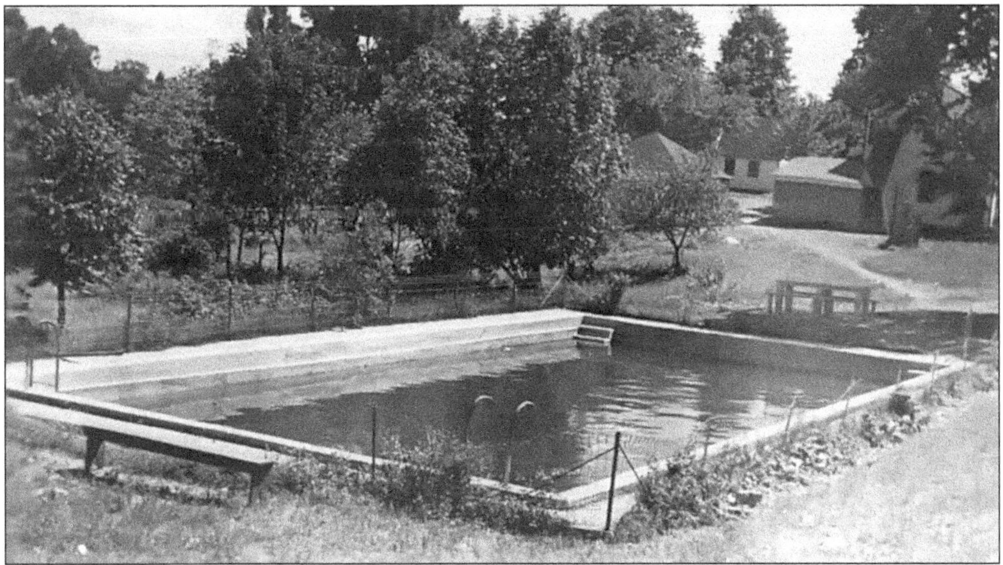

The first swimming pool at the Villa Nueva was located at the north end of the villa's property. A second pool that took the place of this one was built in the shape of a Spanish fan in an area closer to the main buildings and on the edge of the man-made lake. The villa was probably the most well known of all the Spanish villas in New York State. (Courtesy of Shirley Anson.)

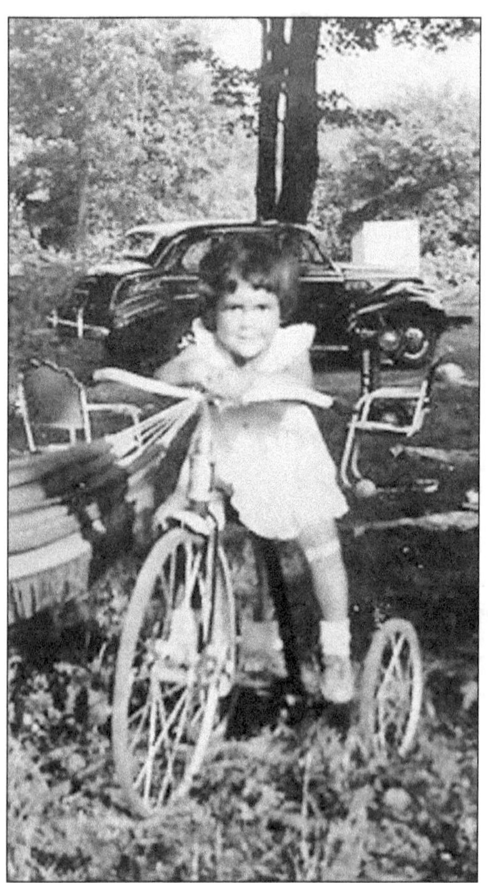

This c. 1949 photograph shows Roxy Santiago on her tricycle at the Casa Roxana. The villa, located on Unionville Road, was owned by her parents, Radames and Josefina Santiago, who had migrated from Puerto Rico to New York City before moving to Plattekill. The Santiagos named the villa after their young daughter. (Courtesy of Roxy Santiago.)

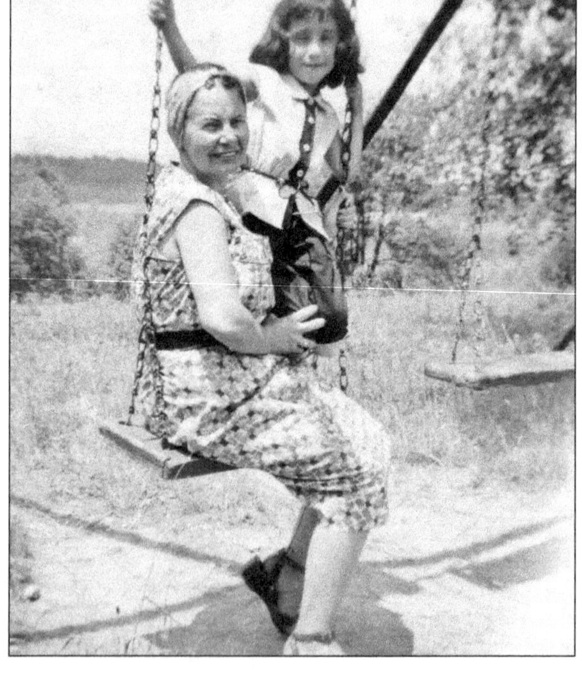

Carmen Baldassari sits on a swing at the Villa Madrid with her granddaughter Dee Rodriguez in this 1954 photograph. The swings were a popular activity, and the same set of swings was enjoyed for many years at the villa by both kids and adults. The Villa Madrid was a villa one went to for the simple pleasure of being in the country. (Courtesy of Sue and Bill Rodriguez.)

Boating was one of the many family-oriented activities available at the villas, as seen in this picture taken at the Rifton Hotel, which was owned by Pilar and Alfredo Diaz, immigrants from Asturias, Spain. A number of the villas had a pond or lake that boats could be taken out on, including Sunny Acres and Villa Nueva. (Courtesy of Luz Damron.)

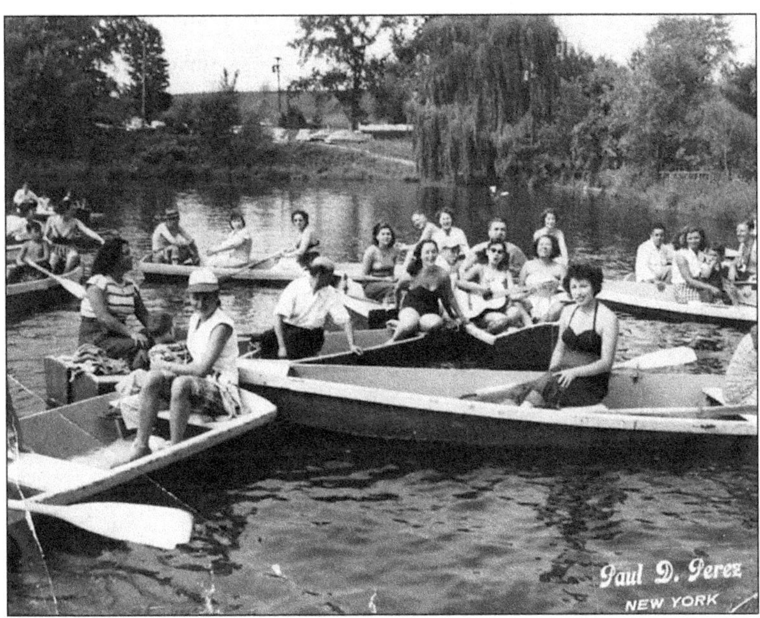

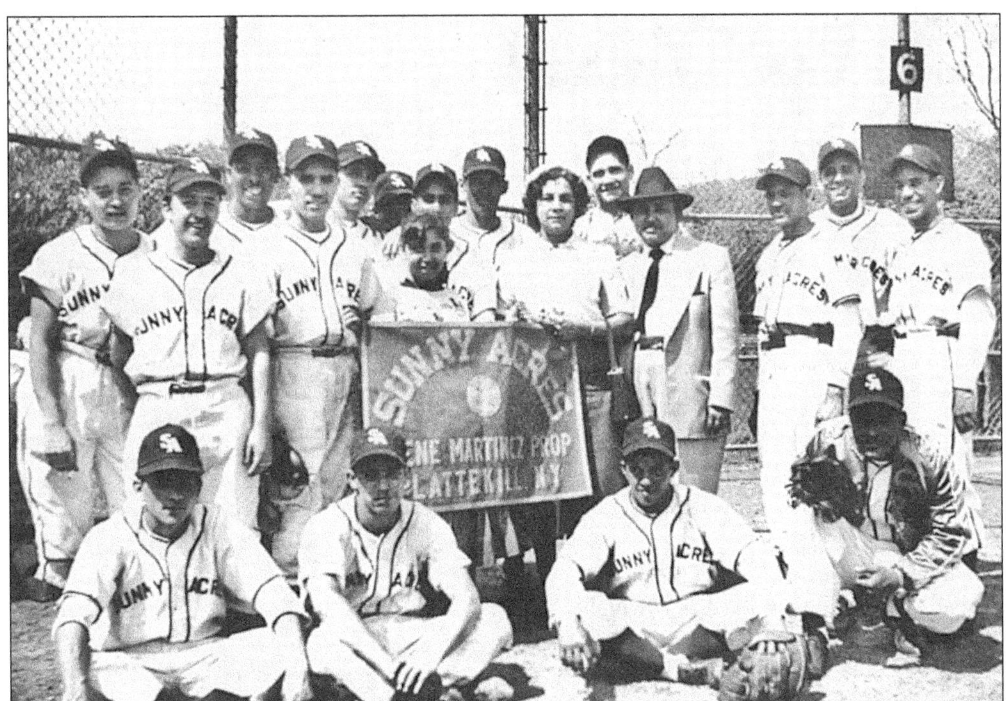

It is a common practice for businesses to sponsor amateur athletic teams in their area, and that was also the case for some of the villas. Sunny Acres actually sponsored a semiprofessional baseball team that played under the same name. In this c. 1950 photograph, Irene Martinez, owner of Sunny Acres, is standing behind and to the right of the banner. To her left is Paco Martinez, her brother-in-law and the manager of the team. (Courtesy of the Martinez family collection.)

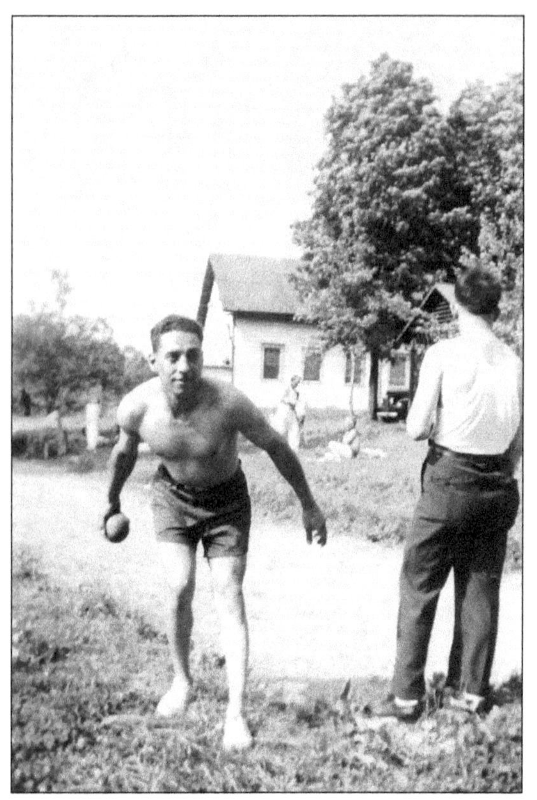

Alberto Gallardo plays a game of bocci next to an unidentified observer. The Hispanic and Italian villas coexisted in the town very amicably. In fact, Villa Baglieri and several other Italian villas were advertised alongside the Hispanic villas on that famous sign of Plattekill businesses that was erected in the center of the village. (Courtesy of Nora Hammond Gallardo.)

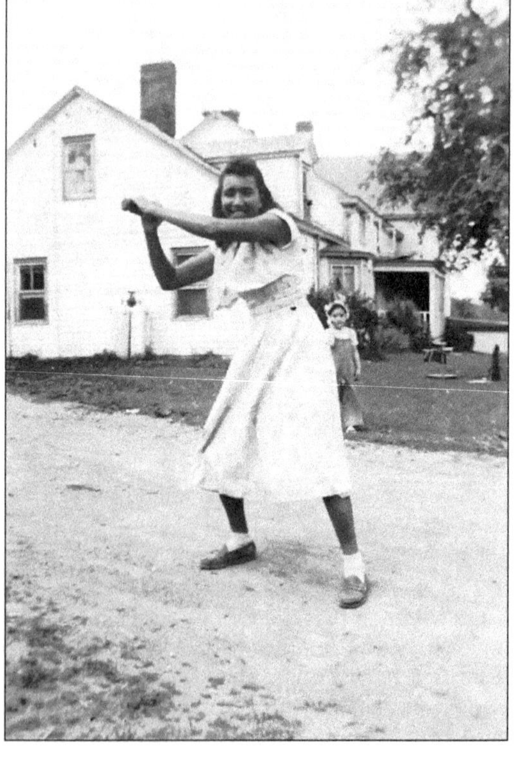

Diana Gallardo is showing off her softball swing stance in front of the main boardinghouse at the Villa Hispana. Diana was the daughter of the villa owners, Alberto and Marta Gallardo. Looking on in the background is Diana's little sister Nora. Diana was an excellent athlete who had tried out for the US Olympic Track Team in the 1950s. (Courtesy of Nora Hammond Gallardo.)

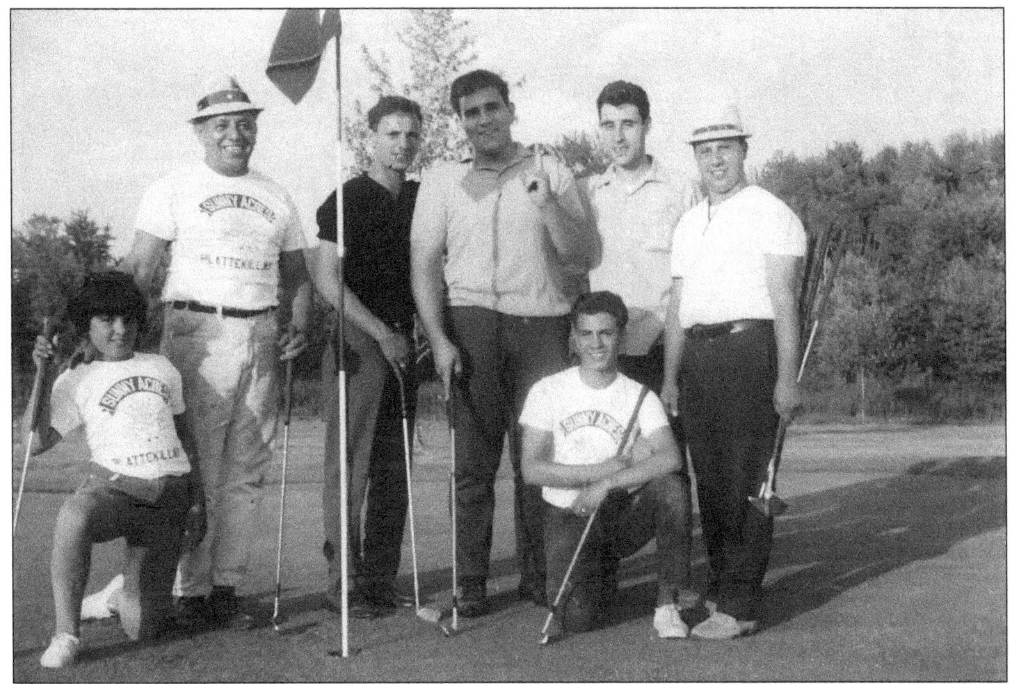

Golf was another activity available to villa tourists. Members of the Martinez family of Sunny Acres, shown around 1963, takes some time off from working at the villa to play a round at Kobelt's Par 3. From left to right are Carla Martinez, Shorty Martinez, Larry Martinez, Louis Suarez, the author, Manny Badillo, and Ron Martinez. (Courtesy of the Martinez family collection.)

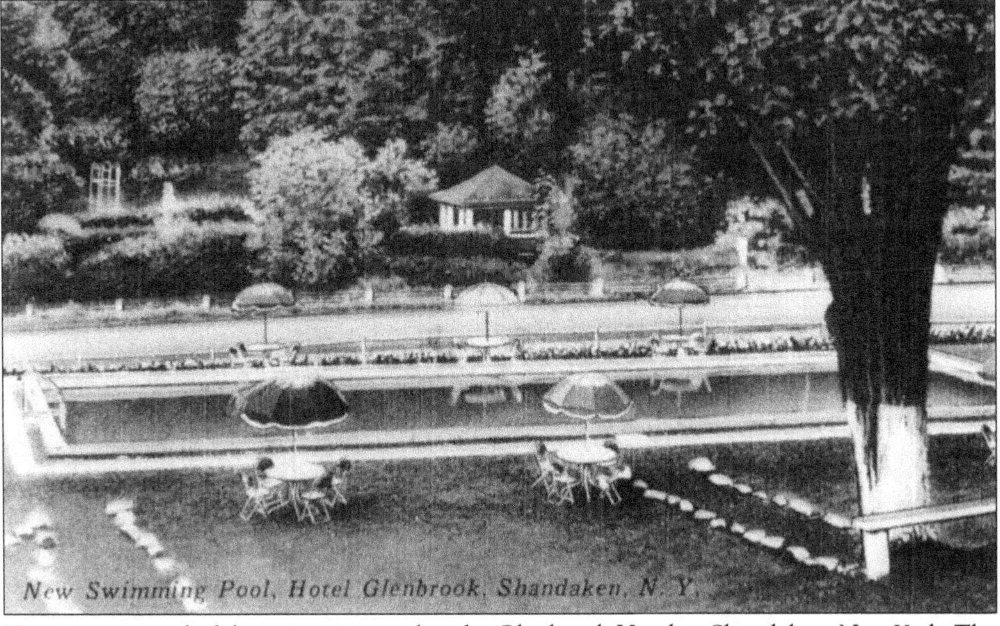

Here is a postcard of the swimming pool at the Glenbrook Hotel in Shandaken, New York. The hotel was located on the Route 28 corridor in the Catskill Mountains. The three partners that were involved in the ownership of the hotel were Ricardo Gil, Carmen L. Garcia, and her daughter, Dolores G. Lopez. (Courtesy of the Martinez family collection.)

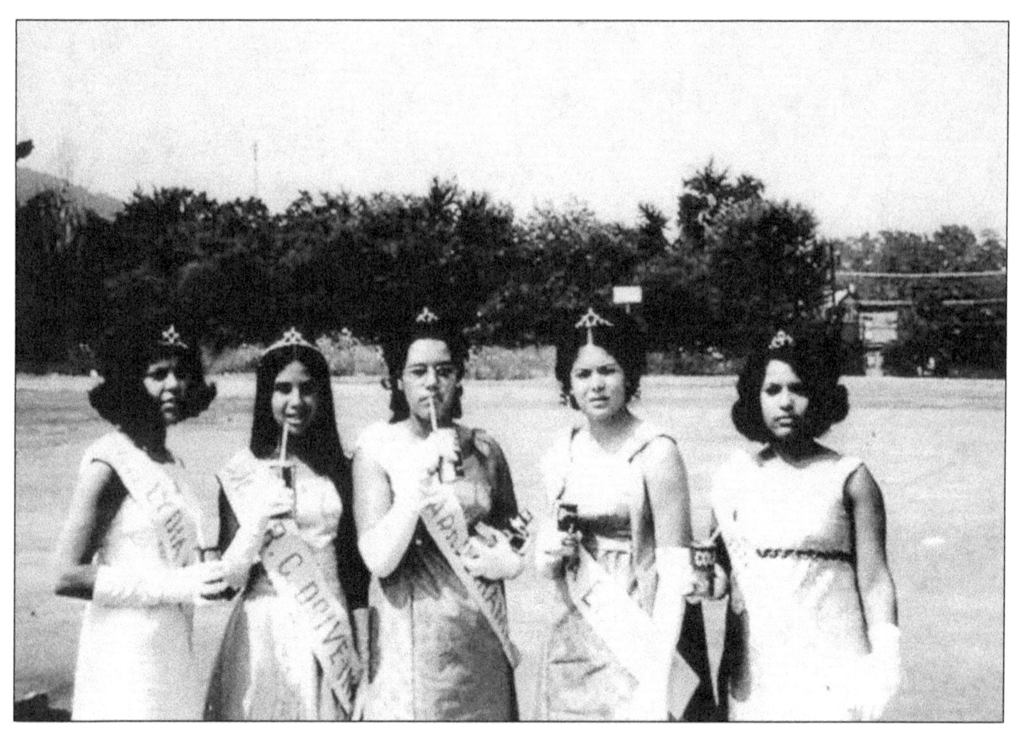

The Puerto Rican Civic Association ran a contest between the villas for the sale of tickets. Of the dozen or so contestants, the ones in this photograph are, from left to right, Elia Ramos, Yvonne Correa, Gladys Guardarramas, Mildred Cintron, and Dagmar Guzman. There were quite a few beauty pageants and contests that took place during the era of Las Villas, and most of those were run by Hispanic organizations who enlisted many of the villas to sponsor the contestants. (Courtesy of Yvonne Correa Morales.)

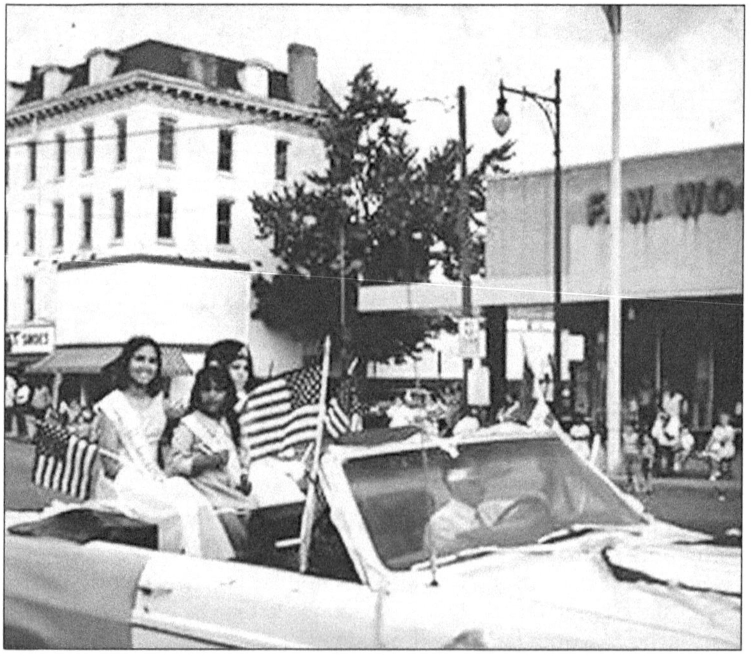

Contestants from a Las Villas ticket sales contest ride in a parade on Broadway in Newburgh, New York, in the 1960s. Newburgh, which is located on the Hudson River, is about 10 miles south of Plattekill and is the closest city to Las Villas. Riding in the back of the car are, from left to right, Yvonne Correa, Anita Guzman, and Margie ? (Courtesy of Yvonne Correa Morales.)

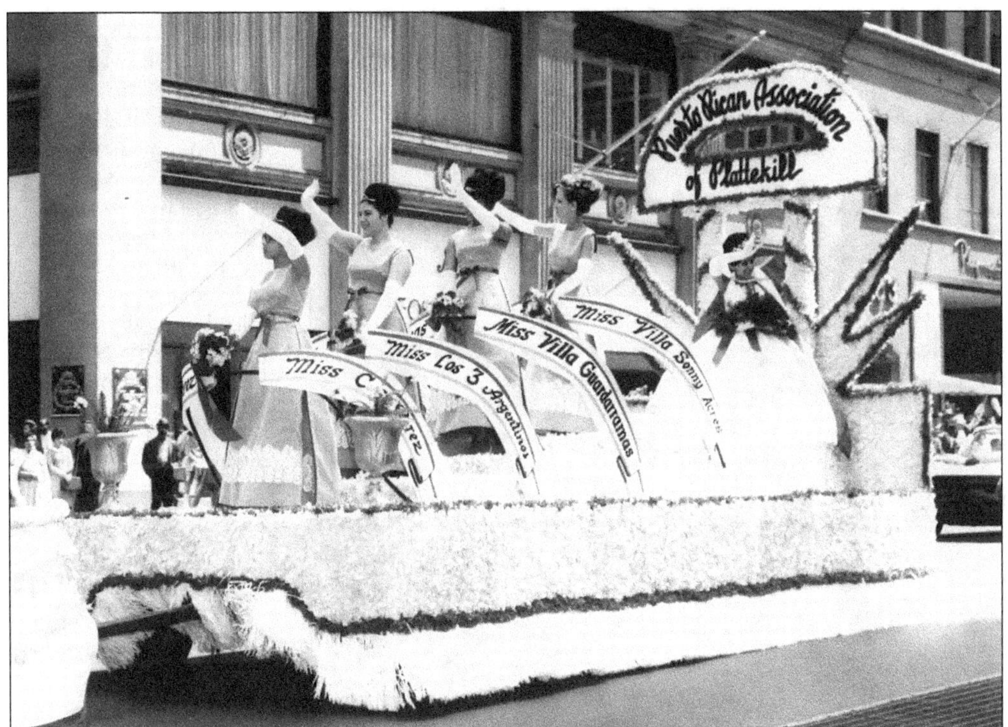

The queen and four finalists from a beauty pageant of the Puerto Rican Association of Plattekill wave to the crowd. Their float is traveling down Fifth Avenue in New York City as they take part in a c. 1965 Puerto Rican Day Parade. The young women are, from left to right, Gloria Velazquez (Casa Perez), Minnie Ortiz (Los Tres Argentinos), Norma Guardarramas (Villa Guardarramas), Linda Comulada (Villa Sunny Acres), and Linda Sifre. (Courtesy of Elizabeth Werlau.)

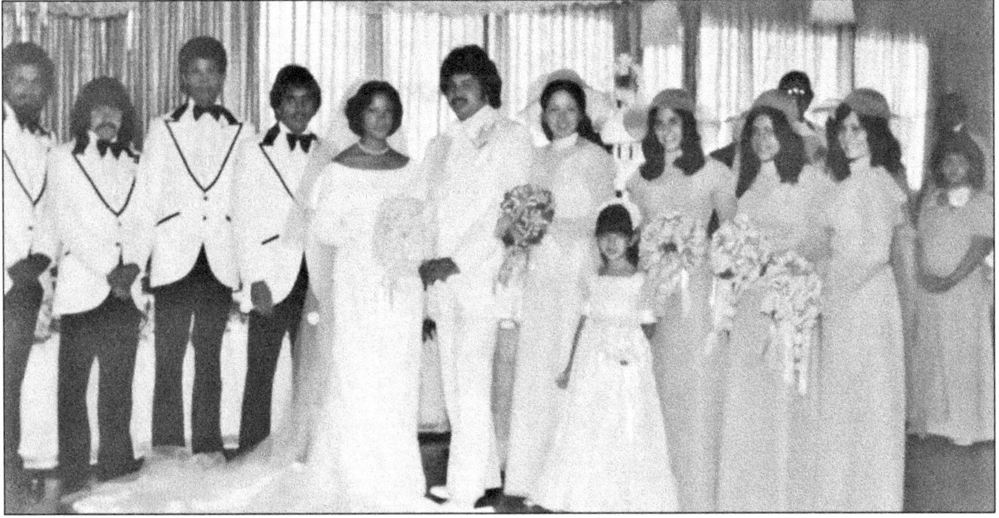
The wedding reception of Plattekill resident Wilfredo Castillo Jr. and Cathi Maisonnett was celebrated at the Villa Nueva on June 22, 1975. The Villa Nueva was not only a resort for summertime visitors to Las Villas, but it also remained open all year long and made its facilities available to local residents who wanted to spend a night out for dinner. (Courtesy of Wilfredo Castillo Jr.)

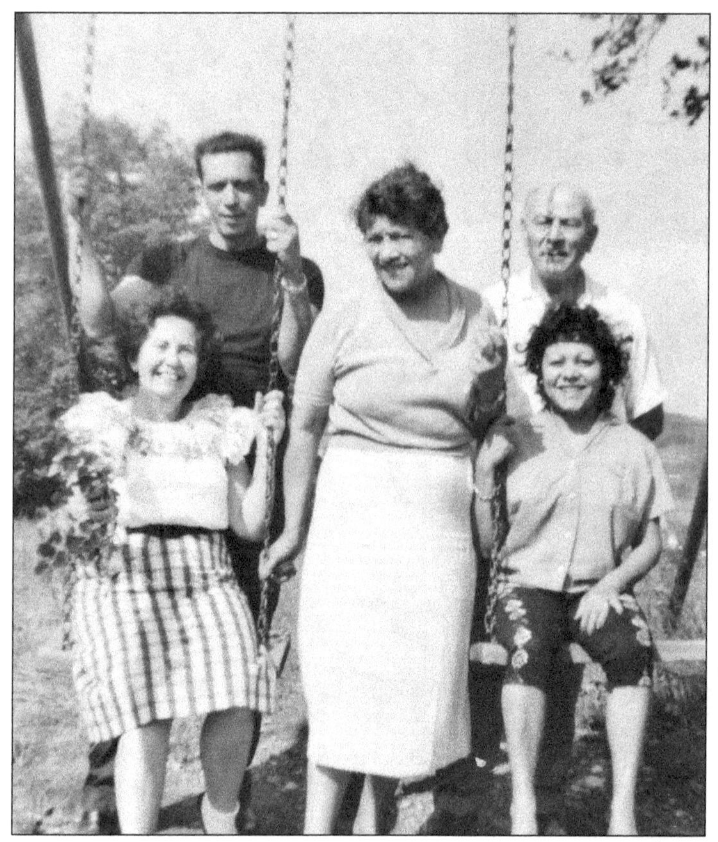

Carmen Baldassari, sitting in the swing on the left, is pictured at the Villa Madrid with other unidentified guests of the villa. The villa sat atop a hill on the Plattekill Ardonia Road in Plattekill and had a spectacular view of the valley below, which was where the Villa Nueva was situated. (Courtesy of Sue and Bill Rodriguez.)

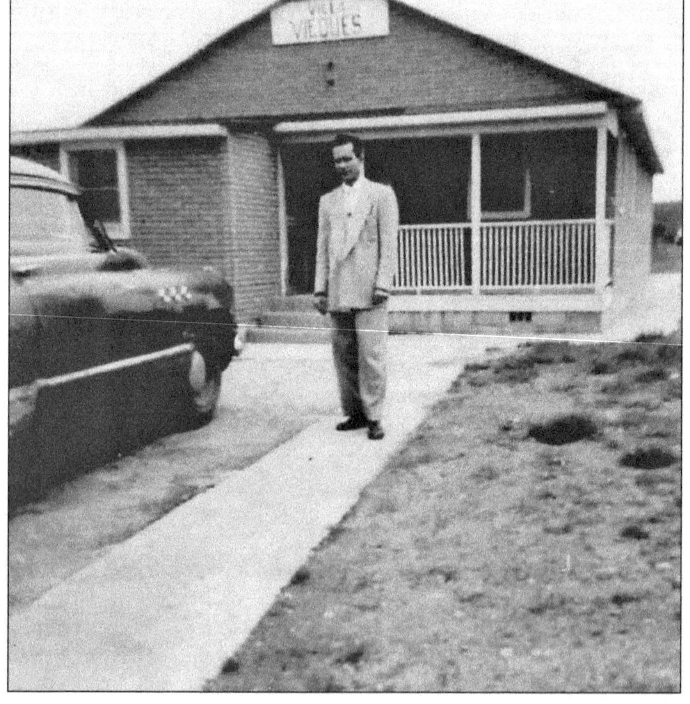

It was very common in the 1950s for a family to dress in their Sunday best and take the family Buick for a drive in the country. For Puerto Ricans and other Latinos, a very popular destination was Las Villas. Damaso Emeric stands in front of the main building at the Villa Vieques. Guests also traveled to this villa on buses. On one occasion, owners Angelo and Leonci Flores were expecting five buses but were soon scrambling to serve nine busloads of people. (Courtesy of Carmen Flores Brigham.)

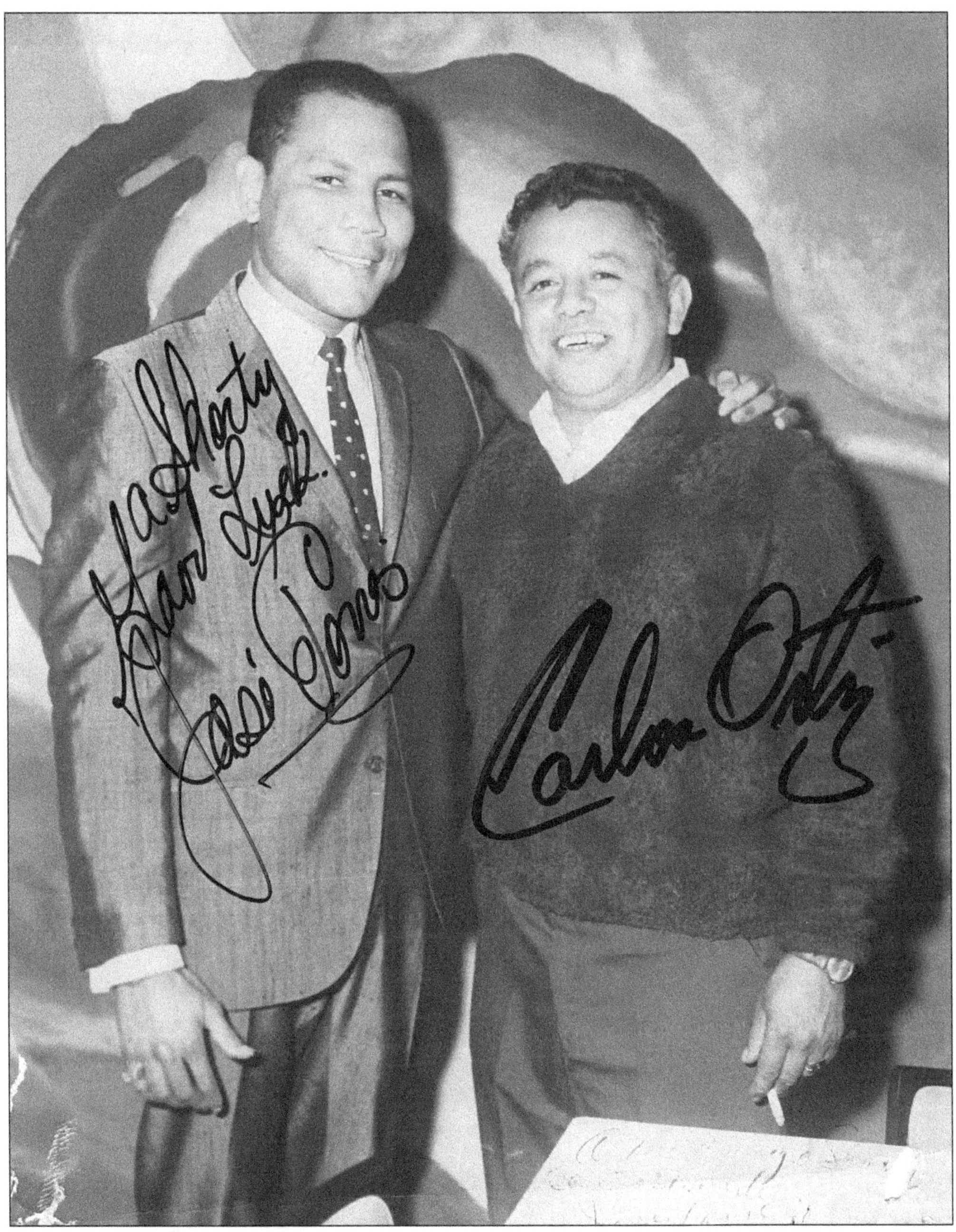

It would not be unusual to see a famous celebrity or sports figure make an appearance at one of the villas during its heyday. This c. 1966 photograph was signed by world champion boxers Jose Torres and Carlos Ortiz. Jose, or "Chegui" as he was commonly called, poses with Shorty Martinez, the owner of Sunny Acres. (Courtesy of the Martinez family collection.)

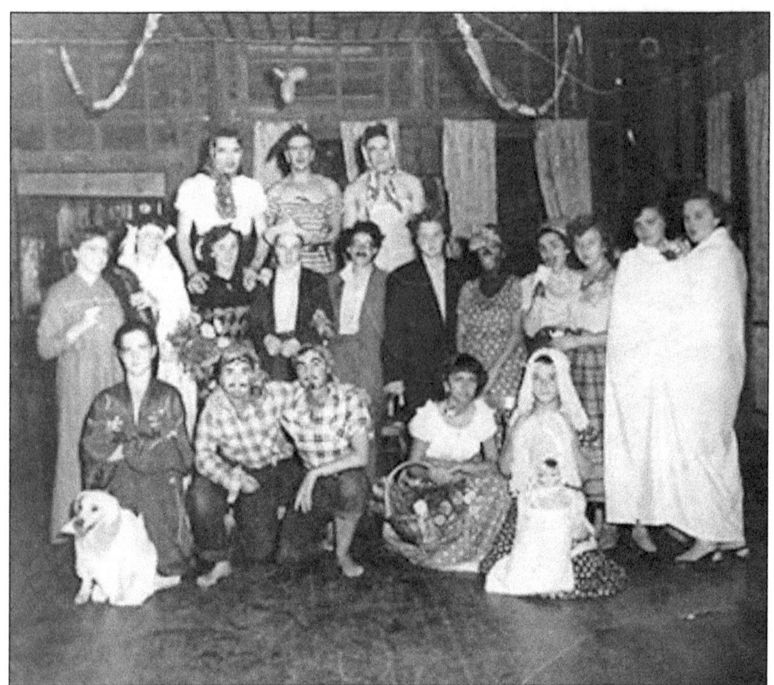

Spanish guests of the Roxmor Inn have some fun by dressing up for a costume party. Spanish groups often entertained themselves with dances and parties, or by performing skits and reenactments. The Roxmor Inn had the look of a mountain lodge and was located in Allaben, a Catskills locality near Phoenicia, New York. (Courtesy of Luz Castanos.)

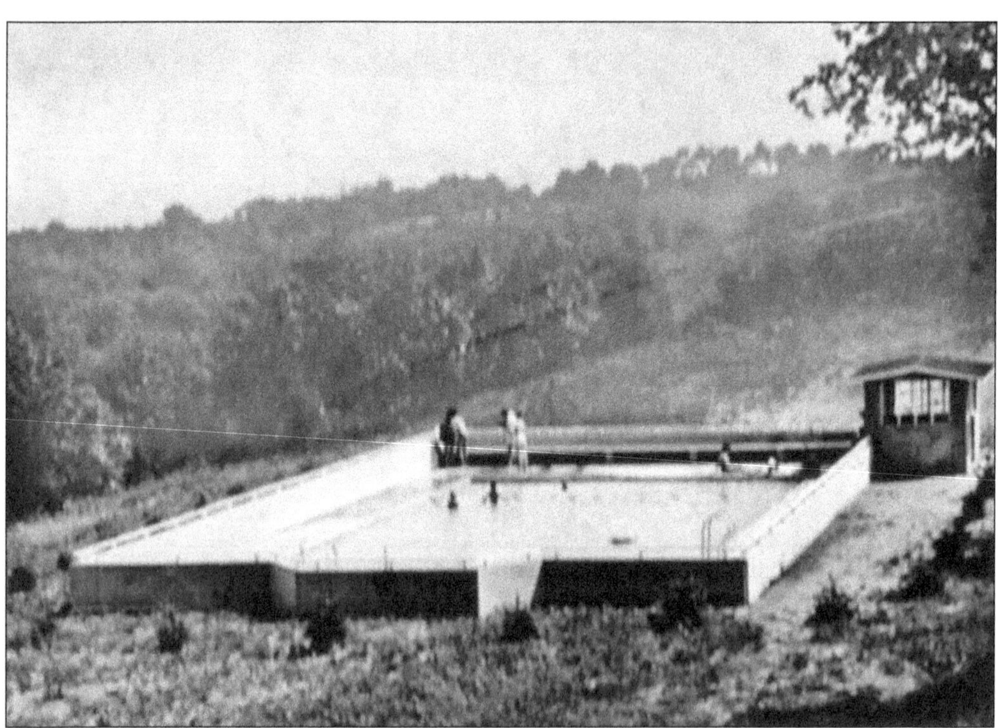

The swimming pool at El Cortijo was located on the crest of a hill behind the villa. In some newspaper articles about Las Villas, the area was oftentimes referred to as the Spanish Alps or, at other times, the Puerto Rican Alps. (Courtesy of the Pliego family.)

Six

ANUNCIOS Y PROMOCIONES
ADVERTISEMENTS AND PROMOTIONS

Even at the beginning of the villa era, the owners of the villas knew about the power of the printed word. Advertisements for the villas have been found from as far back as 1924 or earlier. As long as the villas were in existence, the owners regularly produced promotional materials intended to attract customers. Signposts have been instrumental in directing people to their desired destinations for hundreds of years, and it was no different for finding Las Villas. Of course, these signs came in every size, shape, and color—some professionally made, and some created by the owner or a workhand.

All other forms of advertisements were actively distributed or displayed, either at the villa itself or in other areas where potential customers or interested parties would likely see them. These advertisements were produced in different forms depending on how the owner wanted to use them. Matchbooks were easily distributed and very effective in an era when smoking was so commonplace. There were postcards, business cards, handouts, leaflets, notices, handbills, and flyers in all different colors and sizes. Some of the promotional materials were put out independently by the villa owners themselves, and others were distributed by an organization like the Plattekill Tavern Owners Association, mostly made up of villa owners. The primary mission of this organization was to promote the businesses in various ways for the success and mutual benefit of its members.

Radio spots on Spanish-language station WADO were particularly effective for getting the word out. Newspaper advertisements in the Spanish newspaper *La Prensa* were common because of the wide circulation it had in the Hispanic community. One of the earliest newspapers to carry advertisements for many of Las Villas was the *Brooklyn Eagle*, which covered an area with a large number of Spanish-speaking subscribers. In the 1960s, when Las Villas region was at the height of its popularity, the *New York Times* carried several articles on Las Villas and dubbed the area "the Spanish Alps."

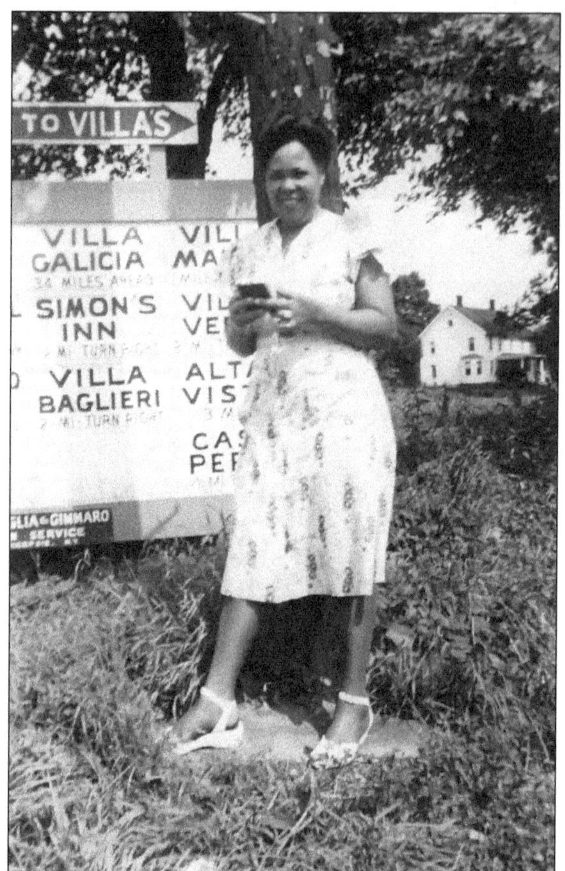

This c. 1947 photograph shows Ana Davoli standing in front of the Plattekill villa sign; she was a frequent visitor to Plattekill and Las Villas. Having emigrated from Cuba to New York City, she had a number of business interests in property located in the area. The sign indicates how far down the Plattekill Ardonia Road one would find the different villas. (Courtesy of Nora Hammond Gallardo.)

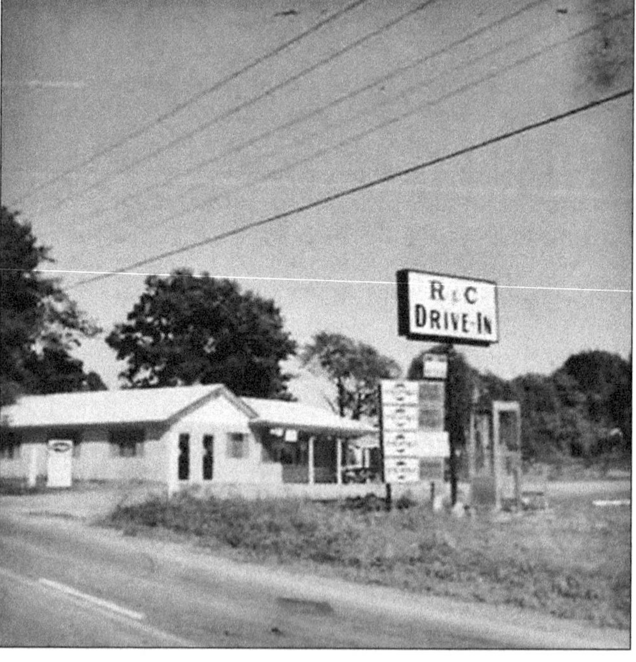

The R&C Drive-In was soon enlarged to include an indoor dining facility, and the name was eventually changed to El Caribe Restaurant. When the bands would stop playing and the villas would close on Saturday nights, the restaurant would frequently be inundated with customers around 2:00 a.m. (Courtesy of Yvonne Correa Morales.)

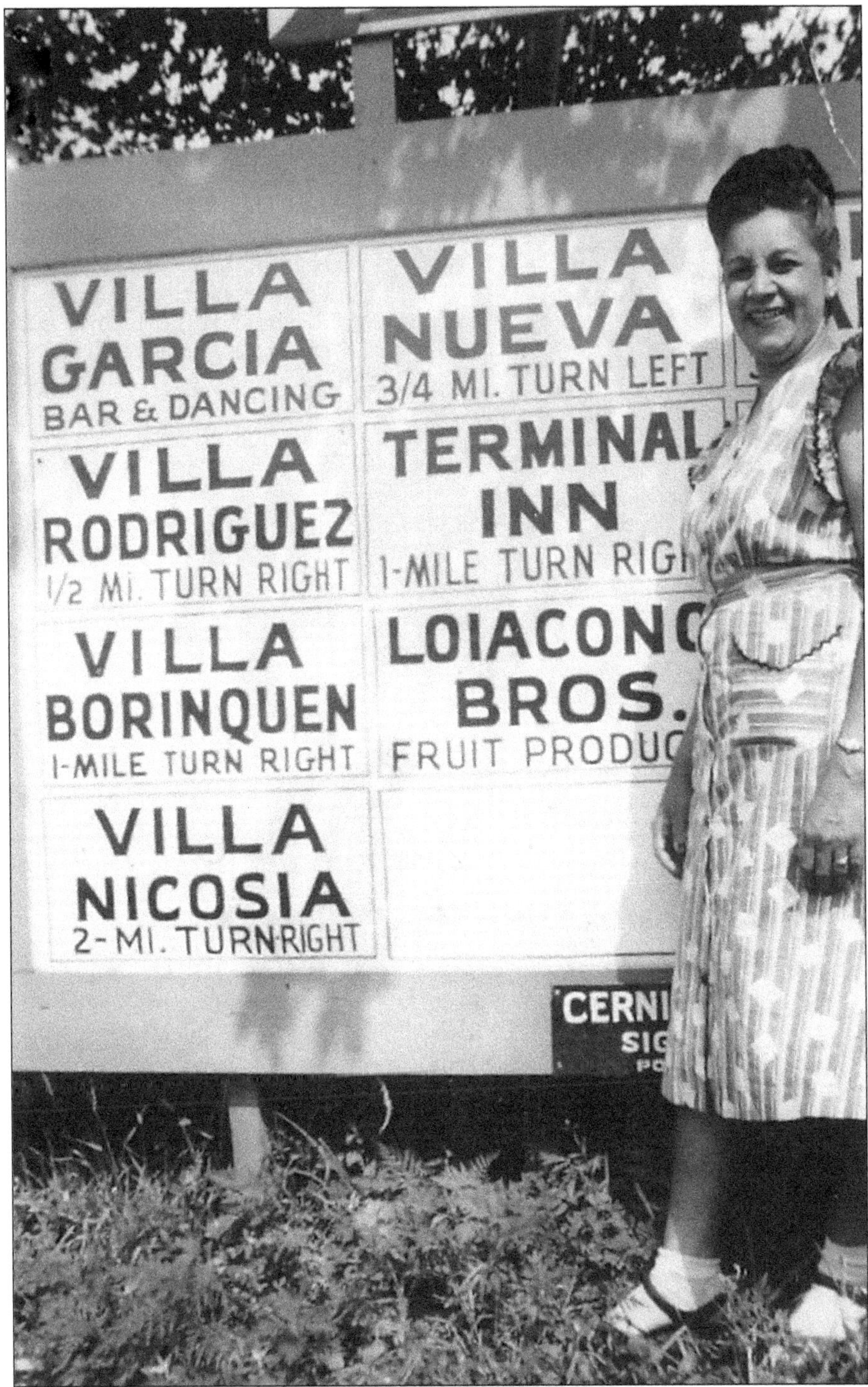

Pictured around 1947, Irene Martinez Anchundia stands in front of a sign that was located on Plattekill Ardonia Road and kitty-corner to Sisti's Plattekill General Store. It stood on the corner and to the right of the present-day post office. It was a forerunner to the sign erected not far from this spot in the 1960s. In 1948, Irene bought a farm that became the villa called Sunny Acres. (Courtesy of Nora Hammond Gallardo.)

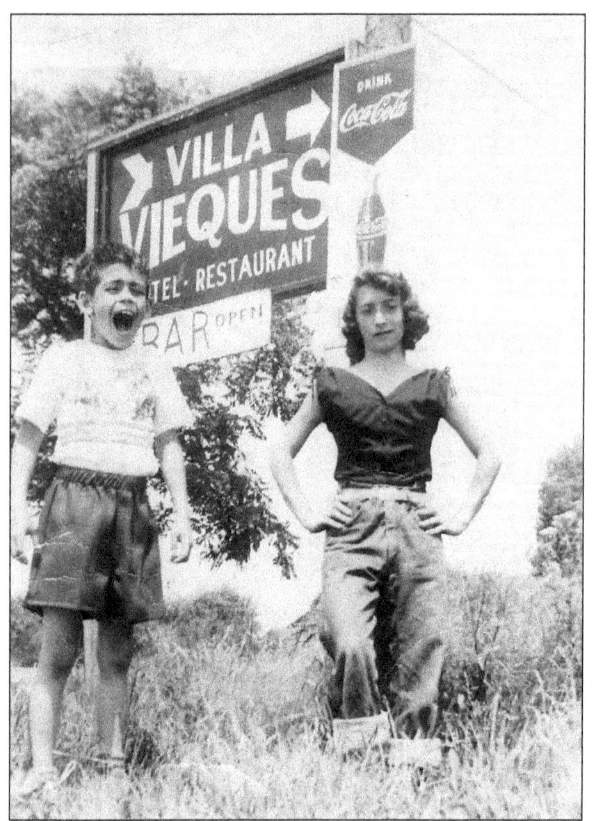

The seemingly irrepressible boy is Eddie Flores, whose parents owned the Villa Vieques, and the unfazed young woman is his sister-in-law Emily Flores. Owners Angelo and Leonci Flores purchased the land in 1950 and built a small bungalow as a temporary residence. In the summer of 1954, they opened the villa for business, catering to mostly Puerto Ricans and other Latinos. (Courtesy of Carmen Flores Brigham.)

Tel. Newburgh: 914 — 564-2381 — 564-9871

Villa Guardarramas

"Donde se encuentran los Viejos Amigos"

P. O. BOX 85 PLATTEKILL, N. Y. 12568

An ideal place for your Summer Vacation in the Plattekill Mountains

Bar & Dancing - No Swimming Pool - Shower Baths . . . . . . Moderate Prices

Bilingual business cards for the villas was very common since their customer base included both Hispanics who were proficient in English and those who only communicated in Spanish. On this Villa Guardarramas business card, what is found in Spanish translates to "where you find old friends." (Courtesy of the Guardarramas family.)

Sunny Acres Hotel-Motel

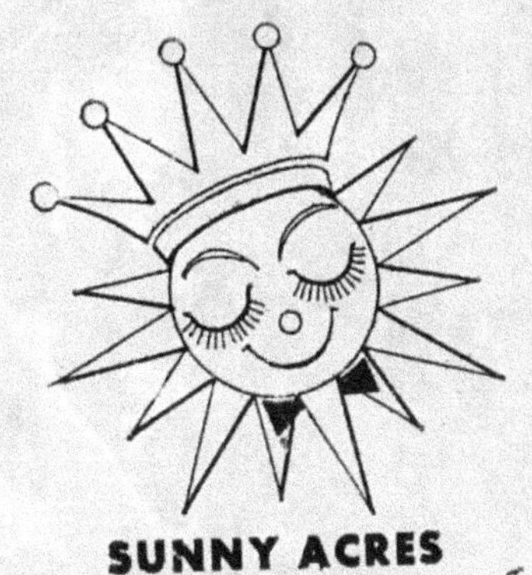

DINING - DANCING

SWIMMING - SPORTS

914 JOHN -- 1-9861

PLATTEKILL, NEW YORK

This mid-1960s business card of Sunny Acres depicts its iconic logo of the smiling sun. It is sparse in terms of details as compared to some of the other business cards. The logo was meant to get one's attention. It has only a few lines of what the villa had to offer and, of course, its phone number. (Courtesy of the Martinez family collection.)

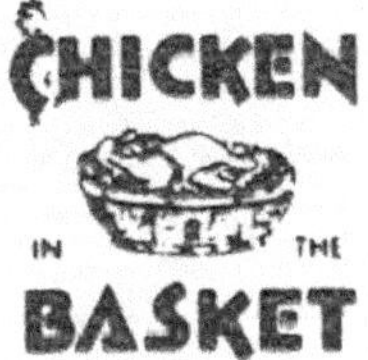

PHONE: (914) 564-2926

LYDIA MY-DREAM RESTAURANT

THE BEST FOOD FOR MILES AROUND

A DREAM FOR YOUR VACATION

LYDIA'S BAR

DIRECTIONS FOR REACHING:

N.Y. THRUWAY TO EXIT 17 NEWBURGH

R.D. #3 UNIONVILLE ROAD PLATTEKILL, N.Y. 12568

A business card for Lydia My-Dream Restaurant is in only English. The business was owned by Lydia and Luis Malave and was located on Unionville Road in Plattekill. (Courtesy of Roxy Santiago.)

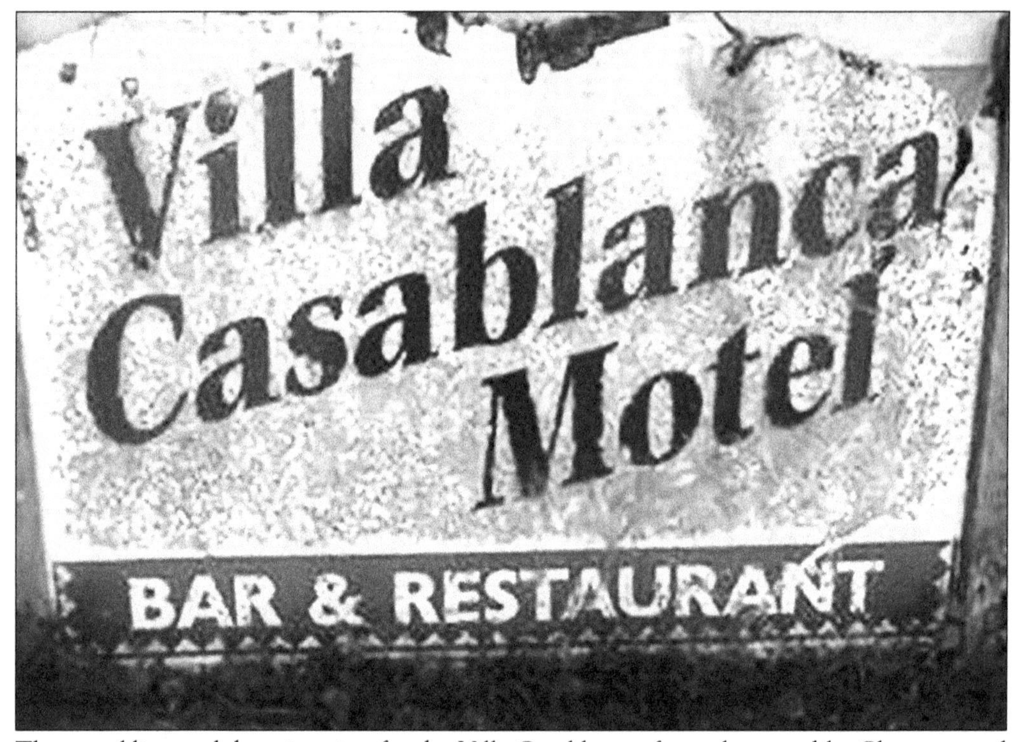

The crumbling and decaying sign for the Villa Casablanca, formerly owned by Clemente and Judy Rodriguez, is now silent testimony to a once lively and vibrant villa scene. Many salsa bands were brought in and played at the Villa Casablanca before the villa era started to decline. The villa was previously called the Villa Garcia and owned by Celestino and Flora Garcia. (Courtesy of Cara Oppenheimer.)

Newburgh Tel. JO. 1-4473 N.Y.C. Tel. TE 1-9958

VILLA SAN JUAN

Sabrosas Comidas Criollas

Lechón Asado, Pasteles

LICORES DE TODAS CLASES

Baile con las mejores músicas

Rentamos Cuartos **Aceptamos Jiras**

Willie & Tula, Props.

VILLA SAN JUAN - PLATTEKILL, NEWBURGH, N.Y.

This business card for the Villa San Juan was completely in Spanish. The cards for the various villas enticed potential customers with detailed descriptions of what they offered their guests in terms of food, music, drinks, and accommodations. (Courtesy of Roxy Santiago.)

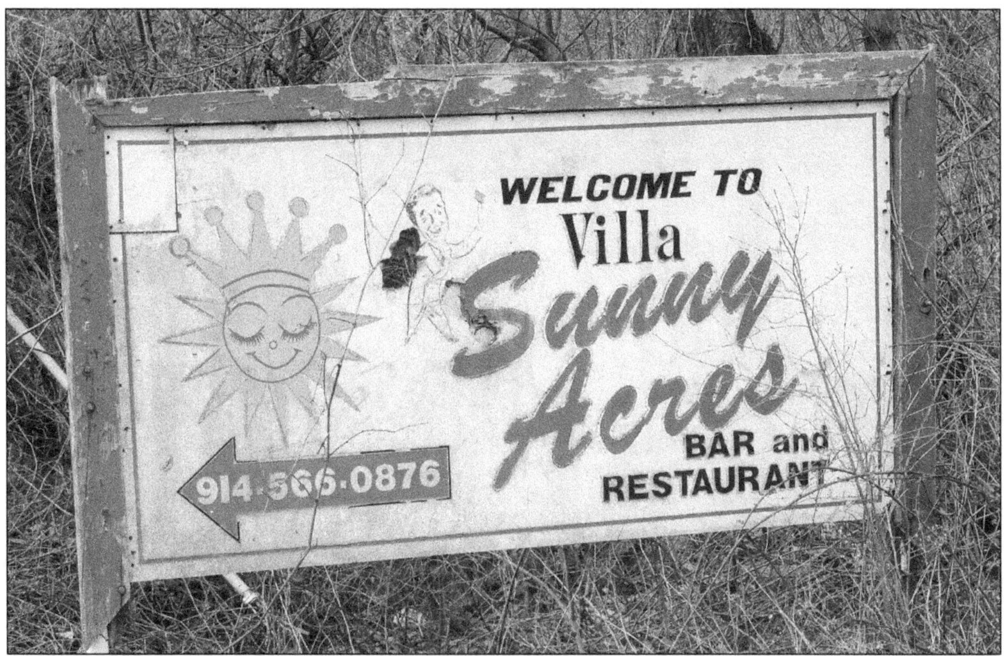

The Sunny Acres sign is clearly showing some aging nearly 50 years after being erected at that same location. At the entrance to Sunny Acres Road, the sign outlasted the villa's main building containing the dining room, dance hall, and bar, which burned down in 2008. The villa had gone through three owners since 1948. (Courtesy of the Martinez family collection.)

Tel. Newburgh 322-J2 "Connie" Hegner, Prop.

VILLA CASITA CONNIE

CLEAN, COMFORTABLE
HOME-LIKE ROOMS

With Hot and Cold Running Water
Best Spanish and American
Cooking in Plattekill
Bar and Dancing

Plattekill (Near Newburgh) New York

The 1960s Casita Connie card is completely in English, which means that most villa guests spoke English or were bilingual by the 1960s. The fact that Casita Connie served Spanish and American food is another indication that the two cultures were beginning to be integrated at Las Villas. Connie herself was Puerto Rican, which would not be apparent by her married last name, Hegner. (Courtesy of Roxy Santiago.)

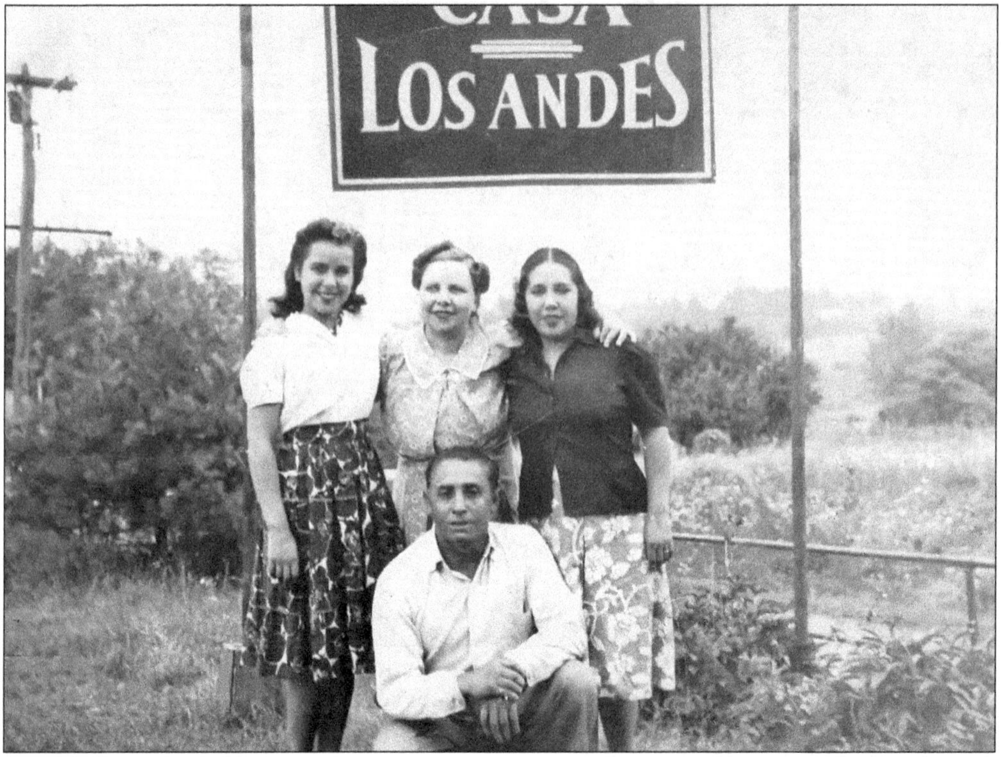

Standing under the Casa Los Andes sign are (kneeling) unidentified; (standing), from left to right, Julie Garzon, Elvira Romero, and Clorinda Luciani. Elvira owned the villa along with her husband, Isidoro Romero. Julie is Elvira's daughter, and the other two were guests at the villa. (Courtesy of Henry "Hank" Romero.)

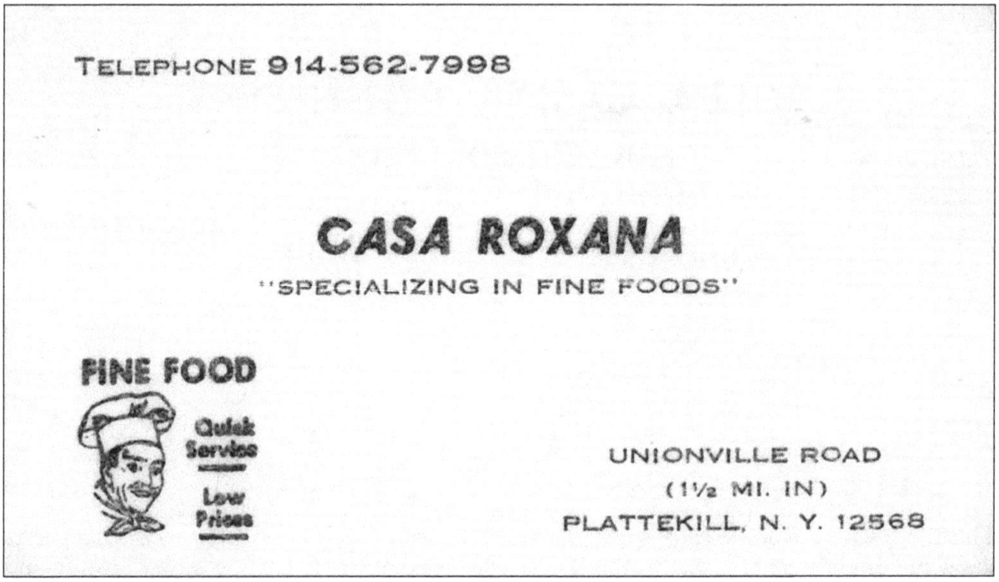

TELEPHONE 914-562-7998

CASA ROXANA

"SPECIALIZING IN FINE FOODS"

FINE FOOD

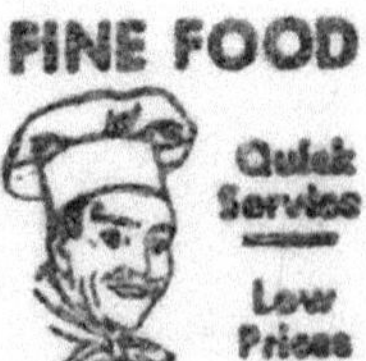

UNIONVILLE ROAD
(1½ MI. IN)
PLATTEKILL, N. Y. 12568

The business card for the Casa Roxana emphasizes the food and service. The designs for the various villa business cards were as unique and diverse as the villas themselves. (Courtesy of Roxy Santiago.)

From left to right, Luis Montalvo and Ana and Jim Davoli were guests at the Villa Hispana and related to the owners, Alberto and Marta Gallardo. The villa was located on Quaker Street, close to the town line that separates Plattekill and Newburgh. In addition to taking in summer boarders, the villa was also a chicken farm. (Courtesy of Nora Hammond Gallardo.)

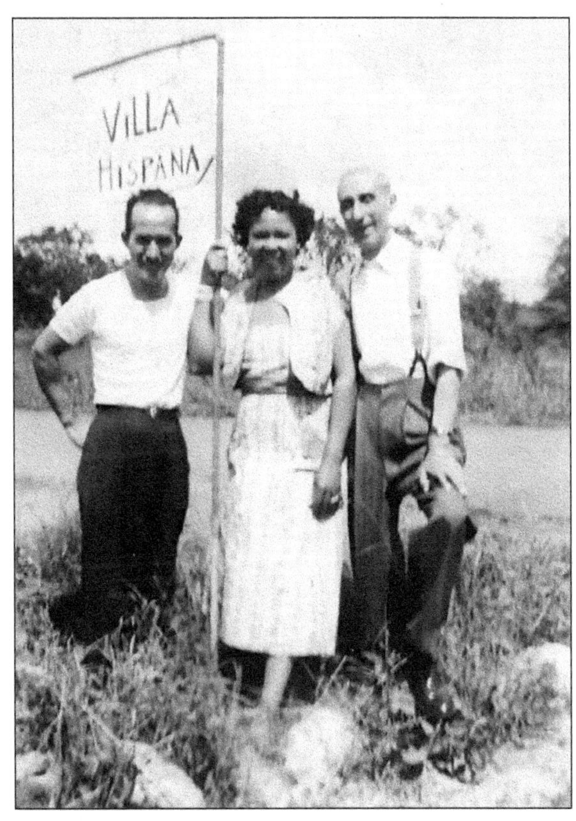

MANHATTAN STREET DIRECTORY

To find the nearest street to any avenue number: Cancel last figure, divide remainder by 2, add number specified in the following key. The result will be street desired.

EXAMPLE: Find the nearest street to 500 Fifth Avenue. First cancel last figure. The remainder is 50. Then divide by 2 and you have 25. Add the key number, which is 17, and the result is 42nd Street.

Avenues	Add	Avenues	Add
A, B, C, D	2—3	Amsterdam	59
First	2—3	Audubon	165
Second	2—3	Columbus	59
Above 600	5	Convent	127
Third	9—10	Edgecombe	134
Fourth	7—8	Ft. Washington	158
Fifth	8—12	Lenox	110
Up to 200	12—14	Lexington	22
Up to 600	15—18	Madison	26—28
Up to 800	19—22	Manhattan	106
Up to 900	23—25	Park	34—35
Up to 1000	26—30	Pleasant	101
Up to 1100	31—36	St. Nicholas	110
Up to 1200	37—40	West End	59
Up to 1500	42—45	Wadsworth	173
Above 2000	24—25	B'way (Deduct)	30
Seventh	12—13	Sixth (Deduct)	13
Above 110th	20		
Eighth	10—11		
Ninth	12—13		
Tenth	13—14		
Eleventh	14—15		

Central Park West, divide house number by 10, add 60.
Riverside Drive, divide house number by 10, add 72.

Telephone Newburgh 775-R1

Casa Perez

HOTEL, BAR AND GRILL

SITIO IDEAL PARA SUS VACACIONES

Modern Swimming Pool

PLATTEKILL, N. Y.

New York Office: 207 E. 149th Street, Bronx, N. Y.
Telephone MOtt Haven 9-8960

The Casa Perez business card has one line in Spanish that states, "Ideal site for your vacations." The back of that card has what they thought would be a handy Manhattan street finder for the New York City guests they generally catered to. Like some of the other villas, the name was advertised differently for some reason. Casa Perez, Casa Villa Perez, and Villa Casa Perez are all variations used by the owner. (Courtesy of Roxy Santiago.)

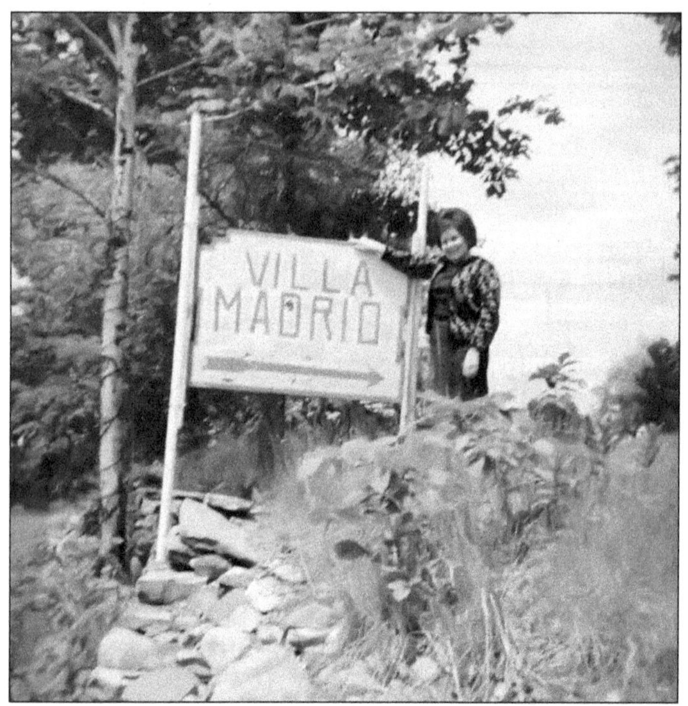

The sign for the Villa Madrid was at the crest of a hill on the side of Plattekill Ardonia Road. The arrow on the bottom of the sign points toward the right-hand turn one had to make onto South Street, where the entrance to the villa was located. (Courtesy of Sue and Bill Rodriguez.)

Para pasarse unas vacaciones en un ambiente
tranquilo y familiar, no hay como la

Villa Hispana

Para Información en Nueva York, Llame al Teléfono
Dayton 9-7173, o a la Villa

Box 153, R. F. D. 2, Wallkill, N. Y.
Tel. Newburgh 368 M 3

Como ir:- Despues de llegar a Newburg, se toma el Wallkill Bus hasta Leplondale, esquina de Quaker Street.

In contrast to the other business cards, this Villa Hispana card from the 1940s, is predominantly in Spanish. It is translated as follows: "To spend a vacation in a calm and familiar setting, there is nothing like the Villa Hispana. For information in New York call by telephone Dayton 9-7173, or to the villa. How to get there: After arriving in Newburgh, you take the Wallkill Bus to Leptondale, at the corner of Quaker Street." (Courtesy of Nora Hammond Gallardo.)

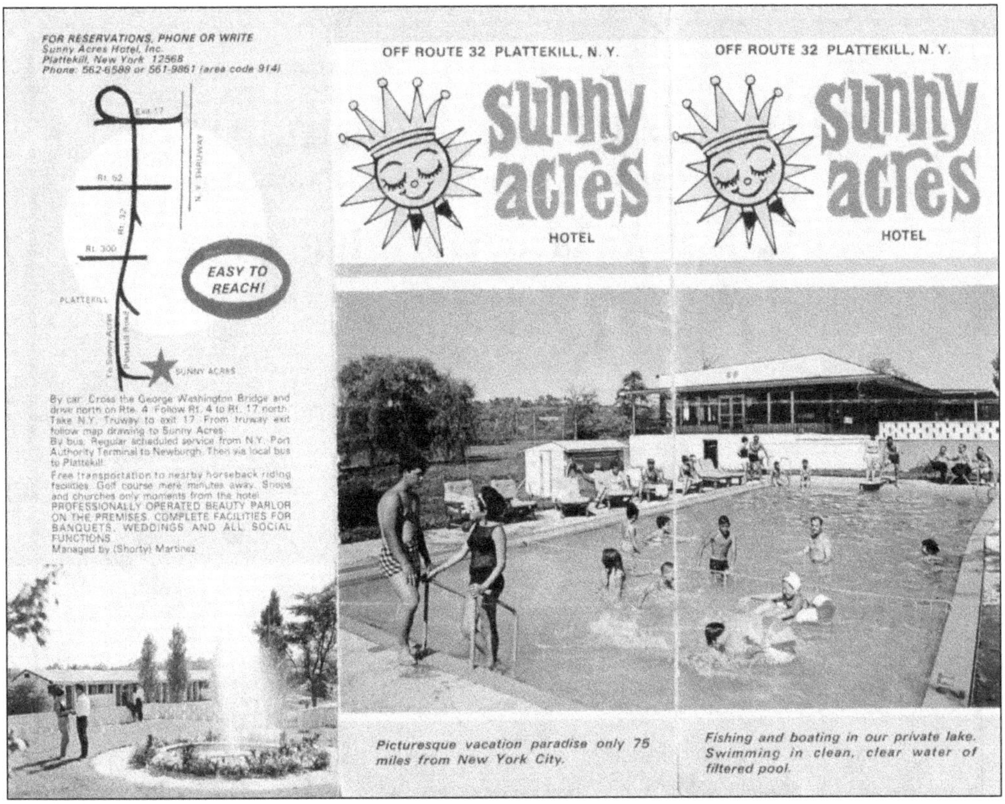

FOR RESERVATIONS, PHONE OR WRITE
Sunny Acres Hotel, Inc.
Plattekill, New York 12568
Phone: 562-6588 or 561-9861 (area code 914)

Exit 17
N.Y. THRUWAY
Rt. 52
Rt. 32
Rt. 300
PLATTEKILL
To Sunny Acres
SUNNY ACRES

EASY TO REACH!

By car: Cross the George Washington Bridge and drive north on Rte. 4. Follow Rt. 4 to Rt. 17 north. Take N.Y. Truway to exit 17. From truway exit follow map drawing to Sunny Acres.
By bus: Regular scheduled service from N.Y. Port Authority Terminal to Newburgh. Then via local bus to Plattekill.
Free transportation to nearby horseback riding facilities. Golf course mere minutes away. Shops and churches only moments from the hotel.
PROFESSIONALLY OPERATED BEAUTY PARLOR ON THE PREMISES. COMPLETE FACILITIES FOR BANQUETS, WEDDINGS AND ALL SOCIAL FUNCTIONS.
Managed by (Shorty) Martinez

OFF ROUTE 32 PLATTEKILL, N. Y.

sunny acres HOTEL

OFF ROUTE 32 PLATTEKILL, N. Y.

sunny acres HOTEL

Picturesque vacation paradise only 75 miles from New York City.

Fishing and boating in our private lake. Swimming in clean, clear water of filtered pool.

A c. 1966 brochure from Sunny Acres showcases the swimming pool on the front and the fountain on the back, along with directions from the New York State Thruway exit to the villa. The sun logo, which was created by the owner, Shorty Martinez, was frequently used and displayed on other villa items such as matchbooks, business cards, and menus. (Courtesy of the Martinez family collection.)

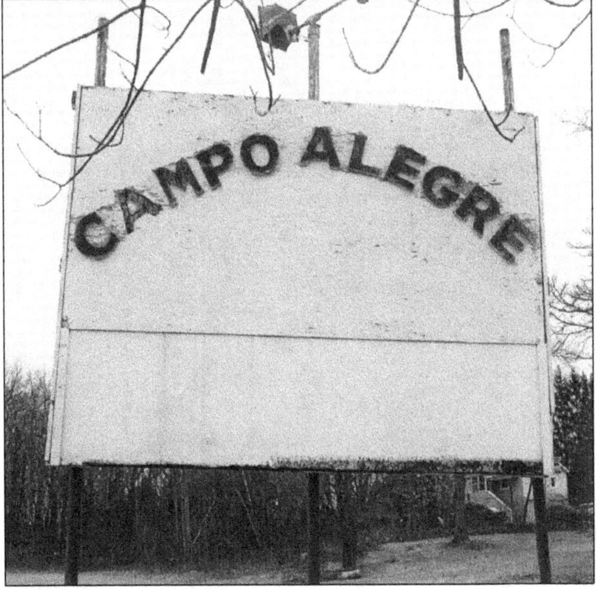

Here is the sign for Campo Alegre on Unionville Road where the villa was located. Campo Alegre was owned by Andres Figueroa and was quite likely the last of the villas to remain in operation, providing great salsa music and great Puerto Rican food. The villa was previously named Casa Perez and had been started in the early 1940s by Daniel Perez. (Courtesy of Elizabeth Ann Rodriguez.)

CERTIFICATE NO. 23

Certificate of Compliance

WITH THE PROVISIONS OF CHAPTER 405, LAWS OF 1922, AND THE

State Standard Building Code

THIS IS TO CERTIFY THAT THE PLACE OF ASSEMBLY

Known as VILLA VIEQUES
(Name of place of assembly)

Conducted as Bar and Restaurant
(Theatre, Motion Picture Theatre, Assembly Hall)

Located at Quaker Street (Address) Town of Newburgh (City, Town, Village) Orange (County)

Drive-In Theatre Cars ____ (No. of Persons)

OCCUPANCY
(Allowed Capacity)

Auditorium ____ (Number of persons) **Balcony** ____ (Number of persons) Seated 164 **Standees** 89 (Number of persons) **Total** 253 (Number of persons)

Is in compliance with the requirements of Article 17 of the Labor Law. This certificate may be revoked unless the premises are maintained according to the provisions of the Labor Law applicable thereto and Rules adopted thereunder.

Carlton A. Kessel
Signature of enforcing officer

Date December 1, **19**72

Building Inspector
Title

THIS CERTIFICATE TO BE CONSPICUOUSLY POSTED AT ENTRANCE SEVEN FEET ABOVE FLOOR

Acquaro Printing Co. — Newburgh, N. Y.

All commercial businesses in the state of New York were required to have a certificate of compliance. This one was granted to Villa Vieques on December 1, 1972, indicating that no more than 253 people could occupy the building at any one point in time. Villa owners would normally display this certificate in a place where it could readily be seen by the public, like at the bar or in the dining room. (Courtesy of Carmen Flores Brigham.)

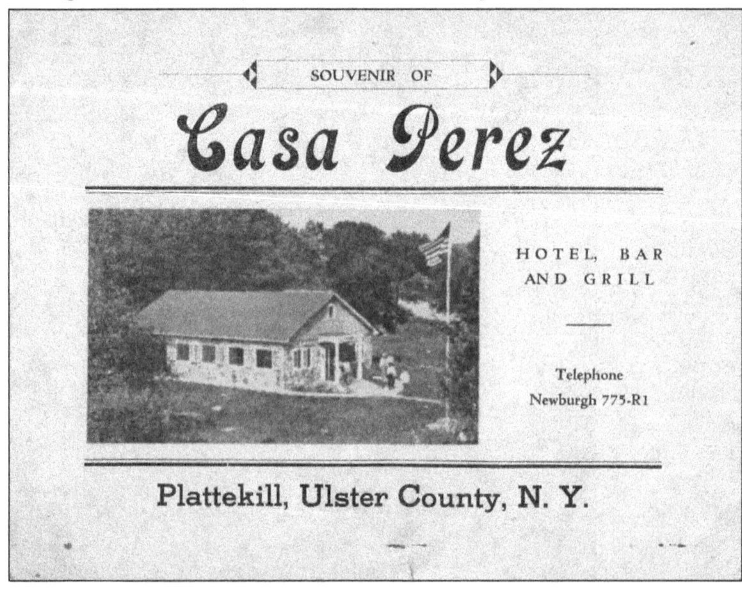

This preprinted cover folder with the Casa Perez Casino on the front was a souvenir from the 1940s or 1950s and contained a photograph on the inside. The photograph would have been taken of a guest, possibly sitting with friends or family, usually in the casino or dance hall. (Courtesy of Shirley Anson.)

A flyer, put out by the Plattekill Tavern Owners Association, lists the relevant contact information for the various member villas and businesses. The association sought to promote tourism in both the town and the region of Las Villas for the mutual benefit of its members. (Courtesy of the Office of the Plattekill Town Historian.)

COMPLIMENTS OF

THE PLATTEKILL TAVERN OWNERS' ASSOCIATION

Largest Spanish Resort Area in the East

Visit the Most Popular Places:

LOS TRES ARGENTINOS
Box 82 Plattekill, N.Y. 12568
Phone: 914 - 561-8979

VILLA GALICIA
Box 69 Plattekill, N.Y. 12568
Phone: 914 - 562-6979

VILLA GARCIA
Box 56 Plattekill, N.Y. 12568
Phone: 914 - 562-8407

VILLA GUARDARRAMAS
Box 85 Plattekill, N.Y. 12568
Phone: 914 - 562-9789

HOTEL-MOTEL CASA PEREZ
Box 14 Plattekill, N.Y. 12568
Phone: 914 - 561-8408

SPANISH BITS RIDING STABLES, INC.
Box 173 Plattekill, N.Y. 12568
Phone: 914 - 565-5980

VILLA SAN JUAN
Box 143 Plattekill, N.Y. 12568
Phone: 914 - 561-4473

SUNNY ACRES
Box 76 Plattekill, N.Y. 12568
Phone: 914 - 562-6588

VILLA VICTORIA
Box 221 Plattekill, N.Y. 12568
Phone: 914 - 561-7728

A Plattekill Tavern Owners Association membership plaque is displayed at El Continental. El Continental was co-owned by brothers Angelo and Enrique Velazquez and their respective wives, Lillian and Gladys. Unfortunately, the villa had a relatively short run—from 1961 to 1965, when a fire totally destroyed the building. In previous decades, the villa had been a bar called Simon's Inn, mostly frequented by the locals of the town. (Courtesy of Angelo Velazquez Jr.)

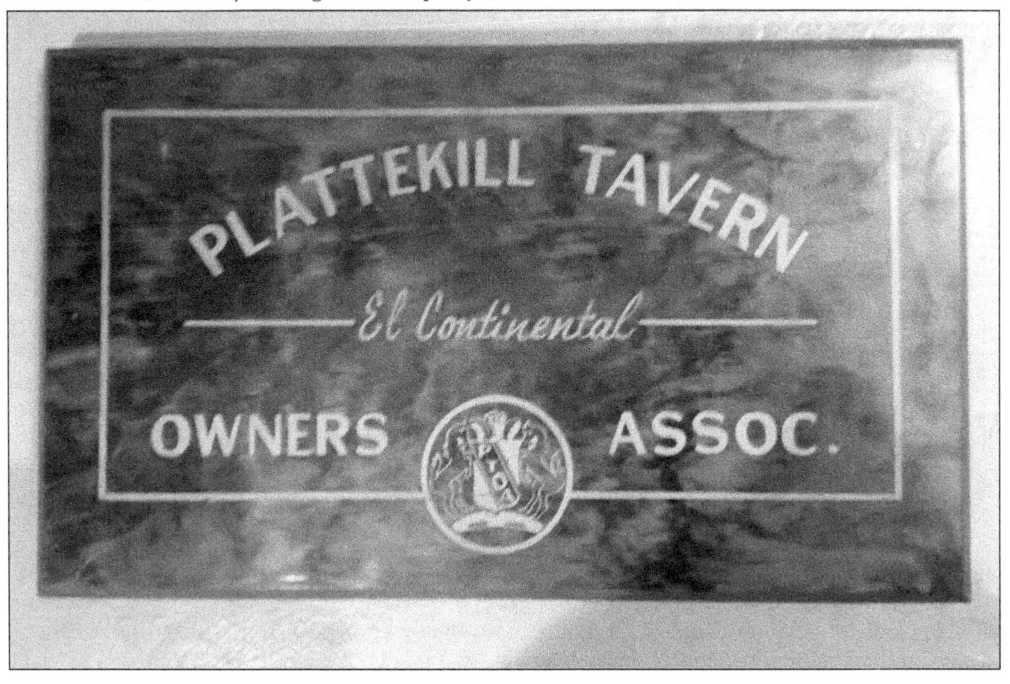

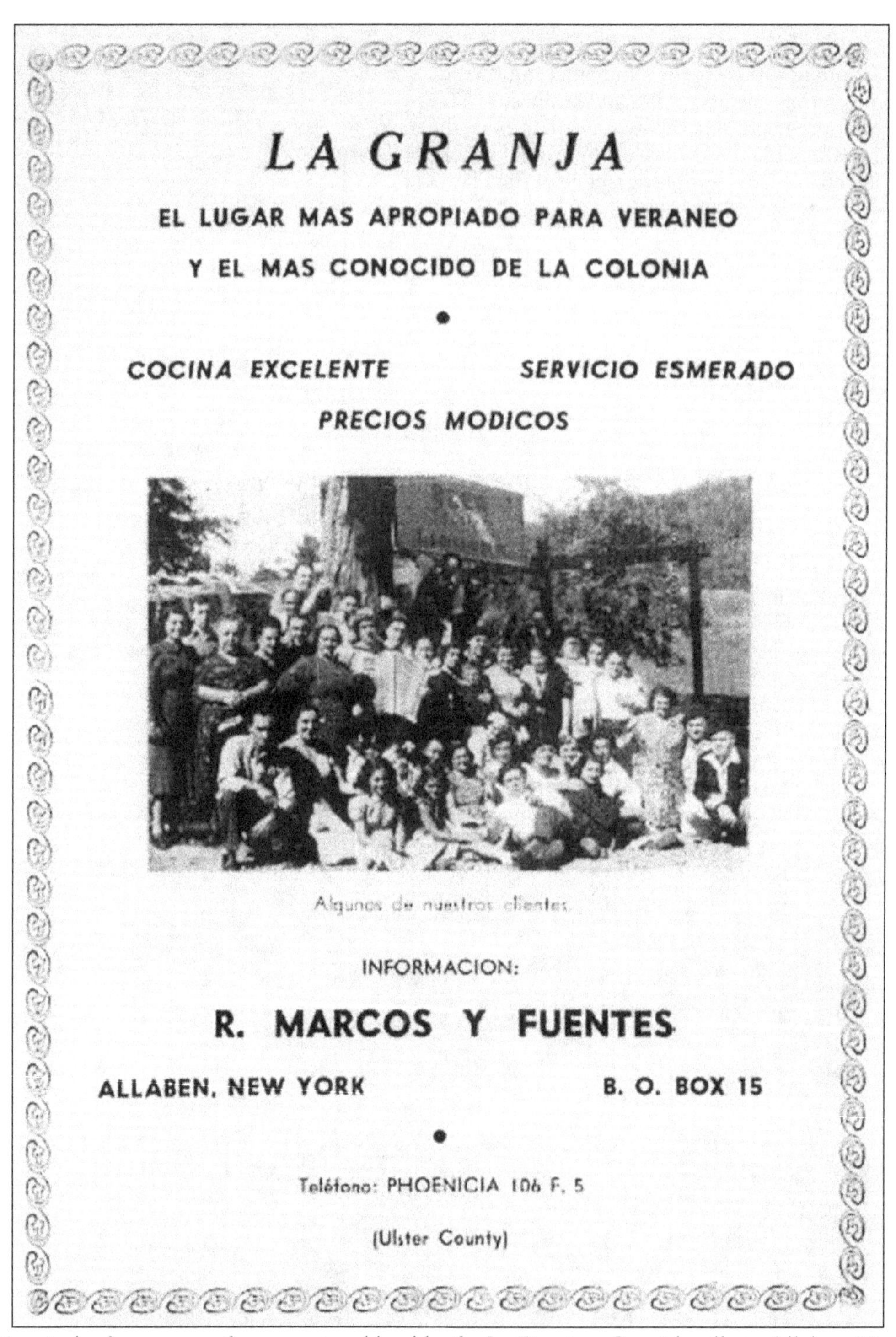

Here is the front cover of a promotional booklet for La Granja, a Spanish villa in Allaben, New York, not far from Phoenicia in the Catskill Mountains. A translation goes as follows: "The most suitable place for summer vacations and the most widely known of the community, excellent cuisine, and meticulous service, reasonable prices." (Courtesy of James Fernandez.)

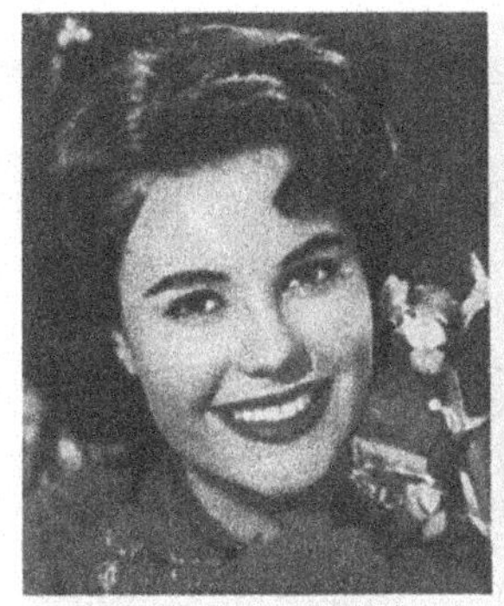
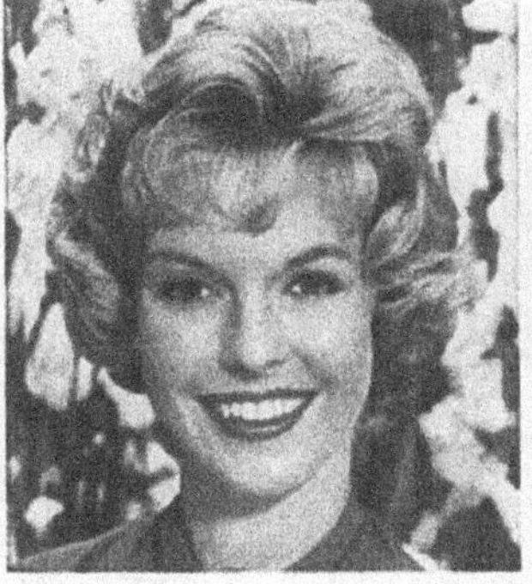
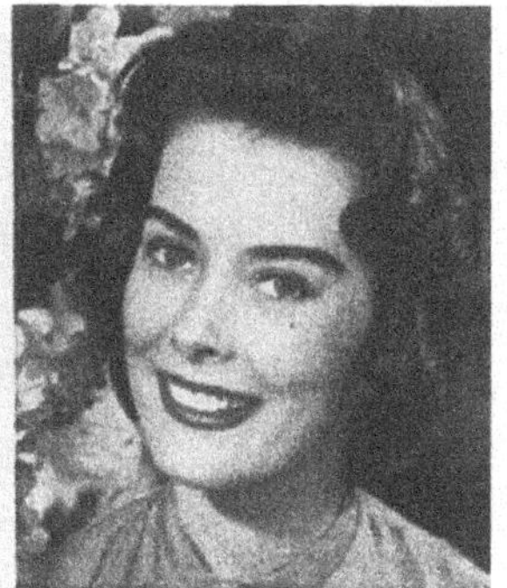

Pat McCloskey Jane Langley Carol Christensen

That happy voting time of year is here again! Time for you to elect

MISS RHEINGOLD 1960!

Choose your favorite candidate—vote for her today at any Rheingold store or tavern

Meet the six lovely young hopefuls—your candidates for the title of Miss Rheingold 1960. These happy finalists were chosen last spring from hundreds of the prettiest girls in New York, Boston and California—by a panel of famous judges.

Here's a partial list of the judges who selected this year's candidates: Bob Cummings, Stevan Dohanos, Irene Dunne, Jinx Falkenburg, Mona Freeman, Art Linkletter, Guy Lombardo, Terry Moore, Rosalind Russell, Leonard Sillman, Jon Whitcomb.

Now it's up to you to name the one winner! With six such pretty candidates in the running, the 1960 election looks close. That's why every ballot is important. Your vote and the votes of your friends could carry your candidate to victory.

$50,000 contract for the girl you elect! The lucky girl who wins the Miss Rheingold title not only wins a year's contract worth $50,000. She'll also enjoy a world of wonderful traveling—and go on to fame as the most photographed girl in town.

Join the fun, vote today! Get in on the excitement of America's second-largest election! Pick the candidate you like best *right now*. Then *vote* for her today or any day through October 3. You'll find Election Ballot Boxes at all Rheingold dealers—over 40,000 in the metropolitan area alone. *Every vote counts—every vote is counted* by an impartial research organization. So the decision is entirely yours. Now, on to the polls to back your candidate!

In all America, there's nothing quite like the Miss Rheingold Election. Just as there's nothing like the satisfying, true-beer taste of the beer itself—refreshing Rheingold Extra Dry. Most people agree—which is why Rheingold is New York's largest-selling beer, and the most imitated beer in America.

COSTUMES BY HARPER'S BAZAAR
PHOTOGRAPHS BY PAUL HESSE

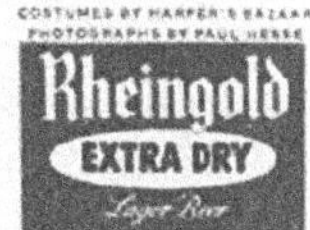

New York's original Dry beer, brewed by Liebmann Breweries, Inc., master brewers

Judi Turner Emily Banks Anne Newman

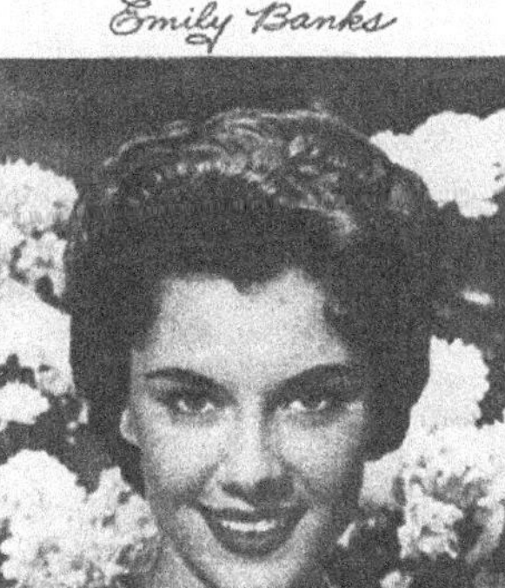
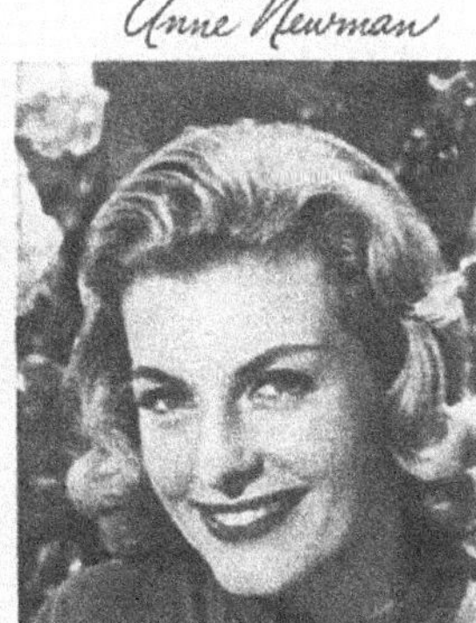

The Rheingold Brewing Company ran a Miss Rheingold beauty contest for a number of years during the era of Las Villas. The company placed ballot boxes in almost every drinking establishment in the Northeast, including Las Villas. On several occasions, the reigning Miss Rheingold made an appearance at the villas, which was covered by *La Prensa*, a Spanish-language newspaper. (Courtesy of Anne Newman.)

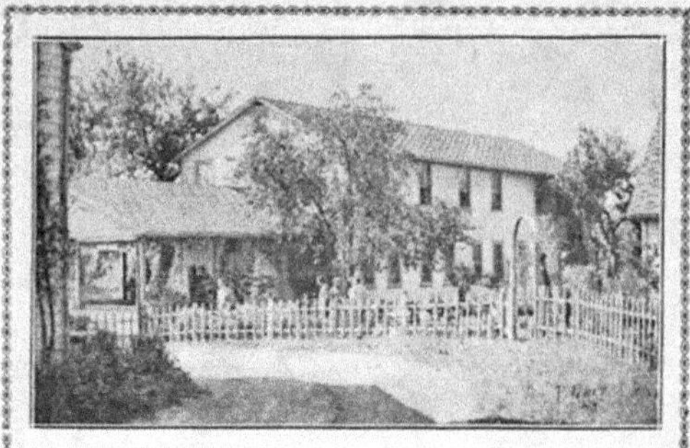

VILLA NUEVA

SEVERINO GARCIA

LA GRANJA MEJOR Y MAS MODERNA EN LAS MONTAÑAS DE PLATTEKILL, N. Y.

La "VILLA NUEVA", lugar predilecto de la Colonia Hispana, con más de 80 acres de terreno y árboles frutales de todas clases, está dotada de todos los adelantos modernos para que el veraneante pueda pasar sus vacaciones con todo confort. En esta Finca se puede gozar de todos los deportes, comida abundante, leche fresca, agua de manantial y toda clase de vegetales, todo de la Finca. Precios sumamente módicos y esmerada atención. Amplias habitaciones, gran comedor, espléndido salón de baile, baños y duchas con agua caliente y fría, etc., etc.

VILLA NUEVA

P. O. BOX No. 15, PLATTEKILL, N. Y. **Tel. Newburgh 926-J2**

This advertisement (left) states the following: "The best, most modern estate in the mountains of Plattekill, NY. - Villa Nueva, favorite Spanish resort, with 80 acres of land and fruit trees. Equipped with modern conveniences for the total comfort of summer guests. Here, one can enjoy all sports, abundant food, fresh milk, springwater, and vegetables from the garden. Affordable prices and attentive service. Spacious rooms, a grand dining room, splendid dance hall, bathrooms and showers with hot and cold water, etc." On the reverse side of the advertisement (below) is a bilingual explanation of directions on how to get to the villa by boat, train, and car. (Both, courtesy of James Fernandez.)

Telephone, Newburgh 9 J 2

VILLA NUEVA

S. GARCIA

El lugar mas apropiado para pasar sus vacaciones en las Montanas de Plattekill, Ulster County. Box 15 Plattekill, N. Y.

Para venir a Villa Nueva: Tomese el Hudson River Boat en 42nd St., Hasta Newburgh: Alli tomen el Buss aVilla Nueva: Trenes: Erie, West Shore a Newburgh: Grand Central a Beacon, Alli tomen el Ferry hasta Newburgh y desde este lugar los traera el Buss hasta la finca. Por Automobile: Crucen el Washington Bridge, tomen Ruta 9 W. a Newburgh, alli ruta 32 a Plattekill. O rutas 4-2-17 y 32. De Jersey City, las mismas rutas. Por Buses: De New York a Newburgh, salen de la Calle 52 West: Newark Terminal, From Jersey City, Journal Square

VILLA NUEVA

Is the ideal place to pass your vacations. Located in the Plattekill Mountains, Ulster Co., New York. For information write or telephone, Newburgh 9 J 2

P. O. Box 15, Plattekill, N. Y.

HOW TO COME: Take the Hudson River Day Line at 42nd St., to Newburgh: By train, Erie, West Shore to Newburgh, Grand Central to Beacon then take the Ferry to Newburgh, in Newburgh take the Buss to Villa Nueva. By Automobile: Cross the Washington Bridge, take Route 9 W to Newburgh, there take route 32 to Plattekill, or take Routes 4-2-17-32. The same routes from Jersey City.

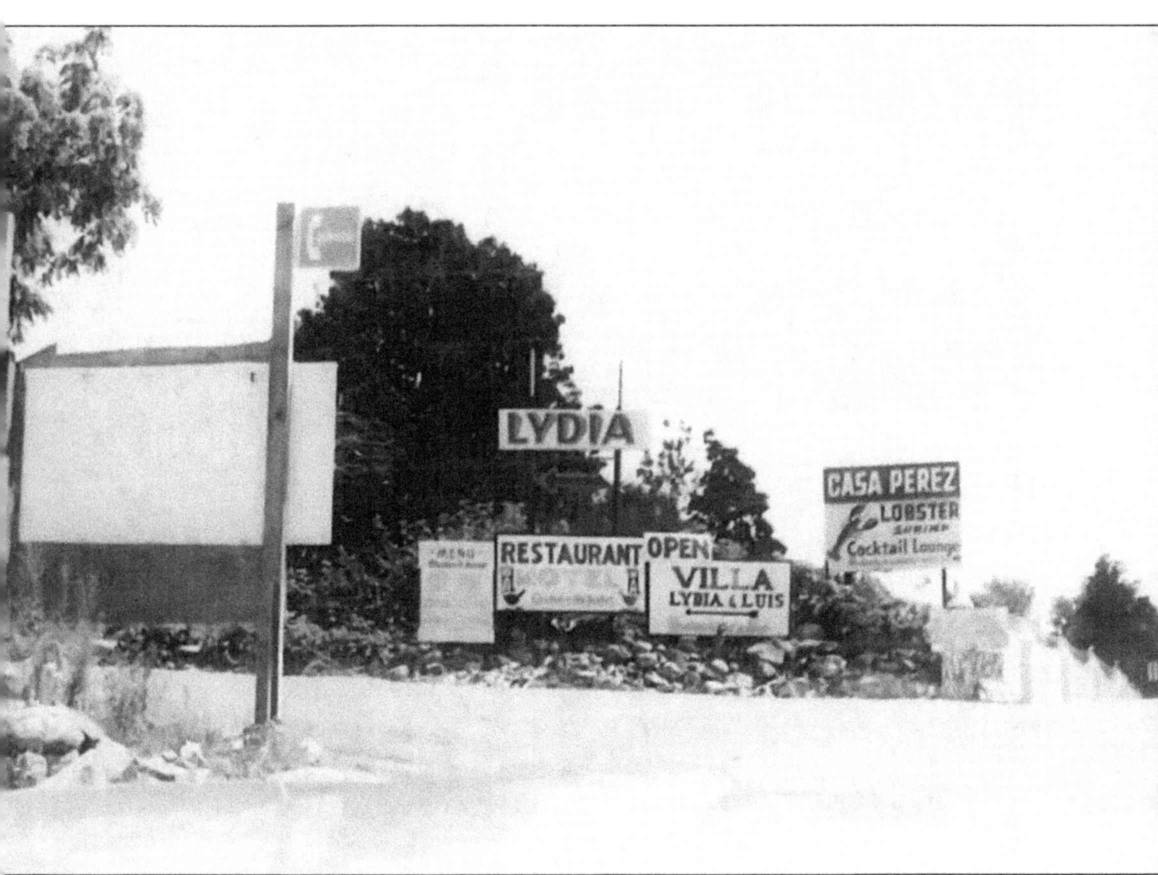

Villa signs clutter an intersection along Unionville Road in the town of Plattekill and compete for the attention of potential customers as they drive by the various villas. On weekends, Unionville Road was most likely the second-busiest road in town, as it was the home to at least a half dozen villas. (Courtesy of Roxy Santiago.)

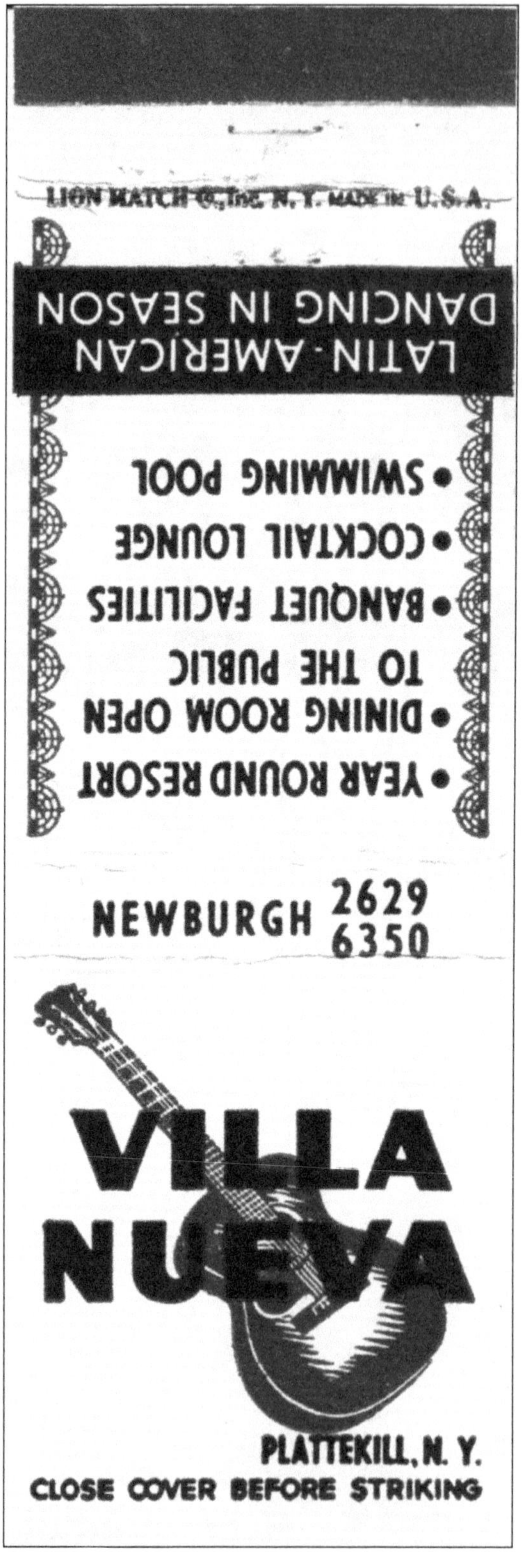

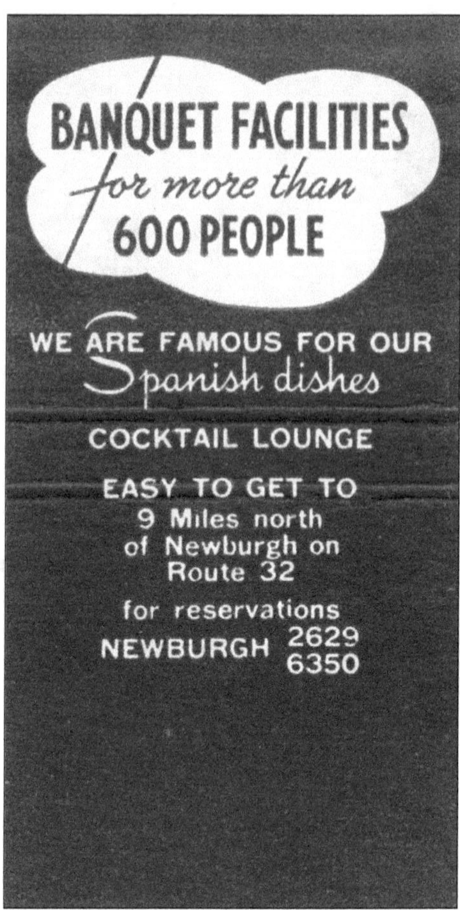

Pictured is an open book of matches (left) with the name of the Villa Nueva printed on the front and a concise list of what it has to offer on the back. On the inside of the matchbook (above) are additional details about the villa as well as a couple of phone numbers and directions on how to get there. Advertising on matchbook covers has always been a popular form of promotion. (Both, courtesy of Elizabeth Werlau.)

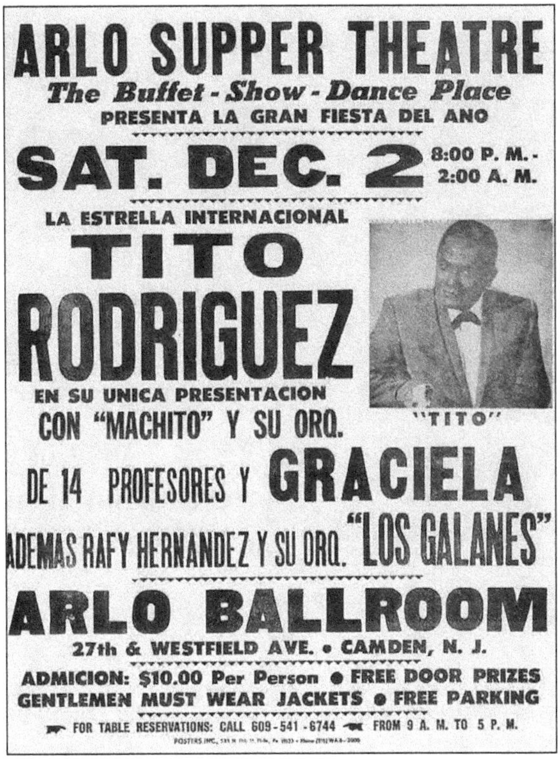

These two posters, with many of the big-name bands of the day, are very typical of others that could be seen in all parts of New York City where there was a large Hispanic presence. The posters advertise upcoming events, the name of the club or location of the event, and the bands that would be performing. (Both, courtesy of Raul Cacedas.)

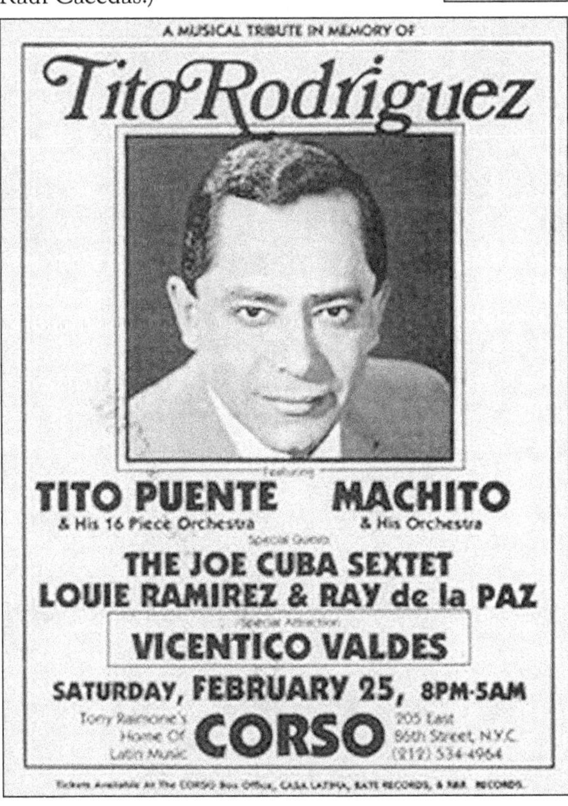